C. Hullmandel lithog.

Georgian Lewes

1714 - 1830

The Heyday of a County Town

Town Crier with Georgian accessories c1870 (Reeves)

Georgian Lewes 1714 - 1830

The Heyday of a County Town

COLIN BRENT

Colin Brent Books

Colin Brent Books

Published by Colin Brent Books
9 Southdown Avenue, Lewes, East Sussex BN7 1EL

ISBN 0 9522423 0 3

Design: Andrew Gammon, Lewes
Printed in Great Britain by Biddles Ltd. Guildford and Kings Lynn

Cover illustrations: Coade stone panels representing Wisdom and Mercy, on the facade of the Shire Hall at Lewes

Endpapers: A balloon ascent by Messrs Green and Gardiner in September 1828, viewed from School Hill at Lewes (Henwood)

Contents

Preface

The last substantial survey of Georgian Lewes was compiled by Thomas Horsfield in the mid-1820s, which encourages me to believe that this volume will not be deemed intrusive or superfluous. It offers a general and, hopefully, succinct history of a county town at the height of its economic and cultural vigour. The more accessible printed and archival sources have been combed; and the narrative is fairly fully referenced and indexed. Being a general survey, there will be gaps, errors and imperceptions, especially as there is little relevant published research. Nonetheless I have tried to set Georgian Lewes in its regional context as a market centre, a shire capital and a focus of professional expertise; I have sampled too its vibrant intellectual, religious and political life, and explored its changing townscape. I hope the book will be useful to local historians, but above all to the many people, resident or not, who value its visual heritage. Hence the book is rather devoid of statistics and "debate", and rather full of people and anecdote. Where possible the maps and engravings derive from Georgian Lewes. Other relevant illustrations will be found in *Victorian Lewes* (Phillimore 1980) and *Historic Lewes* (Lewes Town Council 1985). I have myself undertaken the publication of this book, in order to keep down its price.

I wish especially to thank the following for information: ME Bennett on John Button, John Bleach on Sylas Neville, John Caffyn on smallpox and Elizabeth Hitchener, Judith Cobau on Stephen Philpot, John Farrant on London carriers and Cater Rand I, Jeremy Goring on the Eastport Lane Baptists, RJ Goulden on William Lee, Alan Hill on Lewes bankers, Brian Jenkins on James Drowley, John Kay on John Whitfeld, Elise Knapp on Josiah Welby, Kim Leslie on Elizabeth Hitchener, Richard Saville on Ambrose Galloway, and Willis P Whichard on James Iredell. I am also grateful to Tim Hudson and David Jarman for advice on presentation, and to Joyce Crow, at the Sussex Archaeological Society Library, and Christopher

Whittick, at the East Sussex Record Office, for guidance to sources.

My thanks are also due to Robert Chaplin, Andrew Gammon, Ron Moore, Zena Rector and Alan Shelley for lending illustrations, and to the following for permission to reproduce illustrations: the trustees of Westgate Chapel, drawings by EH New; the British Library, watercolours in the Burrell Collection; the East Sussex County Library, ESRO R/L11/7/6; the trustees of Jireh Chapel, ESRO NI/1/4/1/1, 4/2/1; Lewes District Council, ESRO BLE/TR2/1, LEW/C5/3/5; CJ Davies-Gilbert, ESRO GIL 60; the County Archivist, East Sussex Record Office, billheads, trade cards and printed items in GLY 791/4, A 2714, AMS 5569/26, QAH/8/E3, PAR 378/9/2, PAR 414/9/2/25, 31/2/26, D 358, D 469, A 6077/19/84; Tom Reeves, Tom Paine's portrait; LS Davey, engraving of Lewes Engine House; the Sussex Archaeological Society and the *Sunday Times*, photographs in the Edward Reeves Collection, watercolours, drawings, prints and a silhouette; Eastbourne Borough Council, drawing of the Hermitage. Other engravings are from the *Lewes Journal* and *The History and Antiquities of Lewes* (1824-7) by Thomas Horsfield.

I am most grateful to the Directors of Harveys Brewery for financial help; to Alan Shelley for storing the stock; to Andrew Gammon for his care in designing the book, and to my wife Judith for unswerving help and encouragement.

Lewes bridge

Lewes c1775, based on William Figg's map in Sussex Archaeological Collections

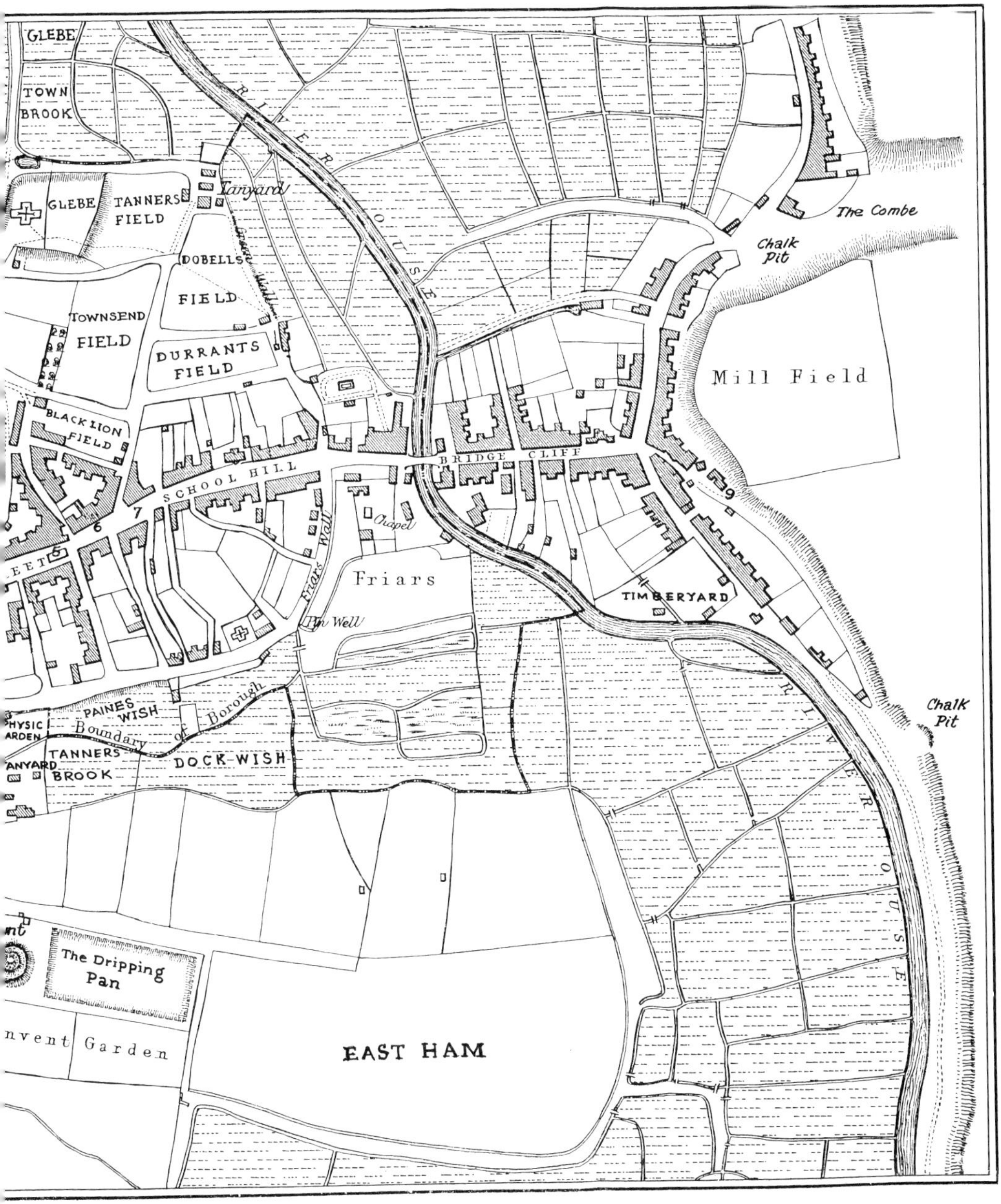

1 Remains of St. Peter's Church
2 The Grammar School
3 The West Gate
4 The Market House
5 The Sessions House
6 The Star Inn
7 Site of St Nicholas's Church
8 Building once the Grammar School
9 Countess of Huntingdon's Meeting House
10 General Baptist Meeting House

St Annes Hill (Horsfield's History)

1
The Mart of Mid-Sussex: Catchment and Communications

Lewes is a fine pleasant town, well built, agreeably situated in the middle of an open champaign country, and on the edge of the South Downs, the pleasantest, and most delightful of their kind in the nation; it lies on the bank of a little wholesome fresh river, within twelve miles of the sea.

DANIEL DEFOE, *A TOUR* (1724).

A county town draws the inhabitants of all vicarages, farms, country houses, and way-side cottages, within a radius of ten miles at least, once or twice a week, to its streets.

VIRGINIA WOOLF, *NIGHT AND DAY* (1919).

In Defoe's time the 2000 inhabitants of Lewes mostly resided in the Borough's High Street. This descended a chalk spur from St Anne's church to the river Ouse, and along it were strung the many facilities that drew in country folk from miles around. After the grammar school and the west gate, on a level stretch, came the Presbyterian meeting house and St Michael's church, where sat the archdeacon's court; then the market house with its whipping post, clock and proclamations board, and the Town Hall which housed the quarter sessions and assizes; here too clustered the wholesale vintners, grocers and drapers, the goldsmiths and gunsmiths, and two commodious hostelries, the *White Hart* and the *Star*; beyond the clock house School Hill plunged past the consulting rooms of wealthy lawyers and physicians, down to the town wharf and the bridge. North of the High Street were a few houses in Fisher Street and the Castle Precincts. Stables, warehouses and barns lined Westgate Lane, Castle Ditch Lane and Black Lion Lane; and near Eastgate Arthur Morris established a stone works about 1727. Further north, beyond Townsends Field and Dobells Field, past Hangmans Acre and Gallows Bank, were some cottages by half-derelict St John's church, and to the east Richard Puxty's tannery at Greenwall. Even further

South Prospect of Lewes, from Richard Budgen's Map of Sussex (1724)

out, on a stretch of whalebacked sheepdown, lay the race course, endowed each year with a King's Plate. South of the High Street lanes and twittens descended sunny slopes between orchards and closes. Houses again were few, mostly in St Nicholas Lane, St Marys Lane, Market Lane, and Keere Street where ancient tenements on the west, held of Portslade manor, faced others built on the Town Ditch in Tudor times. Below the slopes All Saints church and the Quaker meeting house looked towards the Pinwell spring and the Friars wall, its medieval masonry glowing in due season with snap-dragons and viper's bugloss.

East of the Borough, over the bridge and into Pevensey Rape, beyond the wharfs lining the Ouse, the High Street became the West Street of Cliffe. While squeezing past more grocers and drapers, curriers and soap boilers, and past the House of Correction, it crossed several culverted sewers that drained the "sea sand and slubb" beneath. Then at Cliffe Corner, beyond the Fair Place, St Thomas's church and the market house, the road reached a steep chalk slope and divided. East Street (now Chapel Hill) boldly ascended the bluff. Along North Street and South Street the houses quickly gave way on the western side to orchards and timberyards. South of the Borough, beyond watermeadows and the Winterbourne stream, beyond Fissenden's physic garden, Snashall's tannery and the Elizabethan mansion of the Newtons, lay half-rustic Southover, a suburb still overshadowed by the wall and great gate of the priory precincts, and much given to malting and brewing. From its High Street houses spilled into Ham Lane, Eastport Lane, and Puddingbag Lane (now St James Street), a cul-de-sac formed in 1559 when fire destroyed the houses beyond leading up to Rotten Row in the Borough.

Compactly contained within these once medieval limits, Lewes focused the commerce of mid-Sussex. Its markets and fairs, its shops and manufactories flourished because (like Guildford, Winchester, Dorchester and Exeter) the town dominated local traffic by road and river. The Borough High Street, the bridge and the West Street of Cliffe were part of a busy trunk route that followed the ridge of the South Downs, and in dry weather the "underhill" lanes along the scarpfoot beneath. Passing Petersfield, Chanctonbury, Bramber bridge, Devils Dyke, Lewes bridge, Glynde bridge, Firle Street, Longbridge and Eastbourne, this road then crossed the shingle beach to Hastings and Romney Marsh. Through Lewes it funnelled a stream of Trampers - artisans, harvesters, tinkers, showmen, disembarked soldiers and shipwrecked sailors. Among those relieved by a (perhaps credulous) parish officer at St Anne's in the 1720s were

> 40 poore men, some of them were struck Deaf and Dumb and some Blind in Ireland by a very greivious and Turrable Tempest of Thunder and Lightning, which lasted 48 hours;

and

> 24 Saylors who were taken prisoners by the Turks and made them their Slaves, and used them very Barbarous by Burning them in severall parts of their Bodys, Cutting some of Their Tongues out, putting some of their Eyes out, and at last were put into a Turkish Gally and chained down to their Oyres; By Good [if belated] Providence retaken and Brought to England and landed near Chichester.

Other local roads converged on Lewes bridge in the 1720s because the Ouse remained a barrier to wheeled traffic. Downstream the river meandered to the sea through a wide corridor of watermeadows ("brooks"), cut up by irrigation ditches and often flooded in winter. Ferries crossed at Southease and Newhaven; but only in 1784 did a drawbridge replace the latter. Upstream the watermeadows quickly gave way to Low Wealden mud which marooned a packhorse bridge at Barcombe Mill, adapted though it later was for vehi-

Lewes, the South Downs, the Weald and the lower Ouse, from Yeakell and Gardner's Map of Sussex (1783)

cles paying a toll. Not till seven miles upstream, at Sharpsbridge on the southern fringes of Ashdown Forest, did a major highway cross this waterlogged corridor. So road traffic was deflected to Lewes from Hailsham, Uckfield, Danehill and Cuckfield, from Seaford, Newhaven and Brighton.

Yet the Ouse was a waterway, as well as a barrier. It was navigable from Barcombe Mill down to Newhaven harbour, and along Glynde Reach, which made the wharfs near Lewes bridge into a hub of barge traffic. Sea-going craft in or near Newhaven harbour were spotted from St Anne's churchyard or Spital Hill by keen-eyed townsfolk; and Great Storms coated Lewes shrubberies with salt. So important was the bridge to traffic in mid-Sussex that its repair was jointly funded by Lewes and Pevensey Rapes, the Ouse being the border between them. After a tempest swept away its wooden frame in 1726, a narrow but robust arch of Portland stone was substituted.

Besides attracting traffic, Lewes stood near the frontier between the South Downs and the Weald. From medieval times it had been a mart for their surpluses, for Southdown wheat, barley, sheep, wool, chalk, lime and wheatears, for Wealden oats, hops, cattle, butter, cheese, fruit, leather, wool, bricks, tiles, timber, woodfuel and iron, and for seafish landed at Brighton. Their redistribution from Lewes in the 1720s was largely local: oats, woodfuel and hops to Brighton and the Downs; barley, lime and seafish to the Weald. Yet some livestock, wool and hops departed to London, via East Grinstead and Godstone; and other produce crammed the barges descending to Newhaven harbour. In 1701-02 27 cargoes of grain, guns or timber were loaded there for London or Chatham, Portsmouth or Bristol. In 1724-27 49 cargoes, mainly wheat, went to France, Holland or Lisbon.

Lewes also marketed commodities brought overland from London or barged upriver. Cargoes unloaded at Newhaven in 1701-02 included 22 of coal, salt, bottles and butter from Tyneside, ten of groceries, textiles, wines and starch from London, two of iron, spirits, cheese and cider from Bristol, along with scythes and millstones from Hull, pipe clay from Poole and naval prize wine from Plymouth, though salt from Hampshire sank in transit. In 1724-27 21 cargoes arrived from overseas, containing consumer goods from Holland, wine, oranges, lemons and cork from Oporto and Malaga, deals and Swedish iron from Norway, millstones and plaster of Paris from Rouen and Dieppe. This complex exchange of commodities encouraged Lewesians to trade as millers, maltsters, and brewers, as makers of soap, candles, rope, clocks, guns, churns and clay pipes.

The Downland serviced from Lewes by the 1720s was already extensive. To the east its corn market attracted farmers from as far as Beachy Head, having caused other markets to close at Alfriston, Eastbourne and Hailsham; not till Pevensey Marsh did the pull of Hastings begin. But Downsmen to the west resorted also to markets and wharfs at Brighton, Southwick and Shoreham. There Thomas Marchant (c1676-1728) of Hurstpierpoint and his neighbour Henry Campion sold wheat, and bought coal, Lisbon wine, sail cloth and raisins. From Lewes they procured tea, paper, mousetraps, "a male pillion", a hogshead of port, and cash credit. Most Southdown farms were richly endowed by Nature. Near Lewes, at Landport, Malling and Swanborough, their warm well-drained arable fields were tilted

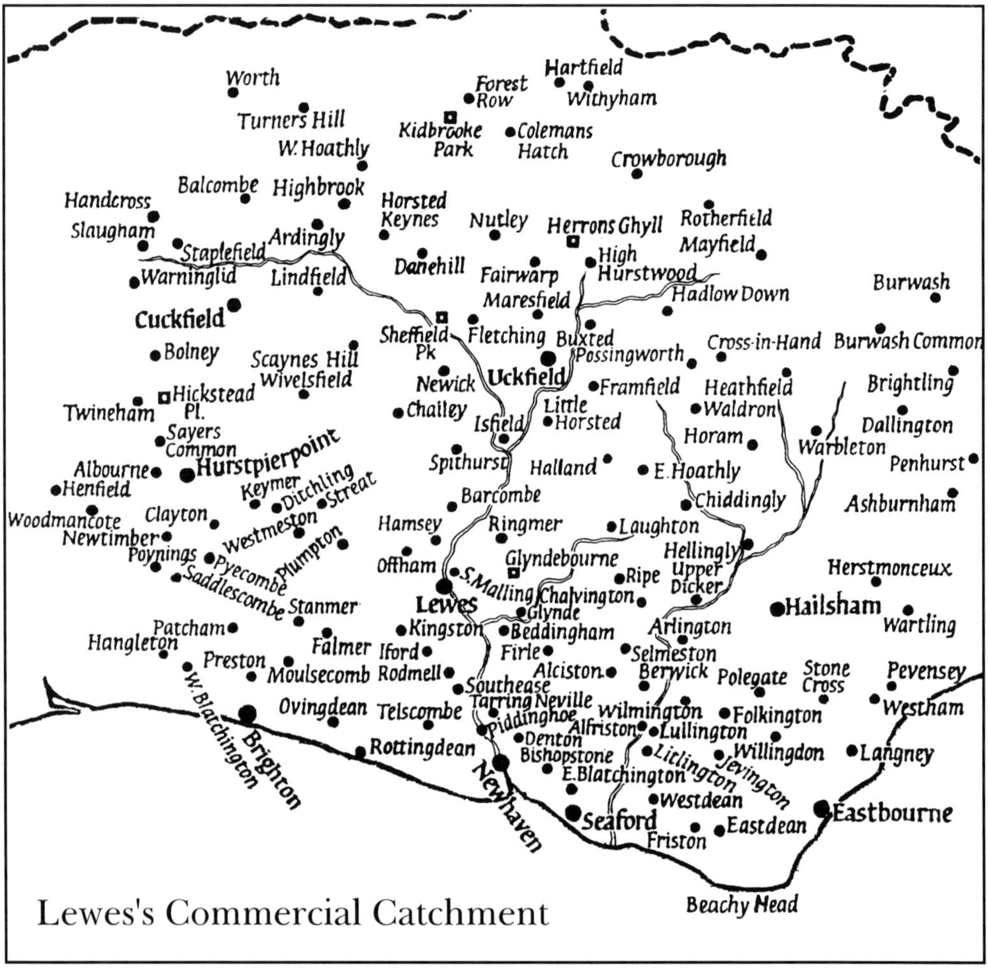

Lewes's Commercial Catchment

between the watermeadows along the Ouse and the "very short, sweet and aromatic herbage" on the thyme-scented sheepwalks above: a pattern repeated down the estuary to Newhaven, and along the Cuckmere and the Adur. Productive cornfields also floored sheltered combes dropping seaward at Falmer, Rottingdean and Birling; while along the scarpfoot, where chalk and greensand mingled, a "slip of very rich and stiff arable" stretched through Plumpton, Hamsey, Alciston and Wilmington, to end at Meads near Beachy Head. The sheep flocks, folded at night on this cornland, formed a "moving dung-hill", manuring it without expense or human toil. This Southdown husbandry yielded wheat and barley, sheep and wool: but beef and dairy cattle were left to Wealden cultivators. It produced too the treeless "champaign country" that delighted pragmatic Daniel Defoe, though not agoraphobic Dr Johnson:

> if one had a mind to hang oneself for desperation at being obliged to live there, it would be difficult to find a tree on which to fasten a rope.

The South Downs also yielded chalk, lime, samphire, rabbits, pigeons and wheatears. A dove-house at Southover contained 3228 nesting holes; and wheatears were a prey each summer to any shepherd hiding a double noose beneath a row

> Of turf-turn'd coops along the sunny brow.

Epicures at Tunbridge Wells prized these tasty "English ortolans" which were sold, fresh or potted, at the *White Hart*.

Very different was Lewes's Wealden hinterland. The vista northward from its castle revealed many miles of sourly undulating Low Wealden clays. Rock hard in summer, "wet and tenacious" in winter, they underpinned in the 1720s a vast patchwork of coppice and deer park, acid furrow, sodden pasture and loosely stinted common, which gave the toiling cultivator hard-won surpluses of wheat, hops and oats, beef and dairy produce. But abundant wood fuel and waterpower did encourage charcoal burners, carpenters, turners, coopers, weavers, glovers, tanners, brickmakers and potters, though iron workers were dwindling fast. Beyond the acid clays stretched the scrub, heathland and warrens of the High Weald; rabbits trapped in Ashdown Forest being also a delicacy at the *White Hart*. From these desolate "forest" ridges, round Pease Pottage, Tilgate, Wych Cross, Crowborough Beacon and Burwash Down, the headwaters of the Ouse, the Cuckmere and the Ashburn tumbled south through sandstone ghylls to waterlog the clays. These barren uplands also set a natural limit to Lewes's trade. Beyond them the Mole and Medway, the Teise and Eastern Rother drained towards Horsham, Tonbridge, Tenterden and Battle. Near this rugged frontier were located several lots advertised in the *Lewes Journal* for auction on market-day at Lewes in 1769-75: farms at Cuckfield, Lindfield and Fletching, oaks at Heathfield and Warbleton, an ironworks at Bivelham in Mayfield, along with acreages in Pevensey marsh.

The Southdown cultivators resorting to Lewes were well placed to profit from several decades of farming prosperity, which continued during the wars against France in 1793-1815. In mid-Sussex the hostilities themselves increased demand for food and fodder, by crowding the coast with soldiers, and with up-market visitors denied the Grand Tour. During the boom many small farmers on the Lewes Downs sold out to local landowners, to the Pelhams, Gages and Trevors, who leased back the land to affluent yeomen, with enough credit and marketing skill to manage 500 acres or more. Their deaths were noted in the *Journal*; and Mark Antony Lower saluted them alphabetically in his *Worthies of Sussex:* the Ades and Arkcolls, the Gorringes and Gosdens, the Woodhamses and Woodmans. John Tourle of Landport, "the richest man on the South Downs", was allegedly worth £300,000 in 1801. John Ellman (1753-1832), the tenant of Place Farm at Glynde, publicized the serviceable wool and toothsome hindquarter mutton of the Southdown flock he tirelessly improved. He tinkered too with oxen and clover, flails and seed drills, winning a Board of Agriculture gold medal. On a visit to Place Farm one Christmas, the great agronomist Arthur Young attended

Glynde church, where William Wisdom noted his hollow eyes and studious aspect. Ellman's Southdown neighbours were also Improvers. At Beddingham Sir Thomas Carr bred two champion heifers which drew admiring crowds to the *Swan* near Smithfield Market. Stephen Grantham at Lower Stoneham shipped 100 prime ewes from Newhaven to Dumfries aboard the *Britannia* in 1823; and Sir Charles Merrik Burrell, who owned Upper Stoneham, gained a gold medal for his remarks on the soiling of cattle. The Lewes-born Mary Anne Gilbert (1776-1845) inherited wide estates at Eastbourne, where she fostered spade husbandry and seaweed manures. From her greatcoat pockets she produced small working models of farm machinery, to beguile genteel neighbours if polite discourse flagged.

Though fertile, the South Downs were not "well peopled". Labourers with families, likely to burden the poor-rates, were discouraged from settling; indeed some farm workers trudged weary miles to work from the back-lanes of Lewes. Because haymaking taxed Southdown resources, the scythers in the watermeadows below the town were too busy to quaff free beer at Firle Place in July 1741. The Southdown harvest needed "foreign" labour. On Midsummer Day in 1802, when the crop was "sufficiently advanced in Ear", Wealdsmen arrived at William Gorringe's 600 acre farm near Kingston Buci, and agreed a price per acre and their rations, mostly mutton boiled with French beans. Sheep-shearers though were an indigenous breed. John Ellman and his fellow flockmasters met at the *Swan* in Falmer to regulate their Government, allowing each (except the Tar Boy) two pints of strong beer and 11 pints of ale daily.

Ellman retired to Lewes, to smart new Albion Street. Other farmers, leasing the Priory lands, resided at Southover. Strong beer, brewed in 1734, was served at John Winton's funeral in 1788. Soon after, Count Henry de Bourbel arrived, a refugee from Revolution, eager to master English agrarian science. Then came John Ellman II, a Wykehamist able to memorize 1200 lines of Latin verse, whose son wrote graphic *Recollections* of late-Georgian Lewes, which Evelyn Waugh spared when ferociously weeding Lancing College library.

The agricultural boom also benefited the struggling peasant farmers who predominated in the Weald. It encouraged enclosure, new root crops, more use of lime, and more acres of wheat. An early Improver was the landowner William Poole (1696-1779) who had chalk, soot, malt dust and soap ashes carted from Lewes to sweeten his arable at The Hooke in Chailey, where Arthur Young admired his seed drill, hollow drainage and potato beds. Yet fallow, and then two years of corn, were still a widespread Wealden rotation in 1800. One commentator moreover distrusted wheat as a cash crop, commending Lord Sheffield's model farm at Fletching, with its neat dairies and fat cattle destined for Smithfield. But even in boom years many Wealden farmers could ill afford newfangled clovers or milking parlours. And though The Broyle and The Dicker were enclosed, many Low Wealden commons survived into the 1830s. Improvers also avoided the barren forest ridges, denounced by William Cobbett as villainous tracts of bare heath, scrubby birch and ugly fir. Being small, Wealden farms tempted Lewesians with capital to invest. In 1753 the dancing-master Stephen Philpot bought 100 acres at Balneath in Barcombe. In 1822 the builder John Morris owned Bachelors Hill Farm (118 acres) at Isfield, where the printer John Baxter purchased Oaklands Farm; indeed a model farmyard he designed was shown at the Great Exhibition.

This wide Southdown and Wealden hinterland shaped the commercial outreach of Abraham Curtis (1711-73), a flaxdresser at Cliffe Corner. He supplied shopkeepers at Firle, Alfriston, Willingdon, Waldron, East Hoathly, Uckfield, Chailey and Cuckfield, with sacking, cheesecloth, rope, thread, bedcords, reins, halters and plough traces. He sent fishing line to Eastbourne and Seaford, shoe hemp to Forest Row, and oakum (for caulking boats) to shipyards at Newhaven and Shoreham. Conversely the East Hoathly shopkeeper, Thomas Turner (1729-93), resorted to Lewes for textiles, groceries, pastry, soap, razors, scythes, breeches, wigs, cauliflower seeds, gunpowder and the discounting of bills, for a book of sermons, for the wine served at Dame Reeve's funeral and the plates screwed on Mr Calverley's coffin. John Burgess (c1751-c1825) of Ditchling came to Lewes to buy alum, Holland, gingerbread, pasteboard, coal and banknotes, and to barter with Quaker Marten for hats, Dowlais and a blanket; a typical Wealden entrepreneur, he was a glover, breeches-maker, bookbinder, goose keeper, potato planter, General Baptist and closet Republican. Also in the 1790s John Trayton Fuller at Ashdown House, near Forest Row, ordered from Lewes ox chains and Norfolk thumb latches, saddle bags and wine, deals and coal, ammonia and wormwood, a square mahogany tambour frame, Dorchester beer, Cheshire cheese, strawberry pottles and a gun with a golden touch-hole.

Familiar with this hinterland was the town's "first Auctioneer" George Verrall, who sold a Lewes butcher's shop in 1756, after a candle had burned four hours. George Verrall II prospered enough to buy The Friars estate in 1804; and his son Plumer's bellicose patter drew admiring audiences in the 1820s. Lewes-based surveyors were also active across mid-Sussex and beyond. In 1757 John Relf measured and mapped an acreage at East Hoathly. Thomas Marchant worked at Northiam (1750), Jevington, Waldron and East Grinstead (1788); at Coombe Place in Hamsey he installed a lifting device above a deep well, perfected after 30 years of trial. Equally farflung were the surveys of Thomas Budgen (1765-1832), briefly a newspaper publisher; of his nextdoor neighbour William Figg who composed church anthems; and of William II who described the Memorials of Old Lewes. In 1816 father and son made a splendid survey of Eastbourne's 4597 acres, though Mr Davies Gilbert (Mary Anne's husband) queried paying twopence an acre for large stretches of empty downland.

The agricultural boom stimulated turnpike trusts to improve the roads across mid-Sussex, so binding Lewes ever tighter to its hinterland. Least urgent was the high road along the Southdown scarp. Setting off along it for Glamorganshire from the *Star* in June 1687, Sir John Ashburnham bowled confidently "over the Downes" to Bramber in a two-wheeled caleche. The Duke of Newcastle in 1762 praised this "good way to the West". Gilbert White (1720-93) often used it to visit his Aunt Snooke and her tortoise Timothy at Ringmer, revelling as he rode in the Natural History: the martins hovering above the Lewes quarries; the ferocious wild bee (Bombus Lapidarius) so rampant on Mount Caburn; the ring-ousels crowding the bushes near Devils Dyke one autumn, but absent the next; and the sheep, horned and white-faced west of Bramber bridge, black-faced and hornless to the east. He also recalled the naturalist John Ray praising the majestic prospect from Plumpton Plain as evidence for the Wisdom of God in His Works of Creation. This "way to the West" was all the busier because no bridge spanned the Adur at Shoreham till 1781, and even then the approach road was flooded by the tides till 1823.

Daniel Defoe enjoyed another whalebacked route, the Lewes to Brighton road, past Cranedown and Newmarket Hill, with its "fine carpet ground" and sea-views, though fierce showers forced the schoolmaster Walter Gale to huddle behind an inhospitable hawthorn. Its name, Juggs Road, marked its use by Brighton fishwives and their panniered donkeys making for Lewes market; in 1765 "Jegsy" Welsh returned via Rottingdean with hemp for a customer of Abraham Curtis. Yet in winter "travelling the downs and bostals" could be hazardous. In February 1764 the journey of Mrs William Green from Hastings to Lewes disintegrated after her chaise mounted the ridge above Berwick:

> We arrived home at half past five o'clock, I, up to the knees in mud, for I walk'd great part of the way, and frighted prodigiously, for just as we were upon the Downs the weather came very Bad, and such a Fog that we could see a yard before us. At Last we met with a Shepherd, and he showed us Furle Mill. After I had walk'd Down that hill, I concluded that all Difficulties was over, but alass, worse was to come, for the nearer we got to Lewes the waters [about Glynde] increased to such a Degree, that we went half a mile, I say, with the Horses swimming.

Far worse were the notorious Wealden roads. Heavy rain soon waterlogged the "bottomless" clay vales and the "mountainous" sandstone ridges, making "the weather" a cast-iron excuse for inaction. Near Lewes Defoe observed a Wealden lady being drawn to church in her coach by six oxen, "the way being so stiff and deep". The movement of cattle, timber and cannon deepened any morass. "Nothing can follow them", remarked John Fuller in July 1743, after 20 of his nine-foot guns had torn apart the Heathfield-Lewes road: "the Country curse us heartily". A journey from Lewes to London, through desolate Ashdown Forest, might take "two long summer days"; and if attempted in winter, pessimists first put their affairs in order. Since the same road linked Brighton with the metropolis, it was an early target for improvement. In 1717 Lewesians joined with mid-Sussex farmers, hop-growers, waggoners, fishermen and higglers in a fruitless petition to be exempted from tolls, when the stretch beyond Ashdown Forest, from Wych Cross through East Grinstead, Godstone, Croydon and Newington, was upgraded. However from 1752 the rival routes between Lewes and Wych Cross, via Chailey-Danehill and Uckfield-Nutley, were improved without contention; indeed John Baker deemed the Lewes-Uckfield stretch "the finest turnpike that can be, not sandy nor any considerable ascent".

Also improved in the 1750s was the Lewes to Broyle Park road which unrolled across Ringmer Green an impressive 30 feet wide. By 1770 Wealden trusts were busy beyond Broyle Park towards Heathfield and Battle, and beyond Uckfield towards Tunbridge Wells; to such effect that in 1829 farmers and hucksters from Hartfield and Speldhurst, parishes within the Medway's catchment, were carting fruit and vegetables to Lewes, and returning with coal and lime. Also upgraded about 1770 was the "underhill" road from Lewes to Longbridge, via Ranscombe Lane, Glynde bridge, Firle Street and Bopeep; likewise the road to Brighton via Falmer, so that vehicles leaving Lewes now avoided precipitous Rotten Row and waterlogged Winterbourne Bottom. In 1813 the scarpfoot lane between Offham and Ditchling was attended to; in 1814 a "very crooked, rough road, with three bad hills", was bypassed at Deans near Piddinghoe, easing access to Newhaven harbour; and in 1819-20 a bold new highway was driven to Eastbourne across Ranscombe brooks, Selmeston fairplace, Wilmington Green and Folkington Common, rendering Glynde, Firle and Bopeep the slumbrous backwaters they are today.

Ashcombe Toll House 1826 (Horsfield's History)

Yet the approaches to Lewes, except from Falmer, were only belatedly improved. The London road via Danehill wound westward up St Annes Hill and past Spital barns. This detour caused the London coach to travel an extra 78,771 yards between 15 April and 18 November 1770, and was ended only in 1822 when a hollow way, running due north, was upgraded at White Hill. Traffic arriving from the east faced severe hazards: a "dangerous declivity" on Malling Hill; the bulks, penthouses and projecting windows obstructing West Street in Cliffe; an elegant but congested bridge; and a "sharp acclivity" on School Hill. However a proposal to circumvent them, by bridging the Ouse near St John's church, forced remedial action in 1827-30. The gradient on School Hill was reduced, and Malling Hill partly bypassed; frontages were set back in West Street; parapets on the bridge were removed, and cantilevered footways added.

The improved Brighton-Lewes-London road quickened stage-coach travel. Till 1762 James Batchelor of East Grinstead kept his family's ancient monopoly on that route, continued "from Father to Son, and other Branches of the same Race". In May 1756 his New Machine left the *George* in the Haymarket on Monday, Wednesday and Friday, taking all day to reach the *Old Ship* at Brighton via the *Star* at Lewes. Some passengers chose his Two Day Stage-Coach, recuperating overnight at East Grinstead in the *Dorset Arms*, also Batchelor-owned. However in May 1762 Messrs Brawne and Tubb launched their New Flying Machine, "hung on Steel Springs, very neat and commodious", which hurtled from Charing Cross at 6 a.m., two hours before Batchelor's conveyance, and sped to the *Castle* at Brighton via the *White Hart* at Lewes. Batchelor responded with a New Flying Chariot and lower prices. This "Meanness and Design" goaded Joseph Tubb to alert customers "how you have been used for a great number of years, when he engrossed the whole to himself". Batchelor's executors sold out in 1763 to Robert Davis, a Brighton-London carrier, who then united with Tubb to "engross" again the route, now used in summer by evermore travellers to the coast. One coach in June 1764 carried a Spaniard crossing to France, a sailor-boy bound for a West Indiaman newly launched at Shoreham, and a pastrycook opening a shop for the summer season at Brighton, by then a growing resort. Ladies' maids leaving there in September 1771 already crammed the Machine when it reached the *White Hart*: indeed their idle chatter much depressed the tourist Sylas Neville.

In May 1788 Messrs Tubb and Davis still monopolized the route with a twice-daily service up and down, using two Machines and two Post Coaches, calling at the *Star* and the *White Hart*. Davies died in 1790, making fond provision for his carriage horses, Tommy and Billy; and in 1794 Tubb retired to Forest Row, after living many years in the Castle Precincts and renting pasture near Winterbourne Laines. By then a new London-Brighton road, via Reigate, Cuckfield and Clayton, bypassing Lewes, had become "the Appian way for the high Nobility of England" visiting the resort; and many Lewesians now patronized a growing stream of ever-faster coaches along it, like the *Red Rover* which in September 1831 brought Gideon Mantell down in under five hours. By 1809 the coaches through East Grinstead terminated at Lewes, and some even took to pulling a springless "rumble-tumble" filled with soiled sailors and artisans. But the London-Lewes coaches did reduce their journey time, from 12 summer hours in the 1790s to under six in August 1826, when the *Defiance*, owned by Messrs Hoare, Simcock and Osborne, competed each weekday with the *Amicable*, owned by Messrs Bryan and Sanderson. On one occasion, near Wych Cross, they careered perilously side by side, axle to axle. However by August 1830 the now united companies offered only a curtailed service: their *Regulator*

The Regulator Lewes Coach

Coach left Lewes at 6 a.m. on Monday, Wednesday and Friday, stopping at East Grinstead for breakfast; and returned at 2.30 p.m. on Tuesday, Thursday and Saturday from Charing Cross, where the *Golden Cross* inn with its three floors of stabling kept a spare coach for the Lewes run. Ultimately, the railways forced Thomas Bryan, the last active partner, off the road.

Lewes's leading coachmakers were the Ades. John I (1742-1822) built the first post-chaise for hire in Brighton; he repaired the curricle of Trayton Fuller at Ashdown House, and became the longest-serving Freemason in his Province. John II shared premises on

School Hill and at Brighton with his sons John III and Durrant. They made a doubled-bodied Improved Low Safety Coach that shuttled between Lewes and Brighton, till their equally reliable *Magnet* replaced it in 1825. That year their Bazaar at Brighton was rebuilt as the largest carriage manufactory in Sussex, employing 60 workmen.

The earliest coaching inn, the *Star*, had belonged to Southover Priory; and visiting bishops and archdeacons still feasted there with the local clergy. Sir Charles Bunbury stayed in 1776, the Earls of Warwick and Shelburne soon after. The landlord's wife, Sarah Dunn 1793-1817, was counted among "the first cooks of her day"; and the owner during her time, the wine merchant Sir Henry Blackman, doubtless kept the cellar well stocked. Its upstart rival, the *White Hart*, was well equipped by the first landlord Richard Verral c1717-37. In the balconied Great Room were four tables, 25 chairs and 15 sconces; in the club-room a billiard-table and 11 prints (perhaps indecorous); in the three best bedrooms "china" furniture, green, blue and yellow; in the garrets a dozen bedsteads; in the stables 120 halters; in the cellars barrels of mild and strong beer, and hogsheads of port wine, red and white; in the cupboards eight Delft plates, 82 pewter dishes, 30 wheatear pots, 33 decanters, 20 punch bowls with ladles, and copper pots for coffee and chocolate; under the beds lurked a cohort of chamber pots, pewter and white.

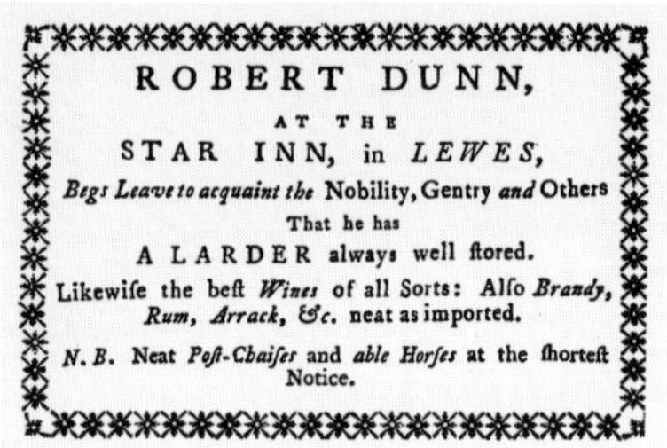
ROBERT DUNN,
AT THE
STAR INN, in *LEWES*,
Begs Leave to acquaint the Nobility, Gentry *and* Others
That he has
A LARDER always well ſtored.
Likewiſe the beſt *Wines* of all Sorts: Alſo *Brandy, Rum, Arrack, &c.* neat as imported.
N. B. Neat *Poſt-Chaiſes* and *able Horſes* at the ſhorteſt Notice.

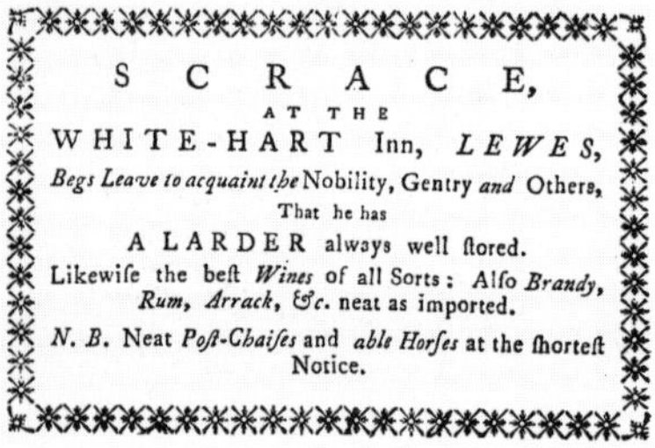
SCRACE,
AT THE
WHITE-HART Inn, *LEWES*,
Begs Leave to acquaint the Nobility, Gentry *and* Others,
That he has
A LARDER always well ſtored.
Likewiſe the beſt *Wines* of all Sorts: Alſo *Brandy, Rum, Arrack, &c.* neat as imported.
N. B. Neat *Poſt-Chaiſes* and *able Horſes* at the ſhorteſt Notice.

Verral's successor, his son William 1737-61, trained in the Duke of Newcastle's household under the master chef, Monsieur de St Clouet. William in his turn instructed the kitchen staff of the local gentry, bemoaning their crude "apparatus", the "poor solitary stewpan", and the sieve fresh from sanding the back stairs. The recipes in his *Complete System of Cookery* (1759), many by Clouet, included PIKE WITH FORCE-MEAT AND CAPER SAUCE:

> Prepare your pike thus: gut it without cutting of it open, but take care it is well cleaned; cut a notch down the back from head to tail, turn it round, and fasten the tail in the mouth, and lay it in a marinade as before: for your farce or forcemeat take the udder of a leg of veal, or the kidney

> part of a loin of lamb, some fat bacon cut in dice, the spawn or melt of the fish, some green onions, a mushroom or two, or truffles, parsley, and salt, a little nutmeg and pepper, add a morsel of butter to fry it, chop it well, and the soft of a French roll soak'd in cream or milk, pound all together in a large mortar, with three or four eggs.

The culinary skill of William's successor, Thomas Scrase 1761-91, is less certain. Sylas Neville was served "the best duck sauce I ever tasted"; but John Byng supped badly on some small soles, and rowdies rattled his bedroom door.

Intrepid Lewes carriers also lumbered up and down the London road. In 1725 Henry Apps settled a grocer's bill at the *Three Sugar Loaves* near St Paul's cathedral for Widow White on School Hill. John Apps in 1679 had brought down the poison which killed a draper's apprentice: his murderer then committed suicide and was buried at the Spital cross-roads "North and South" with "a Stake through his bowels". Commercial cargoes included hops and wool (up) and Seltzer Water (down). In 1740 two Lewes carriers left Southwark each Thursday, from the *Talbot* and the *George*, where part of the galleried courtyard survives. In 1763 three waggons departed weekly; and in 1805 the stage waggons of Shelley & Son, which now monopolized the Lewes-London route, also left the *George* only three times a week, because the new Brighton-Cuckfield-London road carried so much freight. Their Lewes depot was the disused *White Horse*, till John Shelley II in 1813 built Brack Mount House where his waggon-shed still stands. By 1823 the fly waggons and vans of Edward Kenward and Buxted-based John Jarratt were also serving Lewes, from the *Kings Head* and the *Lewes Arms* in Southwark. Indeed Joseph Shelley sold out to Jarratt in 1829. The greater ease of overland traffic, down ever smoother turnpike roads, allowed 2620 tons of flour and linseed oil to be carted to London from the Barcombe mills in 1836.

Uckfield, Lewes, Brighton, Newhaven, and Seaford
VANS ON SPRINGS,

A London-Lewes letter post, via East Grinstead, had started in

1686; but because of the Wealden mud a circuitous route via Kingston, Guildford, Midhurst, Arundel, and Brighton was used instead by 1719, with luckless Eastbourne and Mayfield at the end of the line. By then the town's postmaster was chosen by its political Godfather, the Duke of Newcastle. The perukemaker Edward Tasker 1740-62 preceded his son Thomas, and their barber's shop by the *White Hart* doubtless seethed with news and gossip. Their neighbours, the innkeeper William Verrall and the hatter Richard Palmer, managed the "rides" to Eastbourne and Mayfield. In 1765 Lewesians and Mr Potts from the Post Office met at Claremont, the Duke's mansion near Esher, to discuss resuming a direct post with London along the newly turnpiked roads; they agreed that postboys from Lewes and East Grinstead should exchange bags at Uckfield. This new service carried the burgeoning post between Brighton and London, which brought Thomas Tasker a fourfold increase in salary by 1770, but hastened perhaps his suicide in 1779. His successor was a "correct, honest, worthy" shoemaker, Samuel Dunstone 1778-1822, during whose tenure Brighton, Eastbourne and Mayfield achieved direct links with London.

Despite better roads Lewes's commerce still depended in part on the shipping in Newhaven harbour. Anchored there in 1825, the 36-gun frigate *Hyperion* was much studied from St Anne's churchyard through a spy-glass. From Spital Hill Gideon Mantell noticed

> a fine rainbow stretched through the mist across Firle hills, and the sea by Newhaven harbour caught a gleam of light which shewed a little fleet of colliers lying near it to great advantage.

Yet till 1733 the harbour was impaired by coastal shingle drifting across Seaford Bay, which pushed the outfall of the Ouse ever eastward. As William Camden observed in his *Britannia* (1586), "the South-west wind doth tyrannise, casting up beach infinitely". By choking the harbour and estuary, the shingle also impeded the drainage of the watermeadows up to Lewes and along Glynde Reach to Laughton. In the 1530s Dutch engineers were consulted, and a "new cut" was made, diverting the outfall from Seaford to its ancient site below Castle Hill in Meeching (now Newhaven). By 1664 this New Haven was itself choked, so a coterie of courtiers tried to remodel it as a harbour of refuge and military base "over against the Naval of France", a rival to Dover and Portsmouth. Before the venture foundered an east pier was built, which collapsed by the 1680s.

Though Lewesians then petitioned for a new breakwater to stem the shingle, 13 ships laden with Southdown corn lay trapped in the choked anchorage in December 1730, when the river partly debouched a mile to the east.

Though belated, the Harbour Commission set up in 1731 did quickly build two effective breakwaters, east and west. Ships of 150 tons could still dock in 1754, though more typical was the 55-ton brig *Catherine* arriving in 1790 from Rotterdam with cheese and bulrushes. In 1791-3 the piers were realigned, less directly into the run of the waves. The Napoleonic wars revived schemes for a deep-water naval base, especially after the storm-tossed HMS *Brazen* sank in the harbour approaches. But John Rennie's plan for a 20-acre dock proved too expensive, though in the 1820s the approaches did benefit from the dredging of boulder flints, destined for potteries in Staffordshire and glassworks in Lancashire.

Newhaven Bridge

In 1828 the freighters based at Newhaven averaged 64 tons. By then the decline of corn exports had largely reduced the port's foreign trade to inward cargoes of Norwegian timber, Baltic grain, Iberian wine, Dutch cheese and oats. However coastal freighters were still "constantly trading" with London, Hull, Sunderland, Newcastle, Leith, Portsmouth, Plymouth, Falmouth, Tenby, Waterford, Cork, Bangor, Caernarvon, Beaumaris and Liverpool. They exchanged wheat and flour for consumer goods, coal, iron, oats, butter, cheese, bacon, salt, slate and building stone. Cross-

Channel ferries also docked. After Napoleon's defeat in 1814 Lord Sheffield, who owned Meeching manor, promoted the 116-ton schooner *Wellington* as a weekly summer packet boat to Dieppe - a venture typical of his energy and tact. In June 1826 the General Steam Navigation Company despatched the *Eclipse* twice a week, via the chain pier at Brighton.

Along the Ouse barge traffic faced many hazards till canalization in the 1790s. Floods were frequent and severe; in November 1773 water lapped the 10th brick below the cornice of the *Bear* by Lewes bridge. Lack of water in April 1762 prevented boulders and sand being carried from Lewes to Glynde bridge. When a Great Frost and heavy snow blocked the channel near Southerham Corner in 1775-6, unemployed Lewes lightermen paraded a boat with hoisted sails round the town, and made a "handsome" collection. North-easterly

Lewes Bridge 1781 (Horsfield's History)

winds, and the press gang, also interrupted traffic with Newhaven harbour, causing coal prices at Lewes to soar. Even without such hazards, a 20-ton barge could still take three days to voyage up the "serpentine and languid" Ouse.

After advice from John Smeaton the Commissioners for Lewes and Laughton Levels dredged and widened the channels below Lewes in 1768, though most "Crooks" and meanders remained when the Lower Ouse Navigation Company was formed in 1791. For it William Jessop prepared a thorough canalization, supervised by Cater Rand (1749-1825), a Lewes schoolmaster and civil engineer. Several hundred navvies had realigned the channel from Lewes down to Southease by February 1795; in October salt water reached the bridge, killing fish and polluting wells. Because the tides now flowed faster up and down the river, they also drained the water-meadows and thoroughly scoured Newhaven harbour, making access "easier and safer", though some bargemen bemoaned the stronger currents. The improvement of Glynde Reach in 1796-1803 better drained Ranscombe Brooks and Laughton Levels, even if chair-bottomers were deprived of bulrushes, and bald coots of winter quarters. In the 1820s the River-Superintendent John Ellman further refined the channel to Newhaven, enabling the 120-ton *Kitty* to unload York stone at Lewes bridge, and the *Gage*, a two-masted brig, to moor near Southerham, laden with oats from Riga. In April 1829 the worst floods below Lewes in 20 years dispersed within 48 hours; and in 1838 the engineer William Cubitt secured the removal of Tapsfield's Shallow near the bridge.

The Ouse above Lewes was canalized less smoothly. Barcombe mill remained the terminus for barges in April 1790 when the Upper Ouse Navigation Company began to tackle the 28 sinuous miles between Lewes bridge and the river's source near Slaugham, with cuts to Offham chalkpit and Shortbridge in Fletching. To accommodate barges up to 30 tons, William Jessop planned a minimum depth of four feet between 27 locks, and a width at the water's surface of 24 feet. In July 1791 tolls were levied at the new Hamsey lock. But then the contractors, Messrs Pinkerton, defaulted, leaving a chaos of half-built cuts above Barcombe mill; and though by 1793 barges could reach Sheffield bridge, a general collapse of credit, consequent on war with France, again disrupted work. The Navigation reached Freshfield bridge in 1799 and Lindfield in 1809, and expired in 1812 at Upper Ryelands bridge, 22 miles above Lewes.

Even when this chequered progress was complete, the income from tolls never allowed a dividend. By 1814, on the eve of a post-war Depression, the Company was heavily in debt. Lord Sheffield, a leading promoter, blamed incompetence and secrecy for the "Well-nigh useless and declining Navigation". The locks were even chained during a dispute with the barge-owners. They carried beach, sand, lime, coal and foreign timber upstream into a Wealden hinterland which yielded sandstone, bricks, wool, grain, oak timber and bark. But hopes that coal could be supplied to Crawley and Reigate, more cheaply than from London, proved groundless. Nor was a junction ever made with any London to Portsmouth waterway, though in 1810 John Rennie's scheme for a Grand Southern Canal from the Medway at Tonbridge, through Edenbridge to Horsham, did include a branch from Three Bridges across Worth Forest to the Upper Ouse. In 1825 an 18-mile cut direct to Tonbridge was canvassed, as part of a Newhaven-to-Chatham ship canal. That year optimists also projected a waterway from Lewes to Kemp Town, through Southover and under Newmarket Hill; and another linking Glynde Reach with the river Cuckmere and Horsebridge mill near Hailsham. But a national spate of bank-failures dashed any hope of Lewes becoming the Stourport of Sussex. However the "declining" Upper Navigation lingered on through the 1830s, and transported the bricks for the Balcombe viaduct which carried the London-Brighton railway across it.

At Lewes the wharfs mostly fringed the river on the Cliffe side, where 13 bargemen and lightermen struck work in April 1723, demanding a third share of any profits. In 1755 the bargemen, Richard Mills, William Bunting and James Hillman, were neighbours near the *Ship* in riverside South Street, a thoroughfare obstructed in the 1680s by stacks of timber and the test-firing of Wealden cannon. Wharfs also abutted the back gardens of houses in West Street, along the Ouse to the south and the Great Sewer to the north. In 1801 28 barges were based at Cliffe and Malling, nine at Newhaven, and none in Lewes Borough. The Gastons, who were Cliffe timber merchants, owned six; and William Robinson, "commonly called the Admiral", who rebuilt 79 South Street in 1784, had nine. The rest mostly belonged to the Hillman clan of chalk quarriers and lime burners, including all seven barges trading upstream, and the *Nelson*, at 40 tons the Leviathan of the Ouse. By 1811, with the Upper Navigation approaching Ryelands bridge, the Cliffe and Malling fleet numbered 34. On the Borough bank the Town wharf and other quays, which clustered near the bridge, berthed only a 13-ton pleasure boat in 1804. At Southover, where a few punts for trapping eels were moored, the Cockshut Stream was sometimes dredged.

The hazards of navigation along the Ouse were outstripped of course by those on the high seas, where rough weather sank Lewes-bound cargoes of Hampshire salt and Tyneside coal. And when the south-westerlies raged, the approaches to Newhaven harbour through Seaford Bay became a boiling maelstrom, the marine equivalent of Low Wealden mud. Along its shore in the 1660s official storehouses protected the wrecked merchandise that escaped plunder on its shelving rocks: wine, brandy, molasses, brazil wood, sperm oil, indigo, beaver furs and French silks. A sensational wreck in January 1748 was the *Nympha Americana*, a mighty Spanish galleon, about 800 tons burden, built "chiefly of Cedar". Captured near Cadiz, she broke up off Crowlink, spilling her cargo of "Superfine Velvets, Clothes, Gold and Silver Laces", along with "near 30,000 Pounds Sterling Value of Quicksilver". Greed and pilfered brandy so frenzied the swarming salvagers that sixty (allegedly) "perished on the Beach, Downs and other places". An engraving depicted Mr Richardson of Alciston Falling, and Thc Body of the Doctor Who was Drowned. The quicksilver, officially retrieved, was bought by the Lewes clockmaker Thomas Harben, reputedly at a heavy profit.

Storm off Castle Hill, Newhaven (Horsfield's History)

Corpses were also salvaged in the Bay. Two "cast up on the beach" became a charge on Bishopstone manor in 1773; and his burial of others at East Dean and Friston caused Parson Jonathan Darby 1706-26 to take remedial action, anticipating Parson Hawker at Morwenstowe as a "sailor's friend". Through the cliff near Belle Tout he tunnelled down to the shore a flight of steps, which also opened onto a balcony with a signal lamp, 20 feet above high water. In 1834 Trinity House adopted the makeshift lighthouse that superseded his "Darby Hole". Lewes merchants also tried to lessen the Distress of Shipwreck. In 1787 they stationed mobile cranes along the cliffs between Brighton and Beachy Head, to winch men and merchandise to safety. When the *Pelham*, a Newhaven-registered freighter, sank off Flamborough Head in 1791, eight co-owners headed a subscription at Lewes for Captain Potts's widow and children; and after HMS *Brazen* sank on the Ave Rocks near Newhaven, with 119 of her crew, Lewesians collected for a lifeboat there. Sheathed and lined with cork, her "buoyant powers" a match for any seas, she was delivered from South Shields by Captain Higham in May 1803, and rowed upriver to Lewes bridge for inspection. Larger vessels were urged to

Strike your proud flags; your tops in homage wave
To one small boat, whose purpose is to SAVE!

Though most Lewesians insured their cargoes, the High Calvinist iron founder, Ebenezer Morris, relied on Divine Providence, "not falling down to worship the God of carnal contrivances, the Golden Calf of an insurance office". In August 1837 an inner voice caused him to purchase his pig-iron early, escaping thereby a sudden rise in price. His cargo left port (possibly Bristol) aboard the *William*, along with the *Enterprize* and the *Sisters* carrying supplies for other Lewesians. These two reached Newhaven a fortnight later, but not the *William*, which prompted Pastor Vinall to lead Ebenezer's fellow brethren at Jireh Chapel in strenuous prayer till the vessel arrived, after repairing in a West Country port some storm damage sustained off Lundy Island.

Privateers, many of them based at Dunkirk or Dieppe, also menaced Lewes-owned merchandise. During Marlborough's war in 1704-13 Newhaven's trade slumped heavily; indeed because the Straits of Dover were so infested, Southdown corn jolted overland to London from Lewes. French privateers took the *Birmingham*, freighted with cheese from Gainsborough, in 1779; the *Good Intent*, returning with butter and coal from Tenby, in 1781; the *Lewes*, bound for Lyme

Regis with timber, in 1796; and the *Bacchus*, laden with flour milled at Barcombe for the garrison on Guernsey, in 1800. But the lugger that captured Newhaven's *Captain Broho* and the *Happy Return* in 1780 was American. Two Lewesians, Messrs Cardin and Jarvis, fought back by arming the *Panther*, though she ran ashore at Newhaven in 1746, forfeiting her best anchor and cable to Mistress Gibbon, the Lady of Meeching manor, and the historian's benevolent aunt. Protection by the Royal Navy was much in demand, especially during the Napoleonic wars when the mid-Sussex economy boomed so steadily. In 1800 Lord Pelham secured a cutter, the *Lion*, to patrol the Newhaven approaches, much as Sir John Pelham had solicited some small frigates to deter the pillaging Dutch in 1672. Yet the Navy could itself be a hazard. In 1801 a cutter off the North Foreland fired into the *Welcome Messenger*, bringing groceries from London for Lewes. The press-gang too was a menace. Newhaven harbour "entirely stopped" when the crew of the *Lewes Trader* was seized in June 1741; and again in November 1776 after warrants had "pressed" all the seamen there. Even in December 1826 rumours of impressment deterred Lewes bargemen venturing downstream.

Some Lewes traders invested in Newhaven's merchant fleet which grew from four freighters (115 tons) in 1701 to 16 (1024 tons) in 1828. Already in 1606 the *Eleanor Stansfield* bore the name of John Evelyn's grandmother whose husband dealt in groceries, wine and wheat. In 1687-88 the Quaker Ambrose Galloway often used the *Plain Dealing*; and since the name publicized his Protestant Ethic, he probably owned (or part-owned) her. In the 1720s the *Lewes Adventure* and the *Ringmer* trafficked overseas from Newhaven. Merchants in the town trading with Barbados had the *Lewes* built at Newhaven in 1755. The *Lewes Trader*, awaiting cargoes at Southwark in 1777, was Lewes-owned, likewise a timber-brig stranded near Newhaven in 1786. The Quaker corn merchants, Thomas Rickman & Son, based at Lewes and Barcombe mill, owned the *Hope* and the *Good Intent* in 1785, and fractions of the *Happy Return*, the *Lark*, the *Susanna* and the *Industry*. The portfolio of timber merchant William Gaston in 1792 included a seventh of a snow, an eighth of a brigantine, and a sixteenth of a sloop, the *Gage*. Lewesians investing in the *Pelham*, lost off Flamborough Head, included merchants, grocers, a soap boiler and a banker. The Cliffe iron founders, Polhill & Gibson, commissioned a sloop at Newhaven shipyard in 1811.

Also an investor in the *Pelham* was Parson James Hurdis at

Bishopstone, whose verse depicted the vessels in Newhaven harbour laden with coal, corn, flour, timber and Lewes-bound groceries:

Me pleases much the bustle of the port;
The toil and clamour of the pros'prous bark,
Safe landing on the wharf with brisk dispatch
Her sable cargo from the northern mine;
The neater vessel her capacious lap
Filling with grain, or (stowage ponderous)
The mealy sack of the contiguous mill,
Welcome supply to the far-distant camp,
Or wind-bound fleet of war; the slothful barge
Slug-like conveying from the sloop her deals,
Another from the sloven brig her load
of nauseous grocery, abundant store
For ev'ry village on the banks of Ouse,
And chiefly for yon borough built in air,
Whose ancient castle lifts its brow sublime
To frown upon the flood they cross below.

Bishopstone's Painter-Poet also noted Newhaven's "sounding ship-yard". Mr Dyer built a "fine" vessel there in 1758, and probably launched the *Lewes* for the Barbados merchants in 1755. The *Lewes Journal* in 1782 recalled 40-gun ships being constructed there "in former wars...with utter expedition and safety". 2000 spectators cheered the launch of the *Jamaica Planter* in 1784, followed soon after by a 70-ton sloop for Thomas Rickman & Son. Thomas Tasker built the "iron" sloop for Polhill & Gibson, and James Duly constructed the *Ouse* in 1832, a brig for Lewesians trading with Holland. At Cliffe sea-going spritsail barges were constructed in 1824; and the removal of Tapsfield's Shallow in 1838 preceded the launch of the 400-ton *Lewes Castle* by Rickman & Godlee at their new yard below the bridge in 1839. Earlier, in the 1730s, the Cliffe shipwright James Stanton was "much used" by the Lewes merchant John Whitfeld; and in 1754 Thomas Stanton, probably his executor and a shipbuilder at Rotherhithe, gave a handsome altarpiece to Cliffe church.

2
The Mart of Mid-Sussex: The Exchange of Local Produce

The agricultural and pastoral character of the people on whom [Georgian Casterbridge] depended for its existence was shown by the class of objects displayed in the shop windows. Scythes, reap-hooks, sheep-shears, bill-hooks, spades, mattocks, and hoes at the ironmonger's; bee-hives, butter-firkins, churns, milking-stools and pails, hay-rakes, field-flagons, and seed-lips at the cooper's; cart-ropes and plough-harness at the saddler's; carts, wheel-barrows, and mill-gear at the wheelwright's and machinist's; horse-embrocations at the chemist's; at the glover's and leather-cutter's, hedging-gloves, thatcher's knee-caps, ploughman's leggings, villager's pattens and clogs.

THOMAS HARDY, *THE MAYOR OF CASTERBRIDGE*.

Like Casterbridge, Georgian Lewes "lived by agriculture", by hosting the exchange of Southdown and Wealden produce. It too was "the pole, focus, or nerve-knot of the surrounding country"; and doubtless "corn and cattle-disease" were discussed as doggedly at its dinner parties as they were at Dorchester's. In 1714 the Saturday corn market was held at Castlegate Corner, where the wooden market house, as befitted a regional rendez-vous, boasted a clock, a whipping post, and a board for proclamations. At this hub of public commerce in 1775 the attorney Charles Gilbert received heavy compensation for slander from the attorney Henry Burtenshaw; when the money changed hands all eyes turned from the samples of wheat, barley and clover seed loading the tables. In 1793 the market house was demolished, since dealing was now more snugly done in the Great Room at the *Star*. Much local wheat, after trading at Lewes, was exported through Newhaven: cargoes that Henry Pelham applauded in 1753 as the cornerstone of Southdown prosperity. But exports overseas dwindled by the mid-1780s, so great was domestic demand; and after 1818 they ceased. Coastwise shipments continued, except in "famine" years of soaring bread prices when Southdown corn was needed locally. Flour too was shipped away, much of it ground at the tidemills built near Bishopstone in the 1760s by three Chichester merchants, who also sent wheat from Newhaven to Portsmouth, Plymouth and Liverpool, on board the *Seaford* and the *Chilgrove*. From a powerful watermill at Barcombe, via a warehouse at Bear Yard in Cliffe, Thomas Rickman & Son despatched grain in 1785 to Southampton, Plymouth and Whitehaven, and to Spain, Leghorn and Madeira. Being Quakers, they supplied local bakeries at moderate prices in 1795, a famine year when the Prince of Wales at Brighton heroically renounced white bread. About 1803 they built a second mill at Barcombe, to crush oil from rape and linseed. And great was the local "surprise and alarm" when their successor, Samuel Woodgate Durrant, defaulted in 1829. Among his Southdown creditors cramming the Great Room at the *Star*, to receive 14s 6d in the pound, was another flour-Mogul, William Catt (c1776-1853). A partner at Bishopstone tidemills by 1801, he increased the stones there to 16, and won contracts to victual the coastal barracks and encampments deployed against Napoleon. Though his epitaph at Bishopstone spoke of a "strict adherence to Justice", he was thought to profiteer in famine years; hence the malediction scratched on house-plaster at Southover in June 1817: "Flour 2/11d. a galon...God grant it may soon fall: And Cat may fall with it: is my wish".

By 1714 the three watermills at Southover were defunct; their silted ponds had become Fissenden's physic garden, Shelley's garden, and The Pool, an osier bed north of Pigeonhouse Croft. But the windmills on the Downs above Lewes were usually rebuilt after damage from tempest or fire, though burnt-out Cliffe mill was abandoned in 1760. Malling mill, worked by John Gallop in 1596, became an ultra-modern postmill about 1810. A storm-struck mill on Cranedown rose again in 1798 as a fantailed smockmill; in 1832 a superb Cluniac capital, carved with scenes from the life of St Peter, was found beneath it, a reminder that Southover Priory once owned a mill there. Just across Juggs Road, a postmill with a tailpiece was built by 1781, during the agricultural boom; George Pescod used both till bankruptcy struck in 1825. Three years later a postmill with six splendid sweeps was completed further down Juggs Road towards Nan Kemp's Corner near Ashcombe. By 1828 three mills also graced the environs of the racecourse. Spital mill was rebuilt as a post-and-trestle mill in 1818 by John Kennard who managed the pens at the sheep fair; and Steere's became a smockmill in 1826. The third began life in 1802 as a Subscription Mill on the Town Wall above Westgate Lane, "to grind corn at a moderate price for ready money", and so alleviate Distress in famine years. But in 1819 teams of bullocks drew it on a trolley to a site beyond the Spital crossroads, more open to "trade winds". The brick stump remained in Pipe Passage, and briefly tempted Virginia Woolf, house-hunting in 1919.

Lewes also attracted millwrights. The celebrated George Packham (1792-1872), born at Shortbridge mill in Fletching, trained with Mr Sudds at Cliffe. For Louis Philippe he built a complex of corn, oil and timber mills near Dieppe; and when the fugitive king reached the Bridge Hotel at Newhaven in 1848, wearing a shabby blouse and cap, he summoned Packham from Brighton, and loaded him with silver coin to replenish the royal wardrobe. Samuel Medhurst (1799-1887) constructed Ashcombe mill, and sent machinery to Sheffield mill in Fletching from his yard near the *Black Horse* (now Caffyn's garage); in St Anne's churchyard 11 iron graves commemorate his wife and children. From Foundry Lane in 1828 William Hubbard

Samuel Medhurst (Reeves)

Ashcombe Mill

tendered for a treadmill at the House of Correction: six feet high and over 21 feet long, with 30 tread boards, it could connect with a flour mill outside the prison wall. He repaired Barcombe oil mill, Isfield paper mill, a Lewes bark mill, and a sugar mill at Southover. For Mr Kenward he built a smockmill at Hailsham in 1834.

The chalk quarries at Cliffe, Malling, Southerham, Landport and Offham, so conveniently close to the navigable Ouse, also prospered. During the agricultural boom much lime was needed to sweeten the new acreages of wheat in the Low Weald, "on whose more chilly lap", as Parson Hurdis noted, "Brown harvest loiters". In 1773 James Ticehurst worked an ancient pit off North Street, which became an overspill graveyard for the waterlogged parish of Cliffe. The Hillmans who quarried in Malling owned in 1801 the seven Lewes-based barges carrying chalk into the Weald. Gideon Mantell found his first fossil fish at Robert Hillman's pit off South Street, where 6000 tons of chalk collapsed in 1804, a rehearsal for the avalanche near by in December 1836 which killed eight occupants of Boulder Row, the Malling poorhouse. In 1819 Robert's sons supplied chalk rubble for the bold new turnpike road across Ranscombe brooks. But in 1826 John split away to work pits near Southerham Corner and Malling mill. From a counting-house by the *Dorset Arms* he sent his lime, "well burnt, grey and white", by cart to Blackboys, Cross-in-Hand and beyond, and by barge along the Ouse Navigation. Across the river near Offham George Shiffner of Coombe Place opened a new pit in 1801, finding "the Chalk Rock" very quickly. In 1809 he commissioned the first inclined railway in Sussex, which linked another new pit there and its lime kilns with a cut from the Ouse. Cater Rand suggested this "spirited undertaking", with its double tunnel under the Lewes-Offham road: its

> Machinery, iron waggons, rails and other gear were manufactured at the Butterly Works, in Derbyshire, and put together by Mr. Espin, its superintendent and engineer. A loaded waggon carries a ton and a half at a trip, running down the plane in one minute and a half, and drawing up an empty one.

The sale of Southdown barley at Lewes encouraged malting and brewing there, though by the 1820s demand outstripped supply, and East Anglian barley came in through Newhaven. Brewing also stimulated an informal hop exchange. In 1714 an eighth of England's hop acreage lay in the Sussex Weald, and two gardens blossomed on The

Island at Southover. From Lewes hops were sent overland to the London breweries, and perhaps to the great Weyhill Fair on the Hampshire Downs. Cargoes also passed through Newhaven: to Devon in the 1670s; to Tenby in 1759; to Waterford in 1785, along with Wealden oak bark; and to Christiana in 1833.

At Southover in 1714 at least five malthouses tapped the pure spring water below. From Gables Cottage Richard Dunke had shipped 640 bushels to London in 1668; but production ceased by 1772. The Verrall family engrossed the others. At The Old Brewery House the maltster John (1697-1784) begat the maltster John II (c1725-1808) and the brewer William (1721- 88), who begat the maltster Harry (1763-1849) and the brewer William II (1759-1837), who begat the brewer William III (1798-1890). John II bought Anne of Cleves House and its malthouse, leaving it to nephew Harry who rebuilt the malthouse at The Old Brewery House. William II acquired the brewery and malthouse at Fairhall, and the *Bell* nearby (now the *Swan*). He also purchased the *Dolphin* and the *Pelham Arms* in the Borough, the *Fountain* at Cliffe, the *Cock* at Ringmer, the *Rose & Crown* at Mayfield, and from shopkeeper Thomas Turner, the *Kings Head* at East Hoathly. He held mortgages on other Wealden public houses at Ripe, Rotherfield and Burwash, and at Brighton on the *Star of Brunswick*, the *Norfolk Hotel* and the *Gloucester Hotel*. At Southover William III bought the defunct *Swan*, and in 1828 rebuilt the adjacent malthouse which the Davey family had worked since before 1714. He then annexed the *Star* at Waldron, the first of many Wealden houses. About 1840 he gained a genteel veneer by acquiring Southover manor and the Priory lands, though his tenant there, Parson Harry West, still chose to identify him as "a small-beer brewer" on the final cheque for rent. But nothing daunted him as seigneur of Southover; he presided with aplomb at the Court Leet, the Gas Committee and the Bonfire, a declared foe of Mr Gladstone and of parish spending on public drains.

Verrall's Brewery (Reeves)

Malting and brewing also flourished at Cliffe where the wells pierced through the "slub and sea sand" to the chalk. From the 1750s John Rickman, the Quaker brother of miller Thomas at Barcombe, practised both at Bear Yard, which he bought in 1766 along with the Bear. Then came his son Richard (1745-1801), and grandson John II who opened the *Thatched House* in South Street, and annexed a string of Wealden public houses: the *Ship* at Cuckfield, the *Swan* at East Grinstead, the *Anchor* on the Ouse Navigation at Barcombe with its own Dock or Basin, the *Ship* at Ringmer (also convenient for bargemen), the *Buck* at Laughton, the *Plough* at Arlington, the *Gun* at Chiddingly, the *White Hart* at Hellingly, the *George* at Hailsham, the *Greyhound* at Framfield, the *New Inn* at Hadlow Down, the *Five Ashes* and the *Royal Oak* at Mayfield, the *Wheel* and the *Admiral Vernon* at Burwash. But John II, a cradle Quaker, became also a total abstainer; so in 1817 he sold the brewery and its tied houses to Roff Tamplin and Thomas Wood. He retired to Wellingham House in Ringmer, and being "a particular man", he cautioned his bailiff to stop children playing amid the barns and yards.

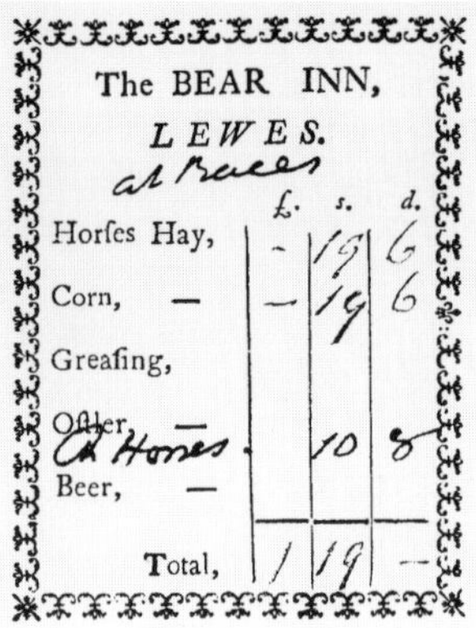
The BEAR INN,
LEWES.

	£.	s.	d.
Horfes Hay,	-	19	6
Corn, —	-	19	6
Greafing,			
Oftler, —			
		10	8
Beer, —			
Total,	1	19	--

Four other malthouses in Cliffe and Malling swelled the crammed commercial portfolio of the clockmaker, ironmonger and banker, Thomas Harben, till his bankruptcy in 1793. Two in Swing Pump Lane were disposed of to Richard Rickman and Harry Verrall; another, opposite the *Dorset Arms,* to George Wille; and a fourth, near the *Wheatsheaf,* to Thomas Berry whose son Thomas opened a brewery near by in 1821, which he sold to Wymark & Son in 1842.

In the Borough William Brett and Obadiah Elliot used a malt-house and brewery between Fisher Street and Cask Lane in the 1730s. A Wealdsman from hop-growing Hartfield, Elliot's weight provoked the wit of Lewes apprentices. He bought the *Ship* in 1769, renaming it the *Brewers Arms.* His son John practised Law, so the brewery passed to Henry Scrase 1775-96, Christophilus Chitty (c1766-1839), Thomas Beard, Charles Chitty 1825-41 and Edward Beard 1825-59. The firm annexed the *Lewes Arms* in 1782 and the *Black Horse* in 1817. By 1825 it controlled the *Brighton Arms* at Brighton, the *Abergavenny Arms* at Rottingdean, the *Greyhound* at Ardingly, the *Norfolk Arms* at Balcombe, the *Swan* at Chailey, the *Bat*

& Ball at Chiddingly, and the *Abergavenny Arms* at Tunbridge Wells. Elliot's descendants in 1802 sold the *Brewers Arms* to its landlord James Wood; in the 1830s Chartists crowded its clubroom and skittle-alley.

Just behind Cask Lane Robert Chester (c1720-69), a Wealdsman from Ewhurst, worked a brewery in Castle Yard, with a malthouse near Westgate Corner. His brother-in-law William Cooper, a hop-grower and grazier from Udimore, then nurtured the enterprise till Robert's nephew, Robert Chester Cooper (c1759-1803), took over. By 1785 the Castle Brewery owned the *Crown*, the *White Lion and* the *Castle* in the Borough, the *Kings Head* in Southover, and the *Ship* at Cliffe. Robert bought the *Wheatsheaf*, and opened the *Stag* and the *Lamb*. He also used a malthouse in St Marys Lane, built in the 1730s by the Duke of Newcastle for a destitute voter, evicted by local Tories. When hops and malt were dear, he shipped in London porter. His son Robert renounced trade to become a Magistrate and Deputy-Lieutenant; so his Langford relatives, Benjamin and John (1784-1850), took over. In 1809 they feasted 15 employees inside a new vessel for storing strong beer which, being Radical Whigs, they christened "Mrs Clarke", after the capacious mistress of the Duke of York, the Commander-in-Chief, whose army patronage she manipulated. In 1825 they opened the *Kings Arms* in North Street, and closed the *Castle*, by then a seedy tavern much used by Trampers, being in the extra-parochial, un-policed Castle Precincts. By 1830 Lewes's brewers controlled all but four of its public houses: the *Brewers Arms*; the *Running Horse* and the *Dorset Arms*, which the Brighton brewer George Wigney snapped up; and the *White Horse*, opened in St Marys Lane by coal merchant John Dennet in 1792, and bought by wine merchant Adam Harvey.

In 1754 Dr Pococke noted Lewes's "considerable" trade in Sussex wool. While watching a cricket match at Alfriston the town's leading dealer, Thomas Friend (c1690-1761), advised Thomas Turner on current prices. In 1737 he bought part of Brighton manor, later the site of Kemp Town. At Lewes he remodelled Barbican House, his High Street home, and acquired the *White Horse*, an ancient hostelry defunct by 1780. His assets passed to a great-nephew and wool merchant, Thomas Kemp (1745-1811) who wedded Ann Read, the heiress of a rich grazier in Romney Marsh. These riches fuelled his election in 1780 as an MP for Lewes Borough, though opponents mocked his trade and his wife's "low Boeotian origins". In 1785 he quitted Barbican House for Coneysborough in Barcombe, a compact Low Wealden estate, where as a gentleman-farmer he sheared his flock twice a year by way of experiment. His Brighton residence he sold to Louis Weltje, the Prince of Wales's kitchen clerk. His son, Thomas Read Kemp, married a daughter of Sir Francis Baring, the banker-chairman of the East India Company, an alliance calculated to bury the most Boeotian of origins.

Thomas Kemp's upward mobility kept pace with a surging wool trade. From 1750 each July for 30 years William Boys, the owner of Ashcombe Farm near Lewes, deposited at the *Bear* a pack for Mr Collins at Devizes. In July 1780 many out-county buyers came to Lewes; they "bought largely on speculation and gave good prices". These climbed even higher as Southdown fleeces improved, and English textile manufacturers pioneered a self-sustained Industrial Revolution. Wool from John Ellman's model flock at Glynde doubled in price between the 1770s and 1800-04. To co-ordinate dealing with out-county buyers, local "growers" launched an annual fair in July 1787. After a dinner at the *Star*, the *White Hart* or the *Bear*, Lord Sheffield, who tinkered with wool statistics and Spanish sheep, would deliver a detailed analysis of market trends. In 1792 120 growers and buyers attended; in 1796 negotiations deadlocked. Prominent among out-county buyers were Messrs Drew, Dyer, Nottage and Gardiner. Once sold, the wool mostly went overland to London: one laden waggon overturned at Sheffield bridge.

Lewes's three livestock fairs were medieval in origin. At the one held in Cliffe on St Matthew's Day in September "great quantities of sheep" were sold in the 1690s; Wealdsmen from Ashburnham attending. About 1747 the Fair Place behind the church became so overcrowded that dealing moved to a field near Malling mill, and then in 1783 to The Paddock, just north of the Borough, though Landlord Hearnden at the *Wheatsheaf* in Malling doggedly staged "the usual and charter Cliffe fair" till 1788. As farming boomed, ever more sheep and lambs converged: 15,000 in 1776 and 30,000 in 1805 when the Duke of Clarence chatted amiably among the wattles. And because John Ellman's improved Southdowns were publicized in Arthur Young's *Annals of Agriculture*, they drew out-county buyers from East Anglia, Bedfordshire, Devon, Wessex, Middlesex, Surrey and the Kentish Weald. In 1809 a meeting at the *Star* of "the most respectable Owners and Occupiers of Land on the SOUTH DOWNS" decided the fair should revert to 21 September (its date before the Calendar Reform in 1752),

> on Account of Croydon and other Fairs being held on the 2nd of October, as on Account of the Buyers of Ewes who live at a Distance, not being able to get them Home in Time to take the Ram.

But some dealers preferred 2 October which gave Kentish graziers time to garner their hops beforehand. So in 1810 over 50,000 sheep and lambs were penned in September, and 10,000 in October. These bustling scenes, so worthy "the pencil of a landskip painter", eclipsed the autumn sheep fair at Selmeston, though "epicures from Lewes" attended it "to feast on the griskins served up by Colman the Cook of St Crispin".

The two cattle fairs were less busy. "Vast droves" of Welsh runts funnelled through Guildford to fatten in Pevensey Marsh, "the Goschen of Sussex", and then funnelled back through Hailsham and Horsebridge towards Smithfield; but they bypassed Lewes and stimulated dealing elsewhere. In the 1690s Nutley's April fair on Ashdown Forest specialized in milk-cows and steers; and Wealdsmen so depended on the November fair at Battle for "winter" stock, that many quitted a county election at Chichester without voting, when the High Sheriff cunningly spun out the polling to coincide with it. The fair at Cliffe on St Mark's Day (25 April: Old Style), specialized in Black Cattle. But in 1819 the largest display in living memory assembled only 500 oxen, bulls and cows, mostly "Country, Devon and Welch" in origin. Out-county buyers were few; some from Buckinghamshire in 1793 were hoping for low prices because several Sussex banks had failed, causing a local cash shortage. The other fair, catering for lean cattle, was held in the Borough on Whitsun Tuesday, the day after the Civic Feast (which in Tudor times had followed the Militia Muster). But again the displays of Welsh runts and Wealden cattle were never more than "good".

However a rising demand at Brighton for meat did stimulate a steady trade in livestock at Lewes. The seawater cure and the Prince of Wales sent the resort's population soaring, to 12,000 in 1811 and to over 40,000 in 1831. Its butchers found Lewes a convenient place to buy Wealden and marshland cattle, so a monthly Tuesday market was begun on Castle Banks in April 1810. It soon became fortnightly, and shifted to the High Street near the *Crown*, causing that "agreeable bustle, which Tradesmen always like to see", despite the occasional bull in a china shop. One drover attending in May 1823 was

Mr Hesman, who set out on Monday morning from the *New Inn* at Pevensey, and collected livestock at Rickney and Hailsham, at the *Bat & Ball* in Horsebridge, and at Laughton pond. Brightonians also frequented the horse auctions at Lewes. Indeed in Thackeray's *Vanity Fair* loungers at the resort in the weeks before Waterloo could eat jellies at Dutton's, watch the Lightning coach arrive from London, or inspect the horses bought at Lewes fair. The Lewes dealer George Drowley c1805-23 kept the spacious Market Street Mews, while Francis Kettle managed the Sussex Mews opposite the *Star*, besides leasing the Riding School in Fisher Street. Their search for "prime specimens" took them to fairs at Lincoln, Pershore, Horncastle and Melton Mowbray.

The town's livestock trade prompted some farriers to practise animal medicine, especially those in the Cliffe near the approaches to the Fair Place. Edward Tooth in 1774 was paid for "care of horses and doctoring cows" at Coombe Place in Hamsey. John Newton followed his father George in 1824 as a Horse-Surgeon, Cutter and Bullock-Leach. Simon Grover & Son proclaimed themselves full-blown veterinary surgeons in 1829.

Local butter was also traded. Ned Penfold was blown from his horse, bringing supplies from Hurstpierpoint in April 1715. At Lewes Thomas Turner bartered butter collected near East Hoathly for three wigs. Cold weather in November 1828 froze the linen cloths of women selling at the provision market, which was started in 1791 to break the town's dependence on higglers of Wealden butter, eggs and poultry. Its success so undermined the ancient weekly market at Cliffe that the market house by St Thomas's church was demolished before 1820.

Butter and livestock, corn and clover, were often discussed at Lewes by the landowners of Sussex when gathered there for the assizes and the summer races. So the town focused a Society they formed in 1771 for the Encouragement of Agriculture, with the Duke of Richmond as President, and draper John Madgwick on School Hill as Treasurer. But Sir John Bridger huffily resigned in 1775, and the Society disbanded in 1778. More resilient was the Sussex Agricultural Society which held its first annual show at Lewes on 31 July 1797, the day between the Brighton and Lewes races, otherwise devoted to Prize Fighting and Low Gaming. After viewing the fatstock, Lord Egremont and the county elite dined at the *Star* with the Prince of Wales, who subscribed merely as "an Inhabitant of

Sussex" and disclaimed any agrarian expertise. Dining there again in 1805, the Prince and fellow members were thanked by Mr Coke of Norfolk for a small Southdown flock, given him for popularizing the breed in East Anglia; afterwards Mr Lestor from Piccadilly set in motion a newfangled threshing machine.

Lewes's vitality as a market prompted its townsfolk to process the by-products of local farming. Supplies of tallow were collected from Newick and Fletching in 1770 (in the sort of hamper used to store executed murderers, earmarked for dissection). The Cliffe tallow chandler, George Verrall 1749-84, supplied soap and candles to Thomas Turner, and his soap ashes went to sweeten the acid clays of William Poole at Chailey. In 1824 his son Thomas celebrated 40 years at 16 Cliffe by advertising starch, soap, candles, and greases for wheels, sails and tarpaulin. Soon after he became the lunatic remembered by Boys Ellman: he

> sat down on the fire [at the *Bear*], and ignited his clothes, and then rushed out and jumped into the river. He got out a little lower down...went home, and changed his clothes. He then returned to the Bear, and found several men dragging the river... being told..."That madman Verrall had purposely set himself alight, and then drowned himself".

Also at Cliffe, in 1811, Thomas Evershed & Partners opened a soap factory. Its noxious fumes soon drew complaints from Mr and Mrs Hooper; devotees of the evangelist William Huntington, they resided nearby to inhale more easily the spiritual fragrance of his sermons at Jireh chapel. Evershed's brothers managed similar factories at Shoreham and Arundel.

A processor of animal skins and hides was Richard Puxty. From his tannery at Greenwall near St John's church he despatched leather to Ostend in 1716, and 1770 bushels of cow hair to plasterers at work on Stanmer House in the 1720s. His son Nicholas retired in 1755 "worth £3-4000", after leasing the drying sheds and bark barns, the beamhouse, millhouse and turfhouse, to William Hammond. This robust Wealdsman refused to license the family vault at Waldron, which goaded the parson to bury there a pauper from the parish workhouse. Hammond's brother settled at Lewes as a currier; and his sister married Thomas Fuller who used the tannery at Southover, which had supplanted a corn mill by 1658. Their son Joseph occupied it till 1832. John Chatfield followed Hammond in

1781 at Greenwall, where he kennelled the Brookside Harriers. His inventory in 1820 included 1568 hides, many skins of calf, lamb, mink, pig and dog (hopefully not Harrier), and a horse mill for grinding Wealden oak bark. Soon after, his son Thomas, a timber merchant, sold the tannery site for housing, though a nearby bone-house and fellmonger's yard remained. Before 1820 William Baxter opened a tannery across the watermeadows at Malling.

Wealden leather was traded at Lewes. Tanners from Waldron and Rotherfield used the market in 1652; and in 1693 the Borough bought a book to register such business. In the 1780s tanners who "attended" the market deposited their takings with local tradesmen, encouraging four of them to launch the Lewes New Bank. Yet market regulation was probably in decay by 1799, when George Grantham, a basketmaker rather than a shoemaker, acted as Searcher and Sealer of Leather: he was also Ale Conner, Clerk of the Fishery etc..

Robert Gilbert (1704-90) occupied a glover's shop and yard on School Hill, and a workshop in a watermeadow near The Friars, besides stocking an outlet at Alfriston. The tanner John Chatfield used the yard from 1763, and bought tallow from the glover and breechesmaker John Burgess, who at Ditchling laid out "a yard to dress skins in", and put "some tobes down into the grown for lime pits". A more eminent breechesmaker was London-trained William Elphick 1790-1826. He settled on School Hill, but traded too in Jermyn Street off Piccadilly. His clients included the fastidious Prince of Wales, and Tsar Alexander (who also bought prize Southdown rams from John Ellman). When Lord Leslie returned a pair of riding breeches, and Elphick sold them cheaply to Parson Harry West at Southover, that abrasive cleric would not settle a bill describing them as "second-hand", till Elphick dragged him to the assizes.

Lewes saddlers traded near the coaching inns. By Fisher Street Corner Arthur Brooke 1780-1828 occupied premises used in the 1730s by Joseph Mosely, who supplied Henry Campion at Danny Park with a "male" pillion and a leather box-cloth for his coach. Opposite the *Star*, near the Sussex Mews, William Newman stitched By Royal Appointment to George IV. He also served the Cavalry Barracks; acted as Secretary to the East Sussex Fox Hounds; and collected the stake money at the summer races. From 1826 Thomas Saxby also ran the Post Office, nextdoor to the *White Hart*. He refused a university education for his son, a brilliant Classical scholar

at the Grammar School, who became his partner in 1838. Also mentally agile was Edward Relfe, author of an *Essay on the Seduction of Women*, who sold a pillion to Thomas Turner, and dined with him (perhaps aptly) on spare rib at East Hoathly.

Between 1762 and 1791 William Barwick, and then William Thunder, managed a shoe manufactory on School Hill. But most production remained smallscale: nearly 40 master shoemakers polling at Borough elections in the 1820s. The majority stiffened the Radical-Whig vote, though Robert Neal 1791-1828, Bootmaker by Royal Appointment, voted Tory. Very much the Dissenting "Radical cobbler" was Thomas Mantell (c1752-1807), who named his third son Gideon Algernon, to honour the Old Testament paladin and the Whig martyr executed by Charles II.

Lewesians also plaited or wove local fibres. In the 1720s William Young sent 259 feet of rope to Stanmer House for the "Engin" of a well, and "to let a man up and down upon occasion". In the 1760s Abraham Curtis dressed flax and hemp at South Street by Cliffe Corner; behind lay a ropewalk, and sheds for spinning and weaving. His account book noted the length of bell ropes in churches across mid-Sussex, an area he supplied with thread, plough traces, netting, sacks, oakum and hemp seed. The raw flax came from his brothers at Ripe and Hurstpierpoint, or by sea from Sandwich. His descendants carried on the firm in Cliffe, and by 1836 its ropewalk, 300 feet long and 40 feet wide, lay behind West Street, opposite the Golden Teakettle; its output included waggon tilts, twine, tarpaulin, hair cloth and shoe threads. Basketmakers were also active. Christopher Spencer used osier beds by the Ouse near Hamsey Place. George Grantham (1688-1765), George II and George III (1749-1836) sold baskets, Tunbridge Ware and Seltzer Water at 59 High Street, though George IV turned the family's "thriving" osier plots below St John's church into a coal wharf about 1810.

Some Lewes children plaited local straw into hats. Indeed when Mr Gold opened a factory in 1802, the *Journal* loyally puffed the local

fibre as "superior for some purposes to Dunstable". More versatile was Mr Kendall's Beaver, Straw Hat, Military and Ostrich Feather Manufactory opposite the *Star*. But cloth weaving was a declining craft. Thomas Hunter, whose ancestors had tended looms at Southover since before 1612, offered in February 1769 to employ a "good hand" there till the harvest. Abraham Curtis meanwhile was supplying flax to Thomas Terry, a linen weaver on St Annes Hill. His successor Thomas Reeves was built a new workshop in 1784, and was the only Lewes weaver listed in the *Universal Directory* (1797).

Wealden timber and woodfuel were traded at Lewes, often in exchange for chalk or lime. Ralph Hogge at Buxted had supplied 75 tons of oak for the Sessions House in 1564. Men from Framfield and Wivelsfield stacked wood on the river bank near South Street in 1679. A Southover dealer bought ash trees near East Hoathly in 1726. Two oaks from Sheffield Park near Fletching were dragged by 48 horses to Landport wharf in 1771; they were then floated to Newhaven en route to the royal dockyards. Charles Wille, a Cliffe timber merchant, claimed "a large connection" stretching for 20 or 30 miles around Lewes in 1837. However Newhaven exported less Wealden timber than Shoreham, Arundel and Chichester, which served wider expanses of "deep, dirty" Low Wealden clay, the oak's ideal habitat. In 1714 the cargoes were mostly make-weights for Southdown corn or Wealden iron: planks, lathes, shipboards, barrel-boards, "trees" for spades or shovels, and such wheelwrights' timber as rims, spokes and felloes. In 1739 a Lewes carpenter advised the Duke of Newcastle about conveying 12,000 pales from Laughton Common, via Lewes, Dover and Thames Ditton, to Claremont near Esher. Some timber cargoes dovetailed with the import of coal to Newhaven from Tyneside. In 1764 Captain Davies of Lewes shipped planks to Newcastle, and a case of acorns for Lord Darlington from Bishop Trevor at Glynde. In 1788 a Newhaven-based brigantine unloaded "broad English oak plank" at Sheerness, then sank while homeward bound with coal. Wealden oak bark, a source of excellent tan, was also exported through Newhaven, to Dublin in 1724 and Waterford in 1785.

In the 1670s Wealden iron was already succumbing to competition from the Forest of Dean, and from Sweden, where men worked "as Slaves", claimed the Sussex ironmasters. By 1714 the dwindling cargoes of Wealden wrought iron shipped through Newhaven went mostly to London, along with cast-iron pots, anvils, anchors, kettles, weights, firebacks, dripping pans, sugar rollers, stoves and "elbows". By the 1730s shipments downriver had probably ceased. However till 1773 Lewes merchants controlled Maresfield forge upstream from the town, which closed only in the 1780s. Ambrose Galloway 1717-37 fed the forge with scrap iron "picked up all over Germany" and shipped in through Holland. Messrs Tidy & Masters supplied Maresfield iron to make palisades at Glynde Place in 1747. Daniel Beard sold English, Swedish and Russian iron at Cliffe in 1762, along with English, German and "Blistered" steel. Joseph Molineux, Lewes's leading ironmonger, also sent Maresfield iron to Glynde, besides stocking Herefordshire cider, "old in Bottles, strong and racy". His son Benjamin gave up the forge in 1773. The Lewes merchants, John Whitfeld and Faulkner Bristow, controlled another forge upstream, at Howbourne near Buxted, fitfully operative till the 1760s.

Wealden guns from the Fuller furnace near Heathfield outlasted wrought iron as an export. Ambrose Galloway (a Quaker activist) barged them downriver from his quay near The Friars, and during the September sheep fair at Cliffe in 1733 he moored a raft of them in mid-stream, firing off salvoes in support of John Fuller's campaign to become a Tory MP for Sussex. His succesors, Messrs Cardin & Jarvis, shipped guns in 1750; and in 1753 71 arrived, destined for the King of Naples and Sicily. Others were exported during the Seven Years War.

Besides Southdown and Wealden produce, Lewes hosted the marketing of seafish, caught off Brighton and carried along the Juggs Road to Fisher Street. Mackerel were delivered in the summer; herring and whiting in the autumn; and plaice, sole, mullet, pilchards, dory, skate, turbot, sand-rays and shrimps in due season. Button's *Directory* (1805) credited Brighton with 100 "strongly built" fishing boats, each crewed by three or four men or boys. In 1827 the fishermen were still so formidable that over 90 special constables were deployed when capstans were cleared from part of the beach.

Supplies to Lewes, though, were sometimes variable. In June 1801 dogfish damaged the mile-long mackerel nets. Plaice grew scarce in September 1829, after shrimp trawlers used nets too closely meshed. Sole became abundant in April 1830 when a new ground off Seaford was fished. Shoals of mullet made their own way upriver to Lewes in September 1823: those that escaped "the deadly net" of Mr Bug Ellis. In 1828 oysters caught off Newhaven were boated up to the bridge. Lewes street vendors included Mr Hogsflesh, alias the Sapient Pig, who devoured rabbits etc. raw for a wager. Wealdsmen bought heavily at Lewes fish market when corn prices rose, though some were supplied direct from the coast by "Wildish rippiers": in 1775 five such salesmen breakfasted at the *Duke's Head* in Seaford on 80 good-sized whiting, washed down with three quarts of strong beer and generous gulps of juniper-flavoured gin. In the Weald itself "innumerable" ponds harboured tench, perch, eels, pike, and the carp supplied to the *Star* in 1717. When Mrs Dabson of Lewes sold 244 more from a pond she rented at Streat, they were removed in three dung carts.

Wille trade card

3

The Mart of Mid-Sussex: Out-County Commodities and Credit

...for tea, a quire of Paper, and two mousetraps...a hundredweight of Malaga raisins...a pond of fish of Mrs. Dabson...a hat from David Douglas...narrow cloath at 6s. per yd. of Mr. Thos. Friend, and 33 buttons with mohair, and canvass, and silk...a book entitled Lex Testamentaria of Mr. Norman...a letter from Mrs. Swaine, demanding her money, principal and interest at Lady-day next...the pillion to Atkinson's to be mended...to Thos. Friend for 3 yds. of calermanco...to Mr. Court for a knife...a bottle of claret...a pair of gloves...Bohea, a pair of spurs, and some Acts of Parliament...silver lace...Avery for a whip for Willy...Mrs. Skinner for three handkerchiefs...things for my mother's funeral.

PURCHASES AT LEWES BY THE MARCHANTS OF HURSTPIERPOINT IN 1714-22.

In 1754 Dr Pococke noted that Lewes lived "by supplying the neighbouring places with the conveniences of life"; and indeed its wide commercial hinterland received from the town an immense variety of out-county merchandise, British and foreign. In 1805 Button's *Directory* stressed that "ready communication" with Newhaven harbour and London rendered it "the emporium from which the adjacent country is supplied", by tradesmen "remarkable for civility and dispatch".

Already in 1702 Baltic deals were carried to Newhaven direct from fiords near Oslo. In the early 1790s shipments from overseas of Deals, Masts and un-cut Timber averaged 1255 tons a year. In 1808 Baltic timber for the new Shire Hall was selected on Thameside, made into rafts at Newhaven, and poled upriver. In 1821 11 cargoes came from London, and one each from Christiana, Memel and Quebec. From the Lewes yards the timber was often tugged, floated or barged upcountry. "Norway oak" was sent to frame an Eastbourne farmhouse in 1727; and while fetching deals from Lewes in 1733, Henry Coppard met with a fatal accident near Twineham. From a spacious yard off South Street William Rice supplied Chiddingly and Rushlake Green in 1763; from others at Landport and Offham he served "the North West part of the Country". From Greenwall in 1838 Thomas Chatfield despatched Memel pine, Christiana plank and American oak to Slaugham, Forest Row, Rotherfield and Waldron. Brighton's rapid growth boosted demand; in 1787 timber was carted there "almost daily", to build the first Royal Pavilion.

Rafting timber up the Ouse

Mounting too were the cargoes of housecoal brought to Newhaven from Tyneside, with a few chaldrons from London. These mostly passed upcountry through Lewes yards, though the Bishop of Durham's steward at Glynde Place pondered dealing with Sunderland direct in 1761, to avoid being "imposed upon" by Lewes merchants. On the South Downs affluent householders used coal before 1714. By 1754 waggonloads were being carted from Lewes to The Hooke estate near Chailey, within the wooded Low Weald. Soon after, coal-burning grates were installed further up-country at Sheffield Park, in time to warm the historian Edward Gibbon. In 1776 coal was piled at Landport wharf for Lord Abergavenny, presumably to heat Kidbrooke Park, his remote fastness near Forest Row. Humbler Wealden homes converted to coal when a boom in lime and brick production drove up the cost of local woodfuel. In 1787 John Burgess at Ditchling bought his first half-chaldron, from Cliffe. At Lewes Thomas Figg began heating his bread-oven with coal in 1792. Brighton too drew on Lewes yards; a resident in 1823 claiming that their coal was cheaper than cargoes unloaded on the beach by the brigs John Constable delighted to sketch. Imports through Newhaven rose accordingly: 2059 tons in 1750, 16,718 in 1807 and 27,567 in 1820. Welsh anthracite also arrived, to dry malt and hops. Privateers seized cargoes from Tenby in 1780.

By the late 1770s Baltic timber and Tyneside coal were congesting the Lewes yards. William Rice occupied the wharfs at South Street, Landport and Offham till his bankruptcy in 1783. His successor,

Gaston's House, Malling Street

William Gaston, owned a yard off Malling Street, with a weather-boarded house boasting two crisply cut doorways. At Bear Yard John Rickman stocked coal, followed by John Godlee (c1763-1841) whose son Burwood superintended the gas works from 1826. (Sir) Henry Blackman unloaded coal, timber and wine at Cliffe wharf (now Harvey's) till 1805, and at Bridgefoot wharf near The Friars till the 1820s. At Cliffe the congestion caused new yards to emerge near the Great Sewer which was extended. On one John Dennett piled coal and millstones from the Peak in 1792. Thomas Berry and Samuel Tooth, dealers in "fir and oak", opened another that year, though established shippers had opposed them "getting a proper place", now that the Ouse Navigation promised healthy profits. New wharfs also spread up the Borough bank north of the bridge. Before 1799 the Barcombe miller Thomas Rickman built on the watermeadows behind Dial House; in 1810 Messrs Chatfield & Grantham were stacking coal and timber on erstwhile osier-beds; and nearby Charles Wille began focusing his "large connection". Below the bridge The Friars estate was partitioned after 1803; the new warehouses included the Viper Store, with a winged serpent above the gable.

As well as timber and coal, out-county iron was increasingly

South Street timberyard (Horsfield's History)

barged upriver from Newhaven. William Fry of Bristol landed eight tons there in 1702. A cargo arrived from Sweden in 1708, with 2675 "Norway" deals. Shipments from Hull in 1775 included Swedish and Russian iron, nails, pots, scythes and shovels. In 1821 Welsh iron was unloaded. At Lewes the ironmongers grew adept at making iron artefacts. In 1685 some "flower pattenwoods" belonging to Benjamin Court were stolen by a Cliffe blacksmith. From 1707 Court displayed his ironware at a fine High Street mansion in showrooms much admired by Parson John Burton. He sent locks and bolts to Stanmer House and to the County Gaol at Horsham, firebacks, curtain rods and a kitchen-jack chain to Compton Place at Eastbourne, and scythes, spades, nails and a stove to Danny Park. After he retired the showrooms became Newcastle House, a social centre for the Duke's

Whig partisans. Court's goodwill passed to Joseph Molineux 1734-71, who controlled Maresfield forge and probably erected the fine shopfront at 61 High Street, now destroyed. His custom stretched to Cuckfield, Forest Row, and across the Surrey border to Godstone. The firm remained "in the front rank of county trade" under Joseph II, William Stuard, Stephen Lowdell, and Edward Grantham who added his family's basket-and-brush business in 1824.

From 14 School Hill William and Mary Roase c1738-63 supplied screws to Danny Park, and 18,000 nails to build a smallpox hospital nearby. They also sold lead, cheese, bacon and ham. The customers included Thomas Turner who meandered home to East Hoathly "not sober", after dining with them on roasted pike. Then came John Richards & Son. They sold Scottish, Swedish and Russian iron, Derbyshire lead, Newcastle Green Glass, Yorkshire ham and bacon,

Cork and Waterford butter, Dutch and English cheeses, though one cargo from Gainsborough was lost to a French privateer in 1779. From Lincolnshire too they imported potatoes, despite a mistrust of that newfangled root which made "No Popery, No Potatoes" a local election cry. From 1800 William Attwood, Nehemiah Wimble and William II carried on with cheese and hardware at Number 14. In 1834 they cunningly commended their Economical Boiler: "the same fire that roasts a sirloin of beef will boil a turkey, a tongue, a plum pudding, and steam three sorts of vegetables". Having bought The Friars, Wimble loyally ceded the dining-room in October 1830 to King William, Queen Adelaide, Captain Fitzclarence etc.. It was the first royal visit to Lewes since Henry III

> was forced by the virtuous Barons, fighting for the liberties of their Country, to seek refuge within the Walls of the Castle,

as Thomas Read Kemp pointedly put it at the banquet. To commemorate brushing the hem of Greatness, Wimble commissioned a 200-piece dinner service.

Besides Economical Boilers Lewes ironmongers made churns, ploughs and palisades for Tomb, Balcony and Park Fencing. And in 1808 Nathaniel Polhill and Thomas Gibson opened a foundry at Cliffe with the casting capacity of a normal London works. Polhill already owned showrooms nearby, salvaged by the ironmonger Henry Harben from his father's bankruptcy. In 1818 Gibson and James Sturt supplied two bell-carriages to Battle parish church. Ebenezer Morris, a butcher's son from School Hill, bought the firm in 1822, and trained for a year at a London foundry near Newgate. When he opened his enlarged showrooms in 1830, a Golden Teakettle, made by Mr Lomas, dispensed eight gallons of punch, before being rehung outside. In 1813 another coppersmith at the firm, Thomas Taylor, made the basking shark which still swings as a weather-vane above Southover church.

Agricultural machinists also traded from Lewes. William English's workshop in 1812 was at Pleasant Place off Lancaster Street; a forbear sharpened five razors for Thomas Turner in 1755. At Southover in 1796 Alexander Cheale improved a device for winnowing and cleaning corn. His son Charles constructed mangles, box-churns, furze-beaters, and cutters to slice straw and turnips. At Cliffe in 1833 George Hards built a Naval Construction Machine, intended to saw curved pieces of wood precisely, and a Naval Pump, little more than 4 feet square, devised to raise 1080 gallons of water per minute.

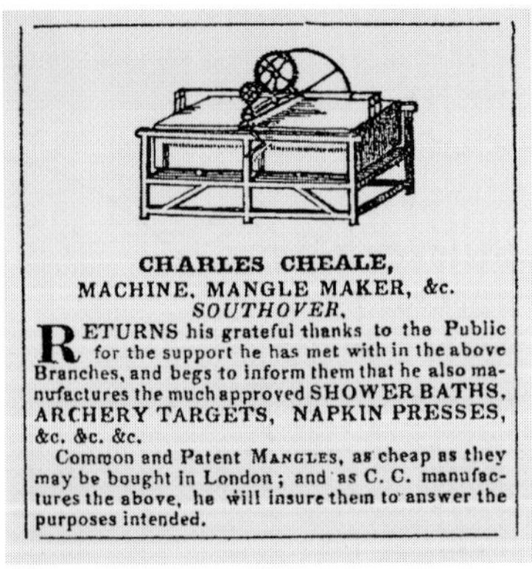

Intricate timepieces were assembled at Lewes. Thomas Barrett (c1665-1752) made lantern and long-case clocks of distinction, and tended others at the market house, the Broken Church, and Streat Place. Abraham Weston (c1675-1746) constructed eight-day long-case clocks, silver verge watches, and a bracket clock "of London quality" in a black lacquer case. For the town-crier's coat he fashioned a brass badge, gold-gilt and bearing the Borough arms. His descendants, like Barrett's, were also gunsmiths; indeed by 1820 exclusively so. Barrett's apprentice, Thomas Harben (1711- 66), who scooped up the *Nympha Americana's* quicksilver, made long-case and hooded wall-clocks. By 1772 his son Thomas, the future banker, employed a London watchmaker to supervise "16 or 17 hands". Such grandiose production aggrieved Richard Comber (c1742-1824), a fine craftsman who made a watch with a rotating hour-ring, and a long-case clock with a second-hand in the arch. He died in a London asylum,

The sign of the White Lion, possibly made by Abraham Larwill, tinplate worker, brazier & wire worker to his Royal Highness, the Prince of Wales. (Chaplin)

but contrived to have his first escort from Lewes committed in his stead. William Kemp (c1722-98) sold John Bridger a gold watch. Clockmakers active in the 1820s included William Hooker at 12 Cliffe, the Original Clock Manufactory; Kemp's partner, John Holman; Isaac Gold, a Radical-Whig friendly with William Cobbett; William Attwood, also a silversmith By Appointment; and Solomon Nathan Berncastel, a Jewish immigrant. He procured Napoleonic medals for Gideon Mantell; and his brother, an accoucheur in Trier, presided over the birth of Karl Marx.

Pipemaking at Lewes depended on imported clay which in 1714 arrived at Newhaven from Poole, along with oil from Newfoundland. Thomas Harman was at work on St Annes Hill in 1657; and John Harman (c1700-70) used a kiln there behind Hill Lodge; pipe fragments survive in the garden. His brother Thomas sold 3384 pipes to Thomas Turner in March 1754. He fired a kiln at Keere Street Corner, continued by the Neeves family, and in the 1820s by John Tanner. By then Henry Pink and William Privet used a kiln off Pipe Passage, possibly started by John Harman II in the 1770s.

From Newhaven cargoes of consumer goods were barged upriver. In the 1720s shipments arrived from Holland, still a crossroads of European trade. They included Rhenish wine, Spa mineral water, Bruges thread, Geneva trays, Westphalian hams, Russian rhubarb, Amsterdam velvet, linen napkins, cheeses, garden seeds, cambric, goose quilts, wainscot, pantiles, bulrushes, periwigs, paper prints, orange trees, brass coffee-pots, tea pots, unlacquered tea tables, close stools and a marble gravestone. Cheeses still arrived from Holland in the 1820s, but by then London had consolidated as an immense warehouse of British and foreign merchandise. Even before the 1720s the metropolis despatched to Newhaven groceries, spices, sugar, molasses, cheese, tobacco, raisins, wines, spirits, haberdashery, German linen, canvas, hemp, alum, paper, mops, bottles, earthenware, starch, copperas, oilman's wares, glue, colours, crocus (a saffron dye), blacking, soap, pitch, tar, cordage, steel, pewter, white lead, shot, coal, deals, masts, ironware and gravestones. In 1701 seven such composite cargoes were unloaded. By 1772 (as the Lewes town-crier publicized) two Newhaven-based sloops were regularly plying to and from Southwark. Waiting to load there in 1777 was the *Lewes Trader*, belonging to William Gaston and Richard Boxall, timber merchants at Cliffe. Thereafter the turnpike roads steadily improved, and more merchandise came overland from London, so two sloops still sufficed in 1815 and 1839. And in 1845, after the railway linked London and Brighton, only the *Mary Ann* doggedly coasted to Harrison's wharf off Tooley Street.

The Lewes merchant most busily importing from Holland and London about 1714 was probably the Quaker Ambrose Galloway (c1650-1718). At his Bridgefoot wharf near The Friars he also stacked timber from Norway and millstones from Hull. Downriver he despatched wheat, malt, guns, shot, iron, saws, hinges, rollers, timber, tan and white osiers to London, guns and plank to Chatham, guns and hops to Bristol, wheat and barley to Holland, Dunkirk and San Sebastian. He sought lateral integration by owning Barcombe watermill and leasing iron forges at Maresfield and Ardingly. His son Ambrose (c1680-1738) kept the watermill and Maresfield forge, and bought the *Bear* and Bear Yard opposite Bridgefoot. Besides trading with London, Holland and Norway, he unshipped oranges and lemons from Oporto, and plaster of Paris from Dieppe. To the builders of Stanmer House he supplied deals, lead, tar, wainscot, pantiles, elm pipes, and stones "to rubb Bricks upon". To Danny Park he sent deals, coal, Newcastle glass, and wines such as Frontignac and Old Mountain. He lent large sums to the County Authorities when the storm-stricken bridges at Lewes and Exceat needed rebuilding in 1726-27. Such indeed was his reputation that John Fuller, a fellow Tory whose guns he exported, asked him to recommend a firm in Holland where Hans Fuller could learn book keeping: the Dutch being neat and frugal, whereas in Iberia and Turkey "the people are all Beaux". Fuller even considered Hans training with Galloway, who left £1000 to the Society of Friends, and an equal sum to Widow Anne Short, along with Dresden china and silverware, including a tea kettle, a lamp and saucepans. To his employee, Richard Cardin (c1702-52), he left his lease of Bridgefoot wharf, and three capacious barges. With a partner Richard Jarvis (c1707-59), Cardin shipped Fuller's guns, resolving in 1743 a dispute about Captain Headly's freight charges. In 1751 they exported guns, shovels, spades and fire-backs, perhaps to Portugal, since the return cargo was to include 36 hampers of White Lisbon wine. At All Saints churchyard their shapely table-tombs stand side by side.

Also a versatile trader was John Whitfeld, a nephew of William Pellatt who owned The Friars. Based at Cliffe wharf in the 1720s, he sent wheat to Dublin, unshipped wainscot, pipe staves and coarse linen from Holland, and supplied deals and lead from London to the builders of Stanmer House. By 1744 he owned a 50-acre estate at Wellingham in Ringmer, settling his tithes there with ten gallons of brandy. In 1746 he acquired Howbourne manor with its iron forge, and collaborated perhaps with Daniel Beard, his neighbour at Cliffe wharf who controlled Maresfield forge. By 1754 the customers for his deals included the gunfounder John Fuller, Mr Medley at Buxted Park and Bishop Trevor at Glynde. But in 1756 a wrangle with the bishop's agent over prices was suddenly cut short when Whitfeld sold all his property and crossed to Holland, where his fate remains uncertain. He fled (rumour had it) because a carter, caught near Barcombe mill with a load of smuggled "Corsica wine", confessed that Whitfeld had used him for many years to carry such contraband to London. Certainly by 1771 his former estate at Wellingham was listed as "Corsica" in the land-tax assessment; and apparently its materials were removed to Seaford by Banker Harben to build Corsica Hall.

Whether replenished by waggon or barge, Lewes grocers supplied "the various country shops for many miles around". In 1714 Walter Brett (1678-1735) managed his father's old-established family firm at Watergate Corner (now the Post Office). There in the 1620s Richard Newton had sold the currants, prunes and spices he imported through Newhaven; he also arranged the baptism at St Michael's of Mary Samboyce, his blackamoor servant, unloaded perhaps with the pepper and nutmeg. William Brett 1735-74 owned a share of the Bridge coffee-house, and was joined at Watergate Corner by his son-in-law Francis Whitfeld 1769-1807, a relative maybe of the fugitive John. Tom Paine, an excise officer in the Upper Town, inspected their ledgers. After Brett died Whitfeld partnered William Verrall, whose father managed the coffee-house over at Newcastle House, and then John Baker from Mayfield, whose death in 1807 caused the venerable emporium to close. The grocer Thomas Gilbert 1770-80 occupied the defunct Bridge coffee-house. His only child, Mary Anne, inherited an estate at Eastbourne, and became the spade-husbandry enthusiast who married Davies Giddy, a President of the Royal Society. Gilbert's successor, Thomas Johnston 1780-1806,

supplied tea, cheese, salt, Irish butter, Newcastle glass and Derbyshire lead to customers at Brighton, Buxted, Waldron and Battle. During race-week he lent his elegant residence (now Lloyds bank) to the Prince of Wales. His son Thomas partnered Thomas Fisher from 1806, and then Edward Monk, a specialist in Irish trade, and a fellow-pupil of Richard Cobden at Midhurst grammar school.

Lewes vintners enjoyed extensive custom. Gabriel Ayres unshipped 31 tons of wine from Oporto in 1727, along with tallow, cork, hams, oil and lemons. His capacious vaults behind 190 High Street were later used as a schoolroom. He supplied hogsheads of port to Danny Park and Compton Place, and arrack to the Duke of Newcastle's household at Bishopstone. Wine and lemons also engaged Richard Jarvis and Richard Cardin II. In 1755 their agent, Captain Thomas Bean of Newhaven, sent them an awestruck letter describing the Portuguese earthquake, written aboard the *Blossom* anchored off Faro near Cape St Vincent. (In Lisbon the cash profits of two merchants had melted away when fire consumed their house.) After two years at sea, Bean was now homeward bound, hoping to sell cork, oranges, lemons and Madeira wine in the Channel ports. In 1754 Cardin II had joined "the Associated Merchants trading from Lewes to Barbadoes or elsewhere". They were based at the Bridge coffee-house, and included the grocer William Brett, the draper John Woodgate, Pastor Ebenezer Johnston, and John Bridger of Coombe Place. Their ship was named the *Warren*, recalling perhaps the Norman Adventurer who governed Lewes Rape. By May 1755 it was outward bound via Madeira to Barbados, where their agent had assembled a shipment of sugar, and doubtless rum as well. He also urged them to despatch a second vessel, freighted with flour, oats, coal, bricks and hoops, and calling at Cork for provisions. In May 1756 Bridger & Co. duly insured the *Lewes*, newly built for them at Newhaven. Captain John Bean was to "touch at Madeira"; and the premium would be reduced if he sailed in convoy. But as the Seven Years War (1756-63) intensified, the enterprise petered out. Cardin II quitted Bridgefoot for London, and his successor John Burtenshaw was bankrupt by 1764.

By 1770 Henry Blackman (c1744-1832) and Edward Campion were supplying Madeira wine and coal from Bridgefoot to The Hooke and Coombe Place. A native of Chichester, Blackman cherished an ebony bowl his ancestor received for sheltering the fugitive Charles Stuart at Hambledon. He was himself knighted in 1782, after presenting a Loyal Address from the Borough. He bought the *Star*, and his daughter married Samuel Shergold whose father owned the *Castle* assembly rooms at Brighton. Edward Campion, a younger son from Danny Park, made way in 1804 for Henry II, receiving £10,000 in compensation. By then the firm's trade reached to Uckfield, Hurstpierpoint and Eastbourne; and among its clients reluctant to settle accounts were the Lewes Freemasons, the Ringmer Artillery Hospital and the churchwardens at Malling. Campion's brother William was a wine merchant at Oporto. He retired in 1789 to Pelham House at Lewes, where his ardent Toryism caused him to be denounced as "A sort of mongrel personage, half Squire, half Visitor", with a head "as round and brainless as one of his Portuguese onions".

Being well stocked with imported textiles, Lewes drapers served a wide hinterland. Parson Moore from Horsted Keynes bought fabrics at William Marshall's "over against the Star". In 1666 he chose hair Prunella for a cassock, and galloon, scarlet serge and red silk buttons for a waistcoat; in 1670 he selected Serge Seraphico for a "Canonicall coat". Thomas Friend, the wool merchant, sent cloth for servants' liveries to Danny Park, till a bitter election campaign in 1733-4 diverted Campion custom to William Durrant (1690-1751), a loyal Tory draper at Eastgate Corner. John Madgwick next traded there, buying wholesale in London and at Maudlin Hill fair near Guildford. Then came three Unitarians, Henry Browne 1789-1822, Henry II, and William Crosskey (c1797-1874). Their emporium survived into the 1980s; as did another at Fisher Street Corner, kept by Thomas Marten c1770-87, the author of *Quakerism No Delusion*, who bartered

hats, bedcovers and Dowlais with John Burgess. His Quaker nephew William 1787-1817 distributed handbills depicting the rigours of the Last Judgement to Lewes's feckless theatre-goers; but William II sold out in 1827 to Joseph Maxfield. At Cliffe the linen draper, John Woodgate c1736-83, also dealt in coal and seed potatoes from Liverpool. He opened Lewes's first circulating library, and collected subscriptions for a stand at the race course.

Woodgate's enterprise ended visits by Scotsmen selling linen goods, who previously lodged at the *Wheatsheaf*, with a minion or two to shoulder the packs. Also itinerant were the Manchestermen. They sold cotton blankets and other "bed furniture" in the 1750s; and their porter John Burren was hustled to Horsham Gaol, for allegedly damning King George in the kitchen of the *White Horse*. Another Cliffe draper, Edward Egles (1762-1838), attempted to manufacture cotton fabric in mid-Sussex, at the timberyard off South Street, at Hempstead mill near Uckfield, and at Balcombe where wrought cotton muslin was stolen from a loom in 1793; but his efforts petered out before 1805. Thereafter Hempstead mill wove and dyed silk, till his executors sold the machinery by advertising in the *Manchester Guardian*.

Dyeing at Lewes was long-established. In 1588 William Butcher of All Saints had coloured a petticoat for a widow at Fletching. At Friars Walk in All Saints, near the watermeadows, resided John Jones cl767-87, John II, and John Gosling who manned the vats from 1827 while his brother-in-law, John III, was training. In 1788 John II opened a fulling mill near Lewes, where people making Linsey and Blanketing could have it processed "in the best manner". John Peckham 1713-47, a dyer in St Michael's, had managed a fulling mill at Fletching. The craft also attracted women. Widow Elizabeth Whapham practised in 1812 at Keere Street; her daughters followed her.

Lewes tailors also served a mid-Sussex clientele. Parson Moore chose Hercules Courtney to sew his Canonical coat. From the 1730s William Bennett, his son and grandson stitched servants' liveries for the Pooles, Gages and Bridgers. Their freehold at 163 High Street included a drying ground on the southern slope below the castle keep. The Palmers were a dynasty of hatters, related perhaps to Samuel, the visionary painter. Richard traded near the *White Hart* in the 1750s, George near the *Star* in the 1780s, and John near All Saints church in the 1820s. At 9 Cliffe Widow Susanna Glazebrook employed a London-trained assistant in 1773 to loop headgear "in genteelest taste". James Harben 1778-94 sold government stamps there as a side-line; and Daniel Harvey, also London-trained, succeeded him. In these realms of Fashion metropolitan experience counted a great deal. Milliners made much of it, and the staymaker Edward Ellis boasted a five year sojourn in the capital, mastering the English, French and Italian modes.

Lewes barbers also strove towards Elegance. In 1711 Samuel Driver kept his silver-topped razors in a leather case. He owned netting tools, ten pewter "blood" porringers, and various books, Bibles and pictures, perhaps to calm nervous clients. Daniel Fabre, a French Protestant refugee dying in 1728, offered a Gallic touch. So did Monsieur Constant, a ladies' hairdresser from Paris, who displayed jewelled caps and modish dresses at the *Dorset Arms* in 1774. Some barbers were also perukemakers. Mr Wallis supplied Richard Stapley at Hickstead Place near Twineham in 1697. Joseph Hartley measured Thomas Turner at East Hoathly; and Stephen Heaver 1755-90 attended Coombe Place. Edward Tasker and his son Thomas also kept the Post Office, garnering the news and gossip. In 1823 barber William Inkpen sold ornamental hair, shell combs and Dutch toys. His shop-sign on School Hill showed Absalom hanging by the hair from a tree, an ass galloping away, and a cautionary verse beneath:

> Oh! Absalom, unlucky prig!
> Had'st thou but worn a periwig!
> For had thy luckless head been shaved,
> Thy life most surely had been saved.

Rags generated by the clothing trades were beaten into paper by harnessing waterpower along the Ouse. The Lewes draper James Lopdell owned a mill in Great Taynter Field near Barcombe bridge, which produced, presumably, the 248 reams of paper shipped to London through Newhaven in 1702. Ambrose Galloway demolished it in 1716. Joseph Molineux, Thomas Johnston and the Lewes printer, Arthur Lee, opened a mill in 1802 by the Hogbrook below St John's church. They offered good prices for rags, and recruited "a few steady women" who formed a stool-ball team. By 1805 it supplied the Prince of Wales. Lee sold out before a second mill was opened near Isfield lock in 1809, when invited guests were serenaded upriver from Lewes in pleasure boats, and consumed viands and coffee on the bank, "*a-la-gipsie*". Both mills were modernized in 1824-5.

Being denizens of a busy market town, Lewesians dealt in cash, credit and insurance. By the 1690s Dr Benjamin White was lending by bond or mortgage across its catchment area, as far as Pevensey, Fletching and Hurstpierpoint. The wool merchant Thomas Friend, with his London and West Country contacts, acted as informal banker to Henry Campion at Danny Park, settling bills etc.. But after the 1734 election Campion switched to William Durrant, the Tory draper at Eastgate Corner, whose son Samuel (1717-82) also handled cash and credit. "Without Trouble by means of Mr Durrant", a Lewes attorney claimed in 1764, any "money" could be shuttled betweem mid-Sussex and London. He acted as Thomas Turner's banker, drawing him a bill for £130 on Sir Joseph Hankey & Co., in exchange for cash and an interest-bearing promissory note. He also lent money, though Henry Bridger of Coombe Place was refused an extra £10,000 in 1763 when Government Stocks were low. One steady borrower was the childless rentier, Edward Trayton, who bequeathed Durrant Southover manor and the Priory Lands in 1761, as "an effectual method of liquidating all his obligations".

Durrant died in 1782, and his estate, rumoured to be worth £140,000, passed to a cousin, a surgeon at Robertsbridge. A year or so before Thomas Harben (1739-1803), along with Thomas and Bannister Flight, opened a Lewes Bank at Newcastle House. Mrs Harben, a Southdown yeoman's daughter, had brought a "handsome" dowry; and Thomas handed over the family clockmaking business to assistants, diversifying into ironmongery and malt. He supplied a great ball to crown the stables at Coombe Place, and annexed malthouses at Cliffe. A silversmith as well, he kept an agent at Brighton to "exchange light gold coin". He also procured slices of government business, becoming a Commissioner to take Special Bail. His brother James, the hatter, became a Distributor of Stamps and a Collector of Post-Horse Duties for the Eastern Division of Sussex. The Lewes Bank also handled the Division's excise revenue, besides displaying Harben's ironmongery, a strange reversal to Benjamin Court's time. There John Burgess bought a "Cast Iron Boat to Greace Rushes In", and the hated Stamps taxing his work as a glover. Posing as a gentleman-banker, Harben now flaunted his new-found affluence. Each St Thomas's Day he bestowed a dole of bread on the deserving poor in Cliffe and St Michael's. In 1788 his phaeton was effusively lent to Mrs Byng, a guest at the *White Hart* with her husband, a senior official at the Stamp Office. At Seaford, a corrupt parliamentary Borough, Harben built Corsica Hall, and bought 13 vote-bearing tenements, hoping to set up his eldest son Thomas as a Pittite MP. Nearby he acquired the manor and advowson of East Blatchington. His sons Henry and James took over the silverware and ironmongery, along with a gunpowder works at Battle.

As a pushy parvenu Harben provoked hostility; indeed after alleged double-dealing at a Lewes election in 1784 (the details are obscure) he was paraded "in effigy on an ass", and berated by Sir Henry Blackman as a jumped-up brazier and tinker, though he responded imperturbably, "I used to gather rabbit skins too". Some rejoiced therefore when the Lewes Bank failed in April 1793, along with others he part-owned at Brighton and Horsham. His estates, burgages and malthouses were liquidated, and his children quitted Sussex. Susan became a matron at the Clergy Daughters' School attended by Charlotte Bronte, who wove her into *Jane Eyre* as Mrs Harden. Henry married the granddaughter of Robert Austen, the grammar school headmaster; his own grandchilden included Joseph Chamberlain (1836-1914).

Harben's premises in Newcastle House passed to the Lewes New Bank, which had been opened in July 1789 nextdoor to the *Star* by the grocer Francis Whitfeld, the ironmonger Joseph Molineux, a soap boiler Richard King, and a rentier Benjamin Comber. Earlier they had informally deposited cash and issued notes for "Tanners and others who attended the Lewes Market". This sound commercial base enabled them to weather April 1793. Indeed they took over deposits managed since 1785 by Richard Peters Rickman, the Cliffe brewer. In 1805 the bank's custom stretched to Eastbourne,

Waldron, Forest Row, Cuckfield and Edburton. By 1814 its new partners, Harry Hurley, Thomas Dicker, Thomas Whitfeld and George Molineux, were well-placed to survive the decay of rural credit after the defeat of Napoleon. Indeed they wound up the stricken East Grinstead Bank, and then leased its premises. In 1822 they opened a branch at The Pantiles in Tunbridge Wells. The bank also rode out the "great commercial convulsion" which shook British credit in December 1825. Lord Gage and 42 other substantial depositors signed a Letter of Comfort, guaranteeing the note issue for six months to a value of £202,000. This averted an avalanche of withdrawals by depositors arriving "almost breathless" with panic. But another Lewes bank, which was opened in 1805 by the corn merchant Samuel Flint, the coal merchant John Godlee, John Wood a Southover rentier, and Nathaniel Hall a Southwick corn broker, did close, though its liabilities were fully met. Other closures reduced rival banks serving mid-Sussex to three: at Brighton, Hastings and Horsham. Not till 1839 did the London and County Bank renew competition at Lewes itself.

In mid-Sussex the long agricultural depression after Waterloo was aggravated by barrack closures, and by the Fashionables deserting its resorts for the Continent. On the Lewes Downs "eminent" yeomen were forced to sell up, and disperse their prize-winning flocks. But worst hit was the Weald. Even before Waterloo local magistrates had lamented the turbulent squatters on its many commons; their turf huts too reminiscent of "Indian towns". In 1820 the *Journal* bemoaned the plight of Wealden family farmers, the decay of their "dairies, spinning wheels and market baskets". A decade later the region was convulsed by "an Incendiary Spirit, originating in the want of Employment for, and the low rates of Wages given to Agricultural Labourers". And about midnight on Thursday the 18th of November 1830 the misery of its hinterland brought Captain Swing to Lewes itself. As the Town Book recorded, a barn near Southover church "was discovered to be on Fire, without doubt from the Act of some Incendiary". The previous August "home" labourers had stoned Irish reapers and their families encamped at Winterbourne.

The collapse of rural prosperity meant Hard Times for Lewes retailers and craftsmen, and rendered the livestock fairs "wretchedly dull". In September 1829 only 18,500 sheep and 14,000 lambs were penned near the Spital crossroads. Even at its busiest a "uniquely dull" Whitsun fair in 1825 attracted no more than 50 head of cattle. Out-county buyers at the wool fair fell away; in 1825 "one solitary lot" was sold. A petition, lodged for signature at the *Star* in 1828, deplored the trade's "ruinous" state, and the import, almost duty-free, of German wool. "Very inferior" too by August 1820 was the Fatstock Show of the Sussex Agricultural Society, despite Lord Egremont's loyal support. Soon after, it gave way to a local pre-Christmas show, for the benefit of Brighton's butchers. They too sustained the cattle market as "a grand depot of consumption", well placed to supply their resort. Indeed in 1819 the corn market was transferred to a Tuesday to coincide, though conservatives still adhered to Saturday; and in December 1828 the authorities at Cliffe launched a rival cattle market, after easing access to the Fair Place by removing the abode of Mr Venus.

From the 1820s the town's commerce also suffered because of improvements to Shoreham harbour, and to the coast road between Newhaven and Brighton. These encouraged cargoes of coal and timber, bound for Brighton, to bypass the wharfs at Lewes. Moreover up-market housing estates were built at Kemp Town in Brighton, Brunswick Town in Hove, Calverley Park at Tunbridge Wells and St Leonards near Hastings; and the local retailers serving them could now poach on the fringes of Lewes's rural custom. From 1841 the growing railway network further damaged the town's retail trade, disrupting the ancient pattern of waterborne traffic, and fostering, in alliance with Lord Burlington, the lusty growth of Eastbourne. By 1830 the *Brighton Gazette* could starkly insist that "too many" Lewesians were engaged in commerce. This was confirmed by the Decennial Census which counted 8900 inhabitants in 1831 and 9500 in 1841, with little increase in 1851 and 1861.

Yet a solid core of marketing, retailing and craft-based enterprise did survive, enough to sustain the town into the 1860s. The grocers Thomas Madgwick & Son, the ironmongers Lowdell & Cooper, the drapers Browne & Crosskey, the tarpaulin-makers Curtis & Son, the machine-makers

David & Isaiah Cheale still attracted rural custom. Lewes Bank opened a branch at Eastbourne in 1854 and Uckfield in 1870. Indeed not till 1896 did Francis Barry Whitfeld, Herbert Whitfeld and Harold Parminter Molineux, merge with 14 other firms to form Barclays. Thomas Chatfield still trafficked timber far into the Weald. At a North Street yard his son Edward (c1815-85) built the *Lewes*, the *Wallands* and other ocean-going ships. John Hillman's son Robert (c1817-84) expanded his father's chalk and lime business; almost 80 quarry workers, a "goodly show of bone and sinew", mustering for his funeral. In 1835 Ebenezer Morris (1801-88) enlarged the foundry at Cliffe, to compete more effectively with the Phoenix iron-works, just established in North Street by John Every (c1797-1887). In 1850 Morris opened a branch at Eastbourne, and supplied the resort with railings and gas-lamp standards. John Every II in his turn embellished Brighton's seafront with "festive, ebullient" band-stands and pierced arcading. Peter Broad's son James (c1824-1900) expanded his father's candle and patent-dip factory off Market Street. Albion Russell (1822-88) from Chiddingly, and his son-in-law Gerald Bromley from Hastings, utilized the town's long experience of boot and shoe making. William Verrall (1798-1890) continued the Southover brewery, finally controlling 35 licensed houses between Brighton and the Kentish border. William Beard (1812-1905) joined the family brewery in Fisher Street. In 1838 John Hillman, Robert's father, opened the Southdown brewery along Thomas Street, designed by Messrs Pontifex. The same year John Harvey (1784-1862), a wine merchant at 6 Cliffe since 1814, bought Cliffe wharf and built the brewery still managed by his descendants. These legacies of Georgian enterprise, along with others in printing and newspaper publishing, allowed Lewes to recover its commercial confidence by the 1860s, and indeed to enjoy four decades of High Victorian vigour.

4
The County Town: Bureaucracies of Church and State

This month and the next will prove busy ones to the innkeepers of this town: who in that space of time will have to accommodate the public at a County Nomination; at a County Election; at a Quarter Sessions; at a Bishop's Visitation; at a Confirmation; at an Assize; at a Wool Fair, at a Bull Fair, and at the Races.

THE *LEWES JOURNAL*, 6 JULY 1801.

Besides facilitating the commerce of mid-Sussex, Georgian Lewes prospered as a hub of administration, focusing a tangle of bureaucracies. Like the markets and fairs, they attracted "the public" and quickened High Street trade. The most ramifying of them hinged on the Justices of the Peace and their Court of Quarter Sessions, the basic organ of local government in Sussex. Its authority, like the High Sheriff's and the Lord Lieutenant's, embraced the whole shire (minus a few Boroughs), but in practice it split the county in two. The Justices in the Western Division (the Rapes of Bramber, Arundel and Chichester) met at Horsham or Petworth or Chichester. Those in the Eastern Division (the Rapes of Lewes, Pevensey and Hastings) always met at Lewes, unless smallpox intervened. Their jurisdiction reached to East Guldeford in Romney Marsh, to ruined Bodiam Castle and Bayham Abbey, almost to The Pantiles at Tunbridge Wells, and to the remote recesses of Worth Forest, though the Cinque Ports and their Limbs were exempted. To administer this sprawling terrain, the Justices resorted to Lewes each quarter, at Easter, Midsummer, Michaelmas and Epiphany; their Sessions House being the Town Hall. Their Court tried offences against the King's Peace, mostly assault, trespass and theft. It also dealt with decayed bridges and highways, deficient weights and measures, and with the endless complexities, legal or carnal, of parochial poor relief. All this required the Court to marshal a regiment of bailiffs, constables, grand jurors, hundredal jurors, petty jurors, parish overseers, attorneys, sureties and witnesses. And if the procedure

The old Sessions House (Horsfield's History)

described in contemporary manuals was observed, its opening was suitably ceremonious: the Sheriff's formal summons; the empanelling of jurors; the entry of the Justices, the Under-Sheriff and then his bailiffs, two by two, with white wands in their hands; the reading of the royal commission by the Clerk of the Peace; the swearing-in of jurors; the Chairman's address from the Justices' bench; a roll-call of constables etc. by the Court Crier; and, never too soon perhaps, an adjournment for dinner.

Lewes's two High Constables attended. Elected each October, along with two Headboroughs, they guarded the King's Peace in the Borough, their stout staves being emblazoned with municipal insignia. In 1813 the watchmaker John Holman sallied into the *Lewes Arms*, "amongst bayonets and swords, at the risk of his life", and arrested three soldiers, Volunteers from Kildare, for attacking a coal-heaver with a pewter quart-pot; yet they were fined a paltry 30 pence each. He also detained two drunken soldiers for battering an elderly seaman to the pavement near the *Crown*, though their victim fled Lewes, rather than tangle with the Law. Holman had more success with Trampers. If they were "deserving", a discharged sailor perhaps, or

Building, formerly the Castle Inn, by the Norman gateway (Sussex Archaeological Society)

a soldier's wife, he shelled out a Borough shilling, and if "distressed for lodgings", he housed them overnight in the east wing of the Market Tower. But he clapped suspected vagrants in the Borough's Black Hole there, till Justice Harrison ruled on committal to the House of Correction. Parson Hurdis met one such, a

Vendress of ballads and the bundled match,

screaming through Bishopstone her "miserable song"; he observed "her cobbled suit"

Of sulphur redolent and of the green
And sobbing ember of the smokey hearth.

Many seasoned Trampers however slipped past the High Constables into the Castle Precincts, an unpoliced enclave outside the Borough's jurisdiction. Indeed the *Journal* condemned the *Castle* tavern there as a "Beggars' Opera", and supplied them with a chorus:

Sub Castro, in safety, how oft have we slumber'd?
How often recruited our strength for the field?
Defying the Traps, when their forces they number'd,
Secure in the Extra-Parochial Shield.

Though the *Castle* was closed down in 1826, "persons of the lowest description" still infested nearby Brack Mount, so suitable otherwise for a tea-room, or an obelisk, giving "an air of grandeur to the town". To delimit afresh their authority the High Constables beat the Borough bounds in 1799, "as anciently trodden and rowed over with the greatest attention", and again in 1813, when the bruised boys were solaced at the *Pelham Arms* with bread, cheese and strong beer.

Happily for Holman, November the Fifth passed without noticeable bloodshed in 1813. Since 1808 the Bonfire had blazed at the town edge on Castle Banks. But earlier a massive pyre was annually built on School Hill, and defended by the populace as a pledge of loyalty to Throne and Altar, sanctified by Time. Local Justices trying to stop this "immemorial" rite were "roughly" used in 1773, and provoked a "considerable" riot in 1785. In 1797 when the faggots and tar barrels stretched 17 feet long, the Justices were outfaced by patriotic ritual: a man with a dark lantern in one hand, a match in the other, and a bundle of shaving hung across his shoulders, approached the pyre; behind him marched 40 others, equipped with kindling torches and singing the National Anthem - once lit, the Bonfire merrily scorched a Ladies' Boarding Academy hard by. Despite a posse of special constables, the fire blazed there again in 1798. However in 1807 five labourers were jailed, and many fined, for piling up the faggots, which did cause the fire to be relocated. Yet "squibbers", often from Brighton, remained a menace. Eleven were indicted in December 1827 for assaulting persons they took to be informers, but they were released after local sources pledged £200 for their good behaviour. In November 1829 a Headborough from nearby Swanborough Hundred was attacked, while striding through the Borough with his stave to reinforce the Peace.

The High Constables also liaised with Quarter Sessions over civil matters, the repair of roads and bridges, the accuracy of weights and measures. Lewes bridge was a charge on both Lewes and Pevensey rapes, so the Court in 1727 levied a rate for its rebuilding. At Hurstpierpoint this demand for £30, "by order of Sessions", caused bitter complaint: "Never were people more heartily curst...it cost about as much once before". In 1799 the High Constables referred to the Court various Nuisances: some "filthy and stinking Gutters running into the Street"; damage by Richard Hobden's waggons to the pitching on Keere Street; the danger to pedestrians of cellars burrowed under the pavement, not least when gratings were maliciously removed at night. They also reported "light Loaves" and deficient

Bushels, Pecks, Gallons, Pots and Decanters.

Customer protection reflected a concern for social order. The Court licensed public-houses. In famine years it was expected to safeguard supplies of bread-corn and reduce profiteering; the Sessions House itself being a stone's throw from the busiest corn market in mid-Sussex. One such "terrible time" was February 1757. The soaring price of bread slashed Thomas Turner's takings at East Hoathly; and after rural buyers threatened direct action, the Justices summonsed several corn-dealers at Lewes for refusing to sell at market prices. Many consumers, especially in the Weald, shared Turner's belief that dear bread arose not "from a real scarcity, but from the iniquitous practice of engrossers, forestalling etc.". In 1794-5 "dearness" coincided with a bitter cold. It froze the paper in the presses of the *Journal*, which now dwelt on the merits of the potato. A thousand Lewesians devoured a rich pea-broth donated by Thomas Kemp. Unrest flared at Brighton market, and militia men mutinied at Seaford. Next winter the beef added to the pea-broth made a "comfortable, hearty meal". At Newhaven British and Baltic wheat was unloaded. Bread prices were high in May 1800. The Baptists worshipping at Cliffe lamented "the enormous price of provisions and the calamities of war". By December "inferior Tradesmen and Mechanics" were "tottering amidst their half-starved families" in a county town chalked with inflammatory slogans. Amid the distress the Justices forwarded to the plump Southdown farmers, gathered at their Saturday market in the *Star*, a letter from the Weald posted at Uckfield. This promised "speedy destruction" to all those "instrumental in keeping up the price of the necessities of life". It warned that "eleven to eighteen thousand desperate men" were ready "to rise at a short notice, armed with missile weapons, that shall set all military resistance at defiance". A second letter promised the overseer of the poor at Southover a decisive rap on his pate. The 40 men, who marched in from Barcombe in February 1801, were content to lobby the Justices for subsidized flour. Other initiatives included charity sermons, benefit balls, "attic" entertainments, cheap rice and potatoes, 20,000 messes of nutritious, palatable soup, and the Subscription Windmill, built above Westgate Lane to ensure "genuine Meal without the Fear of Adulteration" at a moderate price.

Also in 1800 the Bread Act required JPs at Petty Sessions to see that rice, potatoes and herring replaced bread in parish workhouses and outdoor relief. At Quarter Sessions the JPs already tangled with

William Hay (Horsfield's History)

the Poor Law. Indeed William Hay (1695-1755) of Glyndebourne, who chaired the Lewes Bench for 30 years, wrote a tract on its Reform which delighted those exact social scientists, Beatrice and Sidney Webb. The Court resolved many angry disputes between parishes over what constituted a legal settlement. "We cast them", crowed Thomas Marchant at Hurstpierpoint, when Cuckfield was awarded the care of Thomas Mitchell. Cases multiplied as the Division's population grew; 16 awaited the Justices at Epiphany 1826. Paternity problems consumed much bureaucratic energy, in and out of Court. While overseer of the poor, Thomas Turner resorted to the Justices' Clerk at Lewes for a warrant to "take up" an unmarried mother in East Hoathly; he then brought her to Lewes to confess the father's identity, and secured a second warrant to arrest the septuagenarian she named. In 1813 Lieutenant Forster at Lewes barracks was taken up by overseers from Ashburnham. The Justices also regulated apprenticeship. When John Mabb grew deranged, they cancelled his indentures with a Cliffe feltmaker. They clapped in the House of Correction a rowdy youth bound to a Lewes cooper.

A single Clerk of the Peace handled the paperwork at both the Eastern and Western Quarter Sessions. Besides the routine rolls, depositions and order books, Georgian statutes gave him custody of game licences, enclosure awards, plans for turnpike roads and canals, and endless lists, detailing charities, Roman Catholics, pauper lunatics, savings banks, convicted poachers, Friendly Societies, land tax assessments, Freemasons (suspected of "treasonable purposes") and owners of printing presses (seen as founts of sedition). Between 1615 and 1660 the Lewes attorneys William Thomas and William Alcock filled the post. Westerners followed them till Lord Ashburnham, an Eastern Lord Lieutenant, chose the Lewesian James Michell 1756-75. And the Duke of Richmond transcended any Western bias by appointing William Balcombe Langridge 1806-32, a Lewes carpenter's son. He masterminded a new Shire Hall at Lewes, to better house the Quarter Sessions, the Assizes and the Records. He lobbied hard at Westminster for a watertight Act which obliged the Sussex Cinque Ports to share the cost. He assembled bridging loans in advance of a county rate, and because the architect John Johnson was over eighty, he tendered for materials, chose Baltic timber at London, chartered a Newhaven vessel to bring stone from Portland, and accompanied the mason-in-charge to the quarries, where he washed down lobsters and shrimps with "prodigious quantities of beer, cider, wine and negus".

The first Treasurer for the Eastern Division was the Cliffe grocer, John Plumer 1740-61. Then came Charles Gilbert, John Hoper 1801-21, and George his son, all Lewes attorneys. Among townsmen benefiting from rates raised "by order of Sessions" were Elijah Kent, pensioned from the Maimed Soldiers fund in 1720, for losing a leg at the siege of Lille, and pipemaker Henry Apps, reimbursed from the Charitable Uses fund for the curing of his journeyman's broken shoulder.

The bustle at Quarter Sessions, being so good for commerce, made Lewesians the more eager to host the Sussex Assizes. Held twice a year, at Lent and Midsummer, they attracted the shire elite: the peers, MPs and Justices, both Eastern and Western. The two Home Circuit judges toiled into Sussex from Surrey or Kent; and in Stuart times they rarely bypassed the Courthouses at Horsham or East Grinstead, and ploughed on through the "deep and dirty" Weald to Lewes. But from 1713 till 1731 they came most Midsummers. The townsfolk funded their overnight "entertainment" at Benjamin Court's house, and in 1726 cheerfully bore the cost of burying the men "that were hanged". Being a second "public devercion" of the shire elite, the Lewes races were moved from May to Midsummer, to begin after the judges departed. From 1731 till 1799 the judges came every second Midsummer, and then every Midsummer, because a cramped Courthouse lost East Grinstead the Lent Assizes. These went to Horsham which ceded to Lewes its Midsummer Sessions. But the judges began bemoaning the noise invading the Lewes Sessions House on its island in the High Street, despite straw being strewn. So in 1808-12 the chicly Neo-classical Shire Hall was built, with spacious courtrooms, Crown and Nisi Prius, neatly secluded each side of a grand staircase. Such splendour (and the ever-improving turnpike roads through the Weald) secured for Lewes the new Winter Assizes, begun in December 1822. And though Horsham's noble patron, the Duke of Norfolk, spent large sums improving its Courthouse, Lewes annexed the Lent Sessions from 1831.

As befitted a Fount of Royal Justice, each judge brought a viceregal retinue, consisting in July 1789 of a coachman, a postillion, a groom, a trainbearer, a butler, a cook, a marshall, a marshall's servant, a tipstaff and a crier, though they shared a porter. Before their solemn entry into Lewes, they sometimes lodged with the Duke of Newcastle at Halland. At Lewes, after Court's became a coffee-house, they slept in suave bedrooms at grocer Johnston's, The Friars and elsewhere.

Yet despite the entourage and the sermon at St Michael's, despite the Crier of the Court coyly collecting his fees in a neat kid glove "at the end of a wand", and despite the Coade stone panels on the new Shire Hall portraying Wisdom, Justice and Mercy, the Court's proceedings were clumsy, even grotesque. The judges resolved well

Mercy

Wisdom

Justice

enough problems of shire administration: the legality of tolls at Barcombe bridge, or the need to repair Cliffe House of Correction. But the trials for murder, highway robbery and sheep stealing, which so fascinated the shire, often degenerated into Black Comedy. Parson Boys Ellman (1815-1906), a warm-hearted High Tory, remembered them from the 1820s. Baron Graham scribbled down every word of evidence, his octogenarian upper-lip black with snuff. Barrister Plat savagely cross-examined female witnesses till they swooned. A weak-minded youth was executed for burning a barn at Milton Court, but the devious rogue, who "decoyed the poor imbecile to join him", gave King's Evidence and walked free to roam the lanes of Berwick. Another youth, Daniel Leney, hung in 1826, seemed "a mere boy" when pinioned on the scaffold at Horsham. A lodger at Burwash with Hannah Russell, both were convicted at Lewes for poisoning her husband, after arsenic was diagnosed by a worthless surgeon whose expertise Baron Graham warmly commended. Legal twaddling over her marital status delayed Hannah's execution, long enough for the Lewes surgeon, Gideon Mantell, to annihilate the diagnosis, and secure her release. But Leney, so "mild and placid" on the scaffold, no train-bearer, sermon or kid glove could restore.

While Leney swung outside the gate of the County Gaol at Horsham, an obliging hangman stroked the goitrous necks of several women with his warm but lifeless hand: an ancient remedy as grotesque as his trial. Till 1822 the county's executions, or "hanging fairs", had been staged on Horsham Common, usually at noon on a Saturday. A dismal cortege of Under-Sheriff, gaoler, chaplain and hangman accompanied a cart, bearing one or more prisoners and coffins. A crowd, often several thousand strong, patiently munched oranges and gingerbread, and rewarded any lively valediction from the gallows with a collection for next-of-kin. Miss Edith Lavender, convicted at seventeen of infanticide, could only tremble and weep. But Robert Bignall, a notorious smuggler, guarded to the gallows by a squad of Essex Militia, greatly obliged with some verses he had penned on the prevalence of vice; the *Journal* also noted his boots were nearly new. Thunder clouds awesomely gathered as Daniel Hartford, condemned at Lewes for horse-stealing, proclaimed his repentance, thereby securing his child a place in a Philanthropic Asylum. In 1822 3000 spectators savoured a new excitement when a mobile Newgate drop, assembled at Lewes, was set up outside the prison gate. At Edward Broadbent's execution in 1819, because the rope proved too long, earth had been excavated under his feet.

Besides the Newgate drop, other Enlightened reforms modified executions at Horsham. The last woman to be hanged and then burned, for killing her husband, a crime akin to regicide, was 80-year-old Ann Cruttenden in 1776. After 1799 corpses were no longer displayed on gibbets. Splinters from Jacob's Post on Ditchling Common, where Jacob Harris hung in chains in 1734, were long treasured as talismans against epilepsy; and Alfred Lord Tennyson's poem *Rizpah* hymned a Sussex mother who retrieved the bones of her son:

> I kiss'd 'em, I buried 'em all -
> I can't dig deep, I am old - in the night by
> the churchyard wall.

From 1752 executed murderers (unless gibbeted) were stored in tallow chandlers' hampers to await medical dissection, though the skin of Richard Grazemark who raped and killed his daughter, was used for shoe leather, being in places a quarter inch thick, so The *Journal* reported. And "Pressing to death" was last authorized in England at Lewes Assizes in 1735. John Weekes of Fittleworth refused to answer a charge of murder, hoping thereby to save his assets from confiscation. So the Dumb Man was carted to Horsham, and staked to the ground in the prison yard. Still refusing to plead, he was crushed beneath a growing pile of weights, till the 16-stone gaoler climbed on top and killed him.

In 1726, and possibly 1716, Lewes breached Horsham's monopoly of hanging fairs in Sussex. The Gallows Bank where Malefactors died was noted in 1796 as near the Borough Pound on White Hill. By then the profits from Hangmans Acre below were a perk of the Town Crier. However Lewes did host the public whippings awarded at Quarter Sessions and Assizes. Till the 1790s some were inflicted at the cart's tail, often between the west gate and the bridge. Most were at the Borough market-house till its demolition; then at Cliffe "market post"; then outside the new House of Correction. In 1790 Thomas Peckham received over 300 lashes for stealing a bushel of wheat. In 1828 several "respectably attired" women were among 300 spectators who savoured the flogging of six thieves; the Justices deeming that hard labour on the treadmill no longer deterred. Yet Enlightened reform was again at work. In 1820 a statute ended the flogging of women. At genteel Lewes this took place "in private" from at least 1795, when Sarah Mitchell, a prostitute at Brighton Camp, was awarded 450 lashes. A tamer spectacle was the drunkard confined in the parish stocks; at Southover in the 1820s Boys Ellman watched one "babe in the wood" being plied with beer by his cronies.

To reform persons in the Rapes of Lewes and Pevensey they deemed shiftless or vagrant, the Eastern Justices had built a House of Correction at Cliffe in 1609. There two unmarried mothers from St Michael's parish were immured for 12 months in 1767. Local beggars were rounded up and whipped there "with suitable severity" in 1788. The prison was also an outpost for the County Gaol at Horsham. In 1764 two smugglers awaiting trial broke free; and for stealing a jackass John Saunders was held three months between floggings in 1792. Flanked by open sewers, the premises were cramped and doubtless fever-ridden when the tireless Penal Reformer, John Howard, visited in 1782. His progressive theories shaped the design of a new House of Correction opened at North

The new House of Correction (ESRO)

Street in 1793, a project dear to the Duke of Richmond, a liberal Lord Lieutenant. Erected on an "airy and healthy" site, it boasted 32 single cells, a chapel, a bath, a kitchen, a mop manufactory and apartments for the Keeper. Salaries and charges were fixed. Visiting Justices checked the food and daily routine. More single cells were added in 1817, required perhaps by Brighton's rapid growth; and in 1822 a treadmill was installed, which drove a flour mill outside the prison wall in Lancaster Street, thereby neatly linking Retribution and Utility. The hard labour of 15 male convicts could revolve the running stone (39 inches in diameter) 120 times a minute. For female convicts a daintier engine was proposed, able to fill a reservoir and cleanse adjacent streets. The prison's inmates were still very mixed. A cartload of gipsies arrived under escort from Portslade in 1801. 27 convicted poachers were held in January 1826. Robert Bignall was remanded there in 1807, after his arrest at the *White Hart* in Ditchling, though only a fit of cramp on a scaling ladder foiled his escape over the wall. Ready resort to transportation and the lash kept numbers down. In 1830 62-year-old Philadelphia Vinall was shipped away, for stealing two pounds of flour at Maresfield.

Much involved with the Assizes and Quarter Sessions were the High Sheriff, the Under-Sheriff and his bailiffs. They summoned constables and jurors; served writs and collected fines. They provided the judges with an escort, lodgings and a sermon. Aided by a joint Midsummer meeting of Justices, Eastern and Western, they administered the executions at Horsham, and the County Gaol there with its debtors' prison. The Sheriff's own County Court met every four weeks at Lewes or Chichester, and mostly dealt with small debts. At Lewes too it staged the election by freeholders living in Lewes and Pevensey Rapes of an attorney as their Coroner. They chose John Michell (1682-1735) of Lewes and Thomas Attree 1753-64 of Newick, whose son then campaigned on his own behalf. But despite a promising canvass at Uckfield fair, he allowed Francis Wheeler of Cliffe to succeed "without any bustle". In 1785, by 511 votes to 217, Wheeler's son William defeated William Attree of Ditchling, later Solicitor to the Prince Regent:

> Both Rapes, to help the Wheeler out,
> Sent many spokes from all about.

In 1809 over 800 freeholders voted when Wheeler's grandson Thomas vanquished Christopher Kell of Lewes. However in 1817 Wheeler III resigned in disgrace amid charges of extortion and false accounting. George Gwynne 1817-29 and Francis Harding Gell 1829-64, both Lewesians, were elected unopposed.

Apart from cases of treasure trove, the Coroners' inquests make melancholy reading. They tell of opiates misused, imprudent sea bathing, lethal prize fights, scalding barley beer, a blow from a windmill's sail, blizzards engulfing inebriates, and a samphire-gatherer slipping from Beachy Head. At Lewes the postmaster Thomas Tasker hanged himself; lightning struck William Jenner on Spital Hill; Richard Ditch fell from a mast at Cliffe; an avalanche of chalk at Malling crushed John Stanford; and a cesspit at the barracks engulfed a grenadier from the South Hampshire Militia.

The County Court also staged the election by 40-shilling freeholders of two Knights of the Shire to represent Sussex in parliament. The writ decided the venue, whether Lewes or Chichester. However if the county elite agreed on an Easterner and a Westerner, preferably a Pelham and a Lennox, and if this avoided the disruptive expense of a contest, then the writ was managed in favour of Lewes as much the most central. Yet even unanimous elections mustered puissant cavalcades of loyalists on the day. 500 escorted Thomas Pelham from Stanmer Park in 1754. As many converged at Halland in 1761 to salute his patron, the Duke of Newcastle. In February 1767 the deep snow that killed a Lewes newsman also cancelled a by-election ball, but the Duke of Richmond still battled along the Downs from Goodwood to endorse Lord George Lennox. In June 1790 "a grand and extensive procession" swept in more smoothly from the west to support Colonel Charles Lennox. Whenever these loyalists rallied, they expected "entertainment". In 1780 they ate 200 dinners at the *Star* (£120), and 200 at the *White Hart* (£94), besides carousing at the *Bear*, the *Dog* etc. (£52). Musicians, bell-ringers and the Crier of the County Court were rewarded too. Lewes was also the best place for Nominations of Knights of the Shire. After Lord Middlesex's at the *White Hart* in June 1741, he returned before the election to mingle affably at the Midsummer Assizes and races.

A contested county election mobilized many hundreds of freeholders. At Lewes in 1713 2780 divided by rape, between the upper and lower courts of the Sessions House and four waggons parked outside. Despite this crowd control, Mrs Marshall, a spectator from Poynings, was "very much beat and bruised". Almost 4000 voters converged on Chichester in 1774. The Eastern candidate was a Minden veteran, Sir Thomas Wilson of Fletching, an Independent, much averse to election bribery. He faced two Westerners, Sir John Peachey who hoped to defeat him, and the widely popular Lord George Lennox. To preserve their Division's voice, outraged Easterners streamed westward at their own expense. A waggonload from Southover overturned in Michelgrove Wood, though without serious harm; and the 45 who sallied from Cliffe stirred the muse of Dr Delap, then resident in South Street:

> Such spirit late thy sons inspir'd,
> O Cliffe! with British ardor fir'd,
> When, leagu'd in friendly, firm array,
> To Chichester they bent their way.

Because Peachey's few Eastern partisans feared the angry "Mobility" at Lewes, they slunk westward through its back lanes. After Lennox polled 3587 votes, Wilson 1969 and Peachey 1856, the Eastern capital staged a jubilant General Illumination, much as when Montreal surrendered. At Cliffe James Lambert painted elegant transparencies of Lennox, Wilson and the intrepid 45. When the Eastern Victor returned, heralded by 16 running footmen, and escorted by 400 horsemen, Lewes rejoiced afresh. Bells pealed, drums beat, French horns blared. In front of the *Star* Wilson thanked a thousand spectators; and "everyone paid his own".

Less edifying was the contest at Lewes in 1807. Between Tuesday 12 May and Thursday 28 May 5019 freeholders cast 4333 votes for the Westerner Charles Wyndham, 2530 for John Fuller of Brightling, and 2473 for Colonel Sergison of Cuckfield. The Easterners clashed over Emancipation for Roman Catholics and West Indian slaves. The High-Tory Folly-building Fuller opposed both. The moment polling ended, the Mobility tore apart the hustings by the Sessions House and carried the fragments away, claiming "immemorial" custom. It greeted the result - Sergison being the "popular" candidate, by tossing rotten eggs into the balconied Great Room at the *White Hart*, Fuller's campaign headquarters. Sergison then spoke from a window of the *Star*, assuring his partisans that a Sheriff's scrutiny of the poll would overturn Fuller's trivial majority. So they dragged the Colonel and his carriage in triumph up the High Street, to rendezvous at the barracks with Whig confederates marching in from Brighton. Though the Sheriff refused a scrutiny, Fuller's victory had proved expensive. As well as the No Popery favours, he paid for almost 2000 dinners at the *White Hart*, and as many at the *Dorset Arms*, "an East Country House" popular with freeholders from Hastings Rape.

Eastern freeholders toiled westward in 1818, and again in 1820 when Gideon Mantell diagnosed an "immense number" passing through Lewes as Tories "pressed by the Earl of Abergavenny" whose estates focused on Frant. Mantell and two fellow Whigs followed soon after: their hats, horses and postillions heavily bedecked with pink ribbon. To reach another contest at Chichester in 1826, a group of Whigs at Rye hired "an old tub of a vessel", complaining that Paris had "an easier access" than the Western capital. During the voyage they admired the new gas lamps at Brighton and the lobster fishermen off Selsey Bill. From Itchenor quay they rambled through corn fields to the Guildhall in North Street, while their crew drank all the porter on board and absconded. These arduous journeys provoked Easterners twice in the 1820s to promote Bills fixing shire elections at Lewes, but Western influence defeated them.

Because the duties of a Sheriff's year could be tiresome and expensive, the office attracted pushy parvenus. "Low persons" Lord Justice Mansfield called them; and the sight of four ex-Sheriffs, sharing a glass of brandy and water at Lewes sheep fair, disgusted Boys Ellman's father. Yet Sir Ferdinando Poole, long resident at The Friars, served twice with great credit in 1787-89. Each Sheriff recruited a corps of javelin men to escort the Assize judges. Poole clad his in blue coats, buff waistcoats and leather breeches, a Whig colour-scheme complimenting the politics of his racing companion, the Prince of Wales, whose birthday at Brighton they attended, armed with their wooden spears seven feet long. In 1791 they reunited at the *Pelham Arms* for a Javelin Hunt. The corps was limited to 13 in 1822, and its cost transferred to County or Treasury funds. The Deputy-Sheriffs did the donkey-work, and were often Lewes attornies. John Michell in 1720 excused Thomas Marchant from service as an Assize-juror, in return for 30 pence and a pint of wine. He levied fees on the Knights of the Shire elected unopposed at Lewes in 1727, and supplied the data for a poll book after the county contest in 1734. His son William shared the duties with Richard Rideout of Lewes in 1749, though both were jittery about an intended "vigorous prosecution" of local smugglers. Rideout thought he recognized one ring-leader, Little Dick, in a sinister posse he passed on Beeding Hill.

Collecting government revenue was also focused at Lewes. The land tax commissioners (mostly gentry and clergy) met there in 1776 to fix quotas for the Eastern Division. Their managing clerk in Pevensey Rape, the Lewes attorney Charles Gilbert, kept an agreed percentage of the money raised. James Chaffin, a Divisional Collector of Excise, died at Southover in 1787. More junior was Tom Paine who surveyed "the upper part of Lewes" in 1768-74. William Wisdom noted the Democrat's oval face, bushy wig and round hat, his "Bat" legs & thighs. At Lewes Paine penned *The Case of the Officers of Excise*, a plea for their better payment which brought his dismissal from the service, despite its courteous optimism:

> Langour and neglect would give place to care and cheerfulness. Men of reputation and abilities would seek after it and finding a comfortable maintenance, would stick to it. The unworthy and the incapable would be rejected; the power of superiors be re-established, and laws and instructions receive new force. The officers would be secured from the temptations of poverty, and the revenue from the evils of it.

This talent for argument he also deployed in a letter to the *Journal* deploring the inhumanity of the Poor Law, a fitting prelude to the pamphlets, *African Slavery in America* (1775) and *Common Sense* (1776), which he wrote after migrating to Pennsylvania.

Paine conceded that some excise officers on the coast did profit from seizing contraband, though often "at the hazard of their lives". Lewes itself commanded a major corridor for goods smuggled from France to London, and mounted officers based there were on constant patrol. Eight men from the Lower Ouse valley, and two from Whitesmith near Laughton, were indicted at East Grinstead Assizes in 1749 for smuggling goods through Seaford; and though a key witness claimed Officer Skinner had terrorized him into giving false evidence, the geography seems plausible. Caches of tea and brandy were found at Glynde bridge in 1774, and at the *Golden Placket* near Arlington in 1787. Officer Cullen stabled six horses laden with recovered contraband at the *Swan* in Southover, which were promptly abducted. Most smugglers of course enjoyed popular support. Twelve dragoons were needed in 1747 to escort Peirce, a hardened "free trader", from Horsham Gaol to Lewes Assizes. And jurors were often biased. John Burgess lingered at the Sessions House in 1787 to hear Officer Ginden convicted for the murder of a Preston man on the beach, though he was not "much Effected".

As a master glover Burgess was caught in the fiscal web spun at Lewes by the Senior Distributor of government stamps and licences in the Eastern Division. This post, awarded for political partisanship, was enjoyed by the ironmonger Joseph Molineux, the grocer Thomas Gilbert, the hatter James Harben, and his nephew Thomas, the banker's eldest son. At Harben's Bank Burgess bought the stamps and licences allowing him to make and sell gloves. Since he also paid duty on his raw materials, his later enthusiasm for New York State as a free-trading "land of Liberty" was understandable. So was banker Harben's haste to heap courtesies on John Byng and his wife, when that senior official at the Stamp Office in Somerset House passed three disgruntled nights at the *White Hart*. Harben's phaeton speeded Mrs B. to Brighton, where Byng observed "a harpy set of painted harlots", as flagrant as Bond Street in the spring. Possibly these civilities helped Harben's son Henry to become a Keeper of Stamps at Somerset House in 1791.

Also at Lewes the Sussex militia was co-ordinated, to defend a maritime shire vulnerable to invasion. Reports of a French landing at Pevensey Marsh sparked a Great Alarm at Chichester in 1745. Drums beat, the gates closed, bullets were cast and deed-boxes buried. In July 1759 the Lord Lieutenant convened a County Meeting at the *White Hart* to sanction a regiment 800 strong, in two battalions, East and West. But Lord Abergavenny proved a "Dumb and Inanimate" Chairman; the dinner was "dear and bad"; and the county gentry squabbled over the chain of command, though the Duke of Newcastle reconciled them at the Lewes races. Because militia service proved so bothersome and unpopular, a County Meeting in July 1769 voted to pay the government £4000 rather than recruit the shire. When in 1778 a regiment was raised, protests flared round Henfield and Petworth, and a company of the Scots Greys dispersed angry crowds massing near Lewes on "our Downs", as the *Journal* cosily called them. Nonetheless contingents from the three Eastern rapes did parade at Lewes on Tanners Field near Greenwall, "a splendid Campus Martis". (In 1676 they had mustered near the town "upon Henry's mountt".) Their good order owed much to their Colonel, Thomas Hay of Glyndebourne; and something perhaps to amiable Captain Fuller. While on duty at Brighton the future Folly-Builder intrigued Miss Fanny Burney: "He has figure, understanding, education, vivacity, and independence", yet "devotes almost all his time...to a company of light infantry!". He explained his men's tipsy laughter when a gust on the Steine wrecked her finery; they'd just been paid arrears, and couldn't keep even a sixpence in their pockets. When he trimmed their hair they protested, till he bought new feathers for their caps.

Thomas Hay (Horsfield's History)

Popular fear of militia service fed on the regular army's brutal discipline. When in 1747 a deserter was hanged at Lewes, buried, and then dug up for dissection by local surgeons, his comrades snatched the corpse back and buried it in quicklime. In 1765 a civilian crowd heckled the "Barbarity" of a Duty Officer, one Dundas, who forced a drummer to flog harder when a private received 500 lashes for pilfering. Undaunted Dundas then awarded a soldier 300 lashes for losing a sword while aiding an exciseman, who was eager to replace it. Troops were often billeted at Lewes, to combat invasion or smuggling. In 1740 its publicans lobbied hard to remove 80 soldiers before the summer races when bed and board were at a premium. In 1755 an entire regiment was expected. As some recompense a corps of dragoons celebrated the King's Birthday with fireworks and music in June 1763; by October forage was scarce for their 82 horses. Lewesians enrolling as Volunteers risked neither the lash nor the protests of publicans. Blithely in June 1780 an infantry company recruited from the Borough, Southover and the riverside parishes down to Newhaven, marched off to a review at Preston manor, headed by Captain Thomas Kemp, woolstapler.

The wars with France between 1792 and 1815 caused a build-up along the mid-Sussex coast of military camps, barracks, beacons and Martello towers. Manoeuvres on the Lewes Downs were often attended by the Prince of Wales, clad in dashing uniforms cut to his own design. In April 1793 he reviewed the Horse Artillery, before breakfasting at Southover with William Newton, a Lieutenant-Colonel in the Prince's Own Light Dragoons. In September he doughtily mounted guard at Brighton camp; and in October he watched a "desperate sham-fight" at Hollingbury Hill above Moulescoomb, also admired, as the *Journal* archly put it, by "the rising, in a mass" of civilian Beauty and Fashion from Brighton. At Lewes in November the local Beau Monde endorsed the war effort at its monthly assembly in the *Star*, by collecting to equip the Duke of York's army in Flanders with the flannel waistcoats needed to repel "the inclement attacks of a morbid atmosphere". Mrs George Shiffner moreover supervised the stitching of 250 flannel caps. In May 1794 a County Meeting at the Sessions House revived the Sussex Volunteers. They soon included, so the *Journal* reported, a mounted corps of churchwardens led by Sir Henry Blackman, with suitably embossed buttons. Captain Kemp re-embodied his infantry company, now drawn exclusively from the Borough. Its field-day in November was on Malling Down, but ended with an assault on an "elegant cold collation" at the *Castle* tavern (any Trampers beating a swift retreat). In May 1795 a sham-fight, with feasting and sports, was staged on Kemp's Coneysborough estate at Barcombe; in October his company trained at Houndean Bottom with George Shiffner's yeomen cavalry. Such zest doubtless heartened the Sussex Volunteer Committee, meeting at the *White Hart* in January 1796. Next December the *Bear* hosted a militia ballot for Upper Pevensey Rape, while men enlisting at the *Stag* for the navy were promised 20 guineas and "a full share of such SPANISH DOUBLOONS as their fortune and bravery shall entitle them to". Recruits was spurred on by the Illuminations which greeted naval victories over the Dutch in 1797 and 1799, though the unlit windows of an unrejoicing cobbler were smashed.

Mid-Sussex grew acutely aware of its "frontier situation" in 1803, as Napoleon's invasion army massed around Boulogne. Civilians, livestock and vehicles were listed for removal to the Weald. Militia men tended fire beacons on Mount Harry and White Bostal above Berwick. An "improved" weathercock was mooted for the castle keep, to warn if enemy sails were filling. By August 1803 the Borough supplied two infantry companies to the South Lewes Volunteers (the Prince of Wales's Own), captained by Kemp and William Hick, a merchant who once mistook sloe wine for Pexaretta. William Newton, now retired from the Dragoons, formed a third company from Southover and the riverside parishes. They united in January 1804 to execute manoeuvres on Chailey Common with "wonderful correctness". At Cliffe the coroner William Wheeler raised a company embodied in the South Pevensey Volunteers. Even the river cutters along the Ouse Navigation offered to form a pioneer corps under their surveyor Cater Rand. Naturally the news of Trafalgar in November 1805 sparked a heartfelt Illumination. An ambitious transparency at the *Journal* Office showed the *Sanctissima Trinidada* surrendering to the *Victory*, plus "the noble Admiral's ascension to the realms of peace". Landlord James Durnford adorned the *Dorset Arms* with a truculent couplet:

> Nelson still lives in every Briton's heart,
> Know that - and tremble, Master Bonaparte.

Defiance was renewed in December when a pupil at John Button's Cliffe Academy recited to admiring parents:

> With gen'rous fury at their country's call,
> Her gallant sons present a living wall.
> Along her coast the warrior offspring stands,
> Rage in their eyes, and slaughter in their hands.
> From Scotland's coldest shores her banners wave,
> To Cliffs, whose feet the southern billows lave,
> One common fury animates the whole,
> Knits ev'ry nerve, and glows in ev'ry soul.

The military build-up in mid-Sussex quickly brought a chain of new barracks. At Lewes in 1790 40 soldiers were housed in tenements near Irelands Lane; and in 1793 its publicans billeted 230 Horse Artillery, though the War Office supplied hammocks and forage. However in 1796 barracks for 1000 men were built on four acres at Haredean, near Ashcombe toll gate on the Brighton road. Militia men from East Yorkshire held a supper-dance there in April 1797, and in May the Prince of Wales reviewed them on Spital Hill. But the site proved unhealthy, so 30 acres of higher ground near Spital crossroads were leased in 1803. The 52 neat wooden huts, each housing 24 men, were compared to "Sydney Cove in our distant colony of Botany Bay"; and Button's *Directory* deemed them "very conducive" to health and comfort. Yet in February and March 1809 typhus fever infected some 200 inmates and killed at least 23. Even more at risk were the soldiers' families, housed near the Spital crossroads in 15 or 16 single-room huts alongside two canteens (now the *Pewter Pot*). In August and September 1807 the *Journal* reported a bowel complaint that "carried off" over 80 children. Smallpox struck in October 1811. Regularly the Jewish pawnbroker Philip Lyon trudged up from the Cliffe to sell flea-powder. When the families grew destitute after the husbands left for the Peninsula, Lewesians organized a Benevolent Society.

On 6 April 1814 Gabriel, the town bell, tolled briskly to advertise the entry into Paris of the Allied Armies. Jubilant crowds greeted the London coach bringing down the details in the *Gazette*. In June the Allied Sovereigns, Alexander of Russia and Frederick of Prussia, passed swiftly through Lewes. They were "solicitous to catch the Tide" at Dover, as the Town Book tactfully put it, after tarrying at Portsmouth to admire "those impregnable Woodden Walls (for ages the protection of this highly favoured island)". On 7 July, a day of General Jubilee, some 1600 parishioners from St Michael's and St John's assembled on the Wallands to eat 2146 lbs. of "solid food", besides bread and vegetables. 5000 spectators then applauded the rustic sports, "a scene of hilarity, harmony and joy", tinged perhaps with indigestion. In December the barracks were demolished. And in June 1815 Gabriel tolled again, for Napoleon's surrender to Captain Maitland aboard the *Bellerophon*. However the huts by the Spital crossroads survived, being let in 1818 to persons of the "most debauched" kind, "beggars, thieves and whores".

As well as secular officials, Lewes hosted an ecclesiastical bureaucracy. A Spiritual Court, answerable to the Bishop of Chichester, held formal sessions in St Michael's church, and served the whole Archdeaconry of Lewes which included most of the Eastern Division. The Court dealt with church rates, tithes, faculties, marriage licences and probate business, with wills, inventories and administrations. It no longer tangled with lewdness or immorality, but in 1763 a parson thought of using it to extract an apology, perhaps even a penance, after a layman insulted his "Ministerial Function". Its procedures, shrouded in Canon Law, were arcane, expensive and long-winded, even allowing for the immense age of some officials. When Thomas Turner rode in to prove a neighbour's will, the fees mounted steeply, to £1 18s 4d; the "horses, turnpike and ostler" cost ninepence. As a parish overseer he paid a guinea for a licence allowing a pregnant spinster to marry George Hyland without banns being called. The parish also hurried them to the altar with £6 10s in cash, five stone of beef, a wedding ring and a marriage feast. Many rustic couples themselves resorted to Lewes for a licence, and often remained there to marry: indeed half the weddings in the town united "foreigners", till Lord Hardwick's Act ended the practice in 1754. The Court's Registrar was always a Lewes attorney. John Michell also acted as

Coroner and Under-Sheriff. Richard Lardner, whose son-in-law became Archdeacon of Durham, authorized the Duke of Newcastle to rebuild a pew at Bishopstone in 1736. Michell's son William issued George Hyland's licence; and in the 1780s William Raynes lived opposite St Michael's, the "Seat of Judicature". Josias Smith (c1737-1827) died in office worth £80,000, but intestate, which grieved his long-serving domestics.

Each year, after Easter, the Archdeacon of Lewes held a Visitation in St Michael's church, to confer with his clergy from the Deaneries of Lewes and Pevensey. Their churchwardens also came, to take their oaths of office: in Thomas Turner's case the fee was 4s 6d. In June 1806 30 followed the coffin of Araunah Verrall, a veteran churchwarden at St Michael's. Also at the Visitation money was paid in from Briefs. These royal mandates commended victims of fire, flood and tempest to the charity of church-goers. Araunah's father, Edward Verrall, a Deputy-Collector for the diocese, received 17s 6d from Thomas Turner in 1758, plus fourpence in bad copper. Between Visitations the Archdeacons recouped their pastoral zeal in spacious rural parsonages akin to Dr Grantly's at Plumstead near Barchester. Thomas D'Oyly 1751-70 and Matthias D'Oyly 1806-15 abided at Buxted. John Courtail 1770-1806 expired in office at Burwash, aged 92. But Edward Raynes 1815-24, though the pluralist incumbent of Ripe, Firle and Beddingham, chose to reside at Antioch House in Lewes, where he could more easily indulge his ruling passion, whist.

In St Michael's church the clergy from the two Deaneries also met the Bishop of Chichester, dining with him afterwards at the *Star*; and till at least 1798 he summoned their confirmation candidates to a crowded, and perhaps, chaotic sacrament at St Anne's, the largest church in Lewes. In theory episcopal Visitations and Confirmations were every three years. Sir William Ashburnham (1710-98) began well, confirming at Lewes in 1755 and 1758. But "many thousands" of candidates awaited him in 1792; and six years passed before the newly enthroned John Buckner (1734-1824) confirmed "a great number" more. Despite his great age, Buckner tottered to Lewes in 1820 and 1823, dining with Josias Smith, his venerable Registrar. By then candidates also gathered at Hailsham, Brighton, Cuckfield and East Grinstead, relieving pressure on St Anne's. In 1826 and 1829 came Robert Carr, many years Vicar of Brighton, before being promoted to Chichester by his crony George IV, allegedly to pay his gaming debts. Boys Ellman recalled "the solemn rite" with a pious shudder. Festive waggonloads of "great" boys and girls lurched in; afterwards they feasted heartily, and jolted back through the scented fields of summer.

A second Anglican bureaucracy at Lewes managed the Peculiar of South Malling which was subject to the archdiocese of Canterbury. Its parishes stretched from Cliffe north-eastwards to Wadhurst, with outliers at Stanmer and Lindfield. This ecclesiastical enclave held its own Spiritual Court, usually in St Thomas's church at Cliffe, where the Dean visited and the Archbishop confirmed. In 1761 the assembled clergy heard Archbishop Thomas Secker commend the "decent, neat and well Judged" condition of the church fabric, and the careful management of the Church Estate at Cliffe; such trusts, he asserted, were all too often "sacrilegiously perverted". (In fact Andrew Tasker and Thomas Baldy, the long-serving churchwardens, were misusing the revenues.) In 1792 Archbishop John Moore gave a guinea to the parish clerk, the organist, the bell-ringers, and the aged women "who strewed him". In 1810 Archbishop Manners Sutton dined with his clergy at the *Star*, a relaxed moment within the bureaucratic maze that was Georgian Lewes.

St. Thomas's Church (Horsfield's History)

5
The County Town: The Learned Professions

Tuesday 1 May 1764...after breakfast I rode to Lewes upon Mr. Vine's business. I dined at the White Hart in company with about twenty more upon a fillet of veal roasted, a ham boiled, a fore-quarter of lamb roasted, 2 hot pigeon pasties, 2 raisin and currant puddings, greens, potatoes and green salad. The reason of my dining on so elegant a dinner was on account of my having business with Mr. Baley, steward to the devisees and heirs of the Rt. Hon. Hen. Pelham Esq. deceased, who held an audit there today.

THOMAS TURNER'S *DIARY*.

No man can better gild a pill,
Or make a bill,
Or bleed or blister;
Or draw a tooth out of your head,
Or chatter scandal by your bed,
Or give a clyster.

The early bell that summon'd us to school,
The dogs-ear'd Virgil, and the name-carved stool,
The trap, the play ground, and the sportive names,
Dumps, marbles, cricket, and our youthful games,
The birchen rod, the ever-dreaded cane,
Make us almost live o'er those days again.

JOHN VINEY BUTTON, *EXERCISES ON ELOCUTION* (LEWES, 1805).

Its commercial and bureaucratic vigour meant Lewes became a focus for practitioners of Law, Medicine and Education. Indeed its senior officials were usually its leading attorneys. Between them John Michell and his sons, William (1708-71) and James (1721-80), served as Coroner, Registrar, Under-Sheriff and Clerk of the Peace. The family's "Great Benefactor", the Duke of Newcastle, also aided Henry Michell (1715-89) to become Vicar of Brighton. A fine

Classical scholar, he tutored Arthur Wellesley, and argued with Dr Johnson, both thumping the vicarage grate with the fire-irons. The County Treasurer, Charles Gilbert (1736-1816), stewarded manors in the South Downs, the Weald and Pevensey Marsh. He managed the Countess de Bruhl's estate at Frog Firle near Alfriston, and the tithes of Archdeacon D'Oyly at Buxted and Pevensey. His successor as County Treasurer, John Hoper (1759-1845), funded a Sunday School at Beddingham, where he bought Itford farm and built the faintly Gothick Asham House, home later to the Woolfs. His sons John and George, both Wykehamists, served jointly as Bishop's Registrar after Josias Smith died; and George followed John I as Treasurer. Smith managed the Lewes property of Lord Pelham, a trustee of the grammar school, and took charge of its foundation deed, discovered by chance in a London cheesemonger's.

As lawyers these Lewesians became enmeshed in the life of mid-Sussex and beyond. Before becoming Clerk of the Peace in 1806, William Balcombe Langridge (c1770-1832) dealt with militia ballots, the Aliens Act, and settlement cases at Quarter Sessions. As a notary public he interviewed sea-captains wrecked or stranded in Seaford Bay. Yet by the 1790s his purely private practice included mortgages, conveyances and wills, loans, debts and bankruptcies; selling timber at Shipley and the *Star* at Lewes; building a new poor-house at Thakeham; highway robbery at Denton; Parson Dionis Geere assaulting Henry Harben at Seaford; a stage-coach taking to the fields near Cuckfield to avoid a toll-gate; a tenant farmer at Buxted over-cropping his acreage; the transfer of bounty claims from naval recruits to the cordwainer Thomas Mantell; the theft of Artillery Stores at Brighton, geese at Barcombe, a tame duck at Southover. For a dispute in Chancery about downland tenures at Southerham, he quizzed Old Harris the local shepherd. He also acted for a family of yeomen farmers near Mayfield. Its head, Thomas Morris , was accused of sheep-stealing and fled abroad. So Langridge and Thomas's son made a "Journey Dunkerque" in August 1792 (amid the tremors of Revolution) to secure a power of attorney. The son then launched writs against his father's neighbours; but was himself accused of assault, remanded to Horsham Gaol, tried and acquitted. Thereupon he died; his daughter-in-law eloped, and a deed of separation was needed.

Though Henry Burtenshaw held no public office, his private practice also ramified widely. In the 1760s he handled mortgages at

Willingdon and Little Horsted, and securities on the Harbour of Littlehampton. He badgered a Chailey brickmaker over a debt for flour, and George Grantham about rent arrears for an osier bed. He advertised the sale of Coombe Place at Hamsey, Standean Farm in Patcham, and Gravetye Furnace at West Hoathly. As the Steward of Lord Craven's estates in Sussex he grappled with quit rents, fines and heriots, enfranchisement and Borough English, with entail, Widow's Bench and licences to cart marl and dig iron ore; he pondered the commercial impact of the proposed Ringmer-Battle turnpike road. He advised on bathing machines at Brighton, oysters at Shoreham Rock, a gamekeeper's licence at Possingworth, misdirected shipments of coal from Sunderland and butter from London. Brusque and assiduous (hence his quarrel with Charles Gilbert), he loved the finer points of Law: the status of Coal Clubs and standing corn, the serving of writs in Cinque Ports, a tenant's right to thatching straw, the award of prize-money after the capture of Goree, the claim of a Brighton widow, owning three-eighths of a ship, to choose its captain. Thomas Turner consulted him about the Pelham wills at Doctors' Commons because an "ancient" weekly dole of bread and beer, always given to East Hoathly's poor, had been stopped by Newcastle's new Steward at Halland. Any search probably involved Burtenshaw's Bloomsbury-based associate, the Lewes-born John Elliot.

Lewes House and School Hill House (James Lambert: British Library, Addit. Ms. 5671 fo. 46)

Till Brighton consolidated as a health resort, Lewes was unchallenged in mid-Sussex as a fount of medical opinion. In 1714 the physician John Tabor lived at Lewes House; he also owned Howbourne manor near Buxted. Nextdoor in 1715 the physician Peter White used his profits from money-lending to handsomely rebuild School Hill House. His case-load included the Marchants at Hurstpierpoint, the fits of Master Fagg at Glynleigh near Hailsham, and the bruises got at Lewes during a county election by Dame Marshall from Poynings. Among his smallpox patients in 1717 were landlord Wood at the *Bear* and a sea-captain at Newhaven. (White's own father-in-law, Captain Nicholas Tattersal, had carried the fugitive Charles II from Brighton to France.)

Both physicians died before 1729, which helped establish Richard Russell (1687-1759). The son of a Lewes apothecary, he audaciously married in 1719 Mary Kempe, the heiress to Malling Deanery. Then he took a belated medical degree at Leyden, where his thesis on epilepsy satisfied the eminent Herman Boerhaave, whose prescriptions Dr White collected. By the mid-1730s he was much in demand across East Sussex, attending the Pelhams at Stanmer, Lewes and Catsfield, and their Tory arch-rival, Thomas Sergison, at Cuckfield, as well as pregnant Mrs Turner at East Hoathly. However he also developed a seawater cure for scrofula, consumption and glandular disease. This grew so fashionable that in 1753 he built a reception centre for patients by the Steine at Brighton. He believed the ocean to be Nature's defence against all bodily "corruption and putrefaction", instancing the firm gums and radiant teeth of Brighton's fishwives. His patients were made to drink and bathe in seawater, hot, cold or lukewarm. They were gently rubbed with fresh seaweed. They sniffed fumes from boiling "stromboli", a fuel dug on the seashore. And always of course they absorbed the salt-laden sea-air. Russell also wrote an influential Latin treatise on the seawater cure, *De Usu Aquae Marinae In Morbis Glandularum Dissertatio*, published at Oxford in 1750. Its Rococo title-page depicted shells and seaweed, Neptune, Hygeia and a dolphin, and carried a line from Euripides, translating as

> The sea washes away all the ills of mankind.

This reappeared on his modest memorial tablet in Malling church. To meet growing metropolitan demand, "Sea-Water from Brighthelmstone...took off the main Ocean by T. Swaine" was sold by 1756 at the *Talbot* in Southwark, a depot for Brighton and Lewes carriers.

D E

TABE GLANDULARI,

SIVE

DE USU AQUÆ MARINÆ

I N

MORBIS GLANDULARUM

DISSERTATIO.

Auctore RICARDO RUSSELL, M. D.

Θάλασσα κλύζει πάντα τ' ἀνθρώπων κακά.
Mare abluit omnia hominum mala.
Euripides Iphigen. in Taur. V. 1193.

E THEATRO SHELDONIANO,
Prostant venales apud JACOBUM FLETCHER, *Oxon.* & J. & J. RIVINGTON, *Lond.* MDCCL.

Besides seawater Russell promoted the chalybeate St Anne's Well in Hove, a spring famed for the fecundity of the sheep drinking there. (But he did not adopt a well near St Anne's church in Lewes, much resorted to before the Reformation.)

Another pupil of Boerhaave was Edward Poole (1710-92) whose brother owned The Hooke estate in Chailey. He came to Lewes in 1753, but kept no surgery at Brighton till Russell died. Even then he advised John Shelley of Michelgrove that a month's sea bathing might do harm. When he examined Mrs Turner at East Hoathly, his half-guinea fee angered Thomas:

> Really a fine thing it is to be a physician who can charge just as they please and not be culpable according to any human law.

However Poole's marriage to a rich Brighton patient, Widow Sophia Bourryau from the West Indies, slackened in 1765 his quest for cash. The "tender couple", as Parson Davies of Glynde cattily called them, moved into Antioch House, and were soon dashing about in a chariot and pair, with two liveried footmen behind: "only a couple of Flambeaus could render the whole scene still more glaringly visible". Poole's ex-patients probably consulted Joseph Barham on School Hill. His successor in 1769, Thomas Frewen (1709-91), a parson's son from Northiam, had also studied under Boerhaave; indeed his *Physiologia* (1780) refined the Master's theories. As a pioneer of inoculation in eastern Sussex, Frewen was cited at Lewes Quarter Sessions in 1750 as "a common nuisance", for injecting patients at Northiam near a busy highway. However by 1772 he could inoculate Molly Bridger at Coombe Place (ten guineas) without causing public unrest.

When Frewen retired, Thomas Blair became the leading Lewes consultant, attending Lord Gage at Firle in 1795, though after he pronounced apopletic Surgeon Moore a hopeless case, recovery was swift. Blair lobbied hard for a County Infirmary at Lewes to serve the whole Eastern Division. An appeal, endorsed at Quarter Sessions in 1796, was launched at the Star coffee-house. It set out costed proposals based on hospitals at Chichester and Canterbury: a building equipped with 50 beds, £3-4000; 500 in-patients a year, £1000; a dispensary and 500 out-patients a year, £1250. The running costs would be met by parish overseers and Friendly Societies, by Subscribers, church-goers and benevolent "Strangers at Bathing-Places". The appeal chairman, Sir Godfrey Webster of Battle Abbey, pledged £200. But because too little was raised even for a pilot scheme, Lewes failed to consolidate its medical facilities before Brighton's overwhelmed it. In 1826 the Sussex County Hospital was belatedly built between Brighton and Kemp Town, and included a General Sea-Bathing Infirmary. About then the upstart resort boasted nine physicians, 29 surgeons, four dentists, the Vapour Baths of Sake Dean Mohomed, Shampooing Surgeon to George IV, and the German Spa of Dr Struve who simulated the mineral waters of Carlsbad, Pyrmont, Marienbad and Kessellbrunnen. At Lewes the "cold and bracing wave" of the horse-pond below St John's church long remained the only public bath, though overlooked by the "steady" women at the papermill. However in 1810 Thomas Boxall opened a cold bath by the Pinwell spring below All Saints church, charging clients a guinea a season. And in 1818 Amon Wilds emulated Sake Dean Mohomed by erecting "neat" Hot and Cold Baths at Greenwall near his mastic manufactory.

Whereas physicians were masters of medical theory, apothecaries, surgeons and man-midwives were more prosaically concerned with concocting, blood-letting, bone-setting and child-delivery. In the 1720s Lewes boasted at least six such practitioners. Thomas Fissenden tended a physic garden near Southover tannery (possibly a former mill-pond), which the chemist Albert Pam occupied in the 1880s. With his partner, Samuel Wheatly, he sent drugs to Compton Place, Danny Park, and the ducal households at Halland and Bishopstone, custom later divided between Wheatly and William Brett. From Thomas Stonestreat's dissecting-table in 1747 angry soldiers rescued the corpse of Private Oak, reburying it in quicklime. John Snashall handsomely rebuilt 203 School Hill in 1735, and Henry Manning attended Lord Mansell at Newick Park, a fellow Tory.

By the 1760s at least six more surgeons were in practice, besides Richard Martin who treated "the lower sort of people". Henry Manning II served as High Sheriff in 1789-90. John Turner was a Lewes cooper's son, who trained at Southwark. He bled John Bridger in 1759; delivered Lady Poole of a daughter; and dosed a bilious Lord Gage in 1791. John Chambers quizzed Tom Paine "on his non-performance of the connubial rights", so the *Journal* claimed many years later. Thomas Davey, Joseph Ridge and Thomas Mercer, all pupils of John Snashall, were succeeded by their sons. A pupil of Ridge was Joseph Rickman. Born at Bear Yard, he practised in Cliffe about 1800 with his son Thomas (1776-1841), who deserted medicine to study English medieval architecture and build Gothick replicas of it, being the first to separate the Norman, Early English, Decorated and Perpendicular styles. Another Joseph Rickman briefly kept an asylum for lunatics at Southover in 1775.

Thomas Hodson (1762-1841) trained with the London surgeon Dr Cline. He followed Manning in 1787; bought Newcastle House in 1797; and achieved a regional reputation for lithotomy, the cutting of stone out of the bladder. This was pioneered locally by the London surgeon, Dr David Bayford 1778-89, when semi-retired at Lewes for his health. Taught and recommended by Bayford, Hodson had cut 16 times by 1801, and lost only one, elderly, patient. The stone removed from Mr Slatter of Hastings in 1826 weighed three ounces. Rumour had it he could operate under the bedclothes, to save a lady from "exposure". He also ate with relish some over-ripe grouse, buried at Southover by order of Mrs Newton. Such surgery perhaps prompted James Moore to publish in 1794 his *Essay on the Medicinal Qualities of Steel, and its mode of Operation on the Human Habit.* However Moore's pupil and partner, Gideon Mantell (1790-1852), seemingly profited most from Hodson's advice and example. In 1814 Mantell removed a cataract from Mr Cruttenden's right eye. At Chailey he tapped an ovarian dropsy, drawing over six gallons from the largest cyst. In 1819 he removed the shattered finger of a blacksmith at the metacarpal joint; and in 1827 he cut away "a very large fungus haematodes", weighing almost two pounds, from the head of Mr Funnell's boy. He assisted Hodson to amputate above a diseased knee-joint, and to rectify the inguinal hernia of an estate-worker at Firle (who was nursed afterwards by paternal Lord Gage, a pillar of the Chivalric Revival). In 1827 Hodson merely watched as Mantell deftly severed a mangled forearm, with the femoral vein, nerve and artery exposed. And he became a skilled accoucheur, attending over 2000 deliveries by 1828, and losing only two mothers.

Besides defter surgery, Georgian Medicine pioneered inoculation. When a smallpox epidemic "reigned" in 1710-11, a thousand Lewesians fell ill, "about 120" died, and burials reached levels unknown since the Great Influenza of 1638; commerce halted and the Court of Quarter Sessions removed to Battle. Parish overseers confined the infected to their homes; the High Constables ordered stray hogs to be rounded up and hired a "scarvinger" to cleanse the streets. No Borough pesthouse existed, because three isolated tenements in Rotten Row, bequeathed for the use of the poor in 1586, had been quietly privatized. In 1730-31 an outbreak removed the Quarter Sessions to East Grinstead, and then to Battle. After an epidemic in 1741 the Borough raised £421 9s, and built a pesthouse near St Anne's churchyard, which received the corpses from that "receptacle for contagion". In 1758 Cliffe and Malling built their own isolation unit.

By then inoculation was gaining ground, despite Dr Frewen being denounced in 1750 as a common nuisance. Patients injected with "infected Matter" rested indoors two weeks, and then "aired" in isolation for two more. Concerned for their commerce, Lewesians were quick to condemn when the Buxted maltster, Mr Solomon, cut short his convalescence to attend the corn market, and when Jack Wisdom watched a review on Spital Hill two weeks or so after Parson Davies shepherded Glynde through a "general" inoculation in 1767. By 1770 George Sanders, an itinerant specialist, was injecting at Lewes itself. The town's own surgeons preferred to practise outside; Thomas Mercer at Plashett Park, and Joseph Ridge on Broyle Common. However in January 1794 the Borough reluctantly sanctioned its own general inoculation, "an Evil much less to be dreaded than a General Infection". When smallpox struck George Apted's family in St Marys Lane, that cantankerous chandler declared "his House to be his Castle", and would not move to the pesthouse. So a high fence was built round his door. When his neighbours became infected, and refused to budge, the blighted lane was blocked at both ends. Only when the "distemper" spread further did a Town Meeting "solemnly" adopt the lesser Evil. Trade halted for seven days while 2290 townsfolk and some 600 Strangers were injected. George Sanders, temporarily resident at Cliffe Corner, treated over 500 without mishap, so he claimed later when based at Chailey Common. However 45 patients caught the disease and died; they were "of all ages from eight hours to eighty years". 25 women miscarried, and ulcerated arms were common. The *Journal* blamed the weather, and the licentiousness of the lower orders who spurned a spare diet and gorged on meal and strong liquor.

The ravages of the "lesser Evil" prompted Paul Dunvan to propose an Inoculating House in some nearby combe, funded by public subscription, where a surgeon and "sober nurses" could mount a preventative programme. In 1804 a Free Vaccination Hospital was opened, with a county-wide catchment and the Prince of Wales as

Patron, but at Brighton. Vaccination embodied Jenner's use of cowpox to promote a "gentle" immunizing infection, and Lewes surgeons championed it. In 1800 Thomas Hodson denied that a Stanmer woman contracted smallpox from cowpox; and James Moore exposed two vaccinated girls to a person with smallpox. In 1808 the Borough pesthouse, now deemed superfluous, was sold to St Anne's parish for £450, after Thomas Woollgar tracked down the "mislaid" deed of feoffment, and "the Heir at Law to the last deceased Trustee". The proceeds were "let" at 5% to the Borough Improvement Commissioners who retained the interest, till the Charity Commissioners clawed back the £450 and the accrued interest in 1838, to fund a Public Dispensary. The sale was anyway premature, since smallpox still ravaged unhealthy locations: the barracks in 1811; some huts at Ham Lane in Southover, much used by "travelling people"; St Johns Street, Sun Street and Lancaster Street in 1822; Keere Street and White Lion Lane in 1830.

Georgian medicine also tackled the malarial agues so common in and around Lewes. The "wet grounds" along the Ouse and Glynde Reach harboured the fever-bearing mosquito and were noted as "great annoyances" in 1687. Ague-stricken villagers at Glynde in the 1760s sent their case-histories to Old James, a Lewes gardener believed to charm away attacks; whereas the better-informed William Michell took "Jesuits' bark" to throw off a quotidian ague, probably caught near Seaford. Quinine was perhaps present in Thompson's Ague Tincture, advertised in 1782 as curing the year-old tertian fever of a schoolmaster in Pevensey Marsh. Even in November 1827, after the wet grounds were better drained, the ague was "prevalent" at Cliffe, a notoriously insalubrious suburb. Its West Street rested on "Slub and Sea sand" in a "swampy, dirty" situation, beset by clogging vapours. Despite gusts of sea-air in summer, and a grid of culverted sewers, its clogged sanitation begat fevers which spread to the Borough; "the filtration of a jacques" sullied the well-water with "noisome and disgusting particles". Not till 1804 was a parish pump set up near the church porch, sweetly supplied from a chalk spring above the *Fountain*.

Being a medical resort Lewes stockpiled elixirs, panaceas and placebos. A Cliffe perukemaker in 1762 sold the Original Jesuit Drops and Royal Patent Electuary, a sovereign remedy for Venereal Disease, Gleets and Weaknesses. In 1789 a Cliffe watchmaker dispensed his *Pilulae Radiis Solis Extractae*, to combat Female

Complaints, Consumptions, violent Pain in the Bowels, Cholic and Worms of all kinds. The newsmen employed by the *Lewes Journal* carried medicines from a warehouse owned by the proprietors. Credulous townsfolk could also procure a splinter from Jacob's Post at Ditchling, or visit Ashburnham church to venerate King Charles the Martyr's blood-stained shirt. Lewes also welcomed peripatetic healers. Mr Powell, a fire-eater from London, tarried at the *Castle* in 1761 to pull teeth and cure hare-lips. To the *White Hart* came the Chevalier John Taylor, an oculist at once Pontifical, Imperial and Royal, who claimed 80,000 cures:

> Beneath his hand, with hideous cries,
> Through fear, not pain, an Infant lies;
> But in few minutes bless'd with sight,
> Now starts astonish'd at the light; T
> he light that, as with magic power,
> Presents a world unknown before:
> With painful pleasure sighs awhile,
> Then thanks the Doctor with a smile.

Yet the Chevalier failed with George Frederic Handel, and mortally wounded Johann Sebastian Bach.

Less lethal was Lewes's first chemist and druggist, Charles Pitt 1775-1813. Indeed his famous Sauce was impervious to climate, latitude or the passage of time, and imparted to any dish "a matchless taste, a peculiar relish, and a richness of flavour decidedly superior to any other". The fame of his ginger beer and soda water increased when an exploding cork blinded him in one eye. In 1820 his former Chemical Laboratory at 31 School Hill passed to Harry Winton and James Parkinson, a director of the Lewes gas-works.

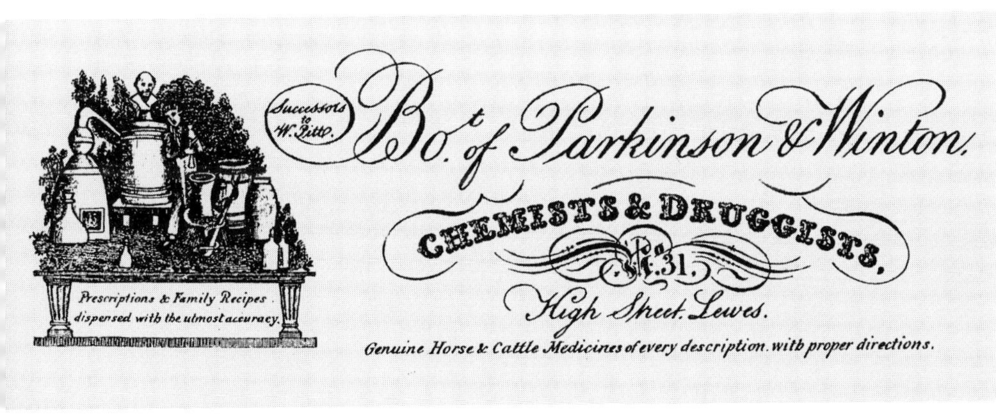

Besides legal, medical (and theological) expertise, Georgian Lewes offered a range of Classical, Commercial and Female Education. At the grammar school "free" boys from the town mingled with fee-paying boarders. Except for Josiah Welby 1725-45, its headmasters were Oxford or Cambridge graduates, and held a Lewes rectory or curacy. Indeed Thomas Peirce 1706-25 spent so much time on parish work that the school trustees cautioned Welby against taking holy orders. But as a cultivated man who translated Dante for the London publisher Thomas Birch, he quickly tired of teaching boys who were "very often dull, and too often incorrigible". Moreover he needed a cure of souls to augment his salary, even though a bequest in 1709 by Mrs Mary Jenkins had increased the £23 per annum willed by Agnes Morley and Thomas Blunt. (In 1775 her bequest yielded £20 10s to the headmaster, £17 15s to a writing-master, and £15 towards books and stationery for the free boys.) So after a study of Clarke's Sermons and Boyle's Lectures convinced him that the Christian religion was "worthy of God", Welby was ordained in 1743, despite the trustees. Though he died in 1745, his resourceful widow Rachel stayed on till 1748, catering for the boarders, while John Bristed, the debt-ridden Rector of St Anne's, taught the boys. About 1714 the Jenkins bequest had also purchased new school premises on St Annes Hill, causing Thomas Peirce to hold a commemorative lesson each year in the old schoolhouse near Southover tannery. This lay disused, except by tinkers, till Colonel Newton bought it in 1808 to round off his pleasure-gardens. The purchase money, £300, swelled the endowment income by £14 7s 4d a year.

The school enjoyed the Duke of Newcastle's protection. Indeed the trustees of the Jenkins bequest, chosen in 1709 and 1721, were Pelhams or their Whig supporters. When Josiah Welby backed the Duke during a bitter Borough election, vengeful local Tories poached his boarders, worsening his financial worries. He and Robert Austen 1748-75 also obliged the Duke by educating as free boys the offspring of his Lewes partisans. John Elliot, the brewer's son, went on to practise Law and research Antiquity, while innkeeper Verrall's boy became "a great Proficient" in Latin, arithmetic and "Writing several good hands", enough, his father assured the Duke, to merit a clerk's post in "The Treasury, Customs, War, Pay or Stamp Office". The fee-paying fathers of the boarders included a parson from Etchingham in 1716 and a surgeon from Essex in 1729.

The guardians of Nicholas Gilbert, an Eastbourne attorney's son, paid a dancing-master and a barber-wigmaker in 1715-18, as well as the writing-master and usher. Arthur Iredell (1758-1804), who became Rector of Southover, was a Bristol merchant's son, and Lord Macartney's cousin. Iredell's brother James (1751- 99), a native of Lewes, was perhaps a pupil too. He became Attorney General of North Carolina, and his pamphlet, *The Principles of an American Whig* (1775), advocated American Independence, just prior to Tom Paine's *Common Sense* (1776). Also "at School at Lewes" was John Hamilton Mortimer (1740- 79), the Augustus John of his times, a superb draughtsman with a flamboyant life-style. His father was an Eastbourne corn dealer and customs officer who claimed descent from the Earls of March, so perhaps he chose the grammar school, not a commercial academy.

Free boys averaged 12 under Robert Austen and James Castley 1775-78, but only six under William Gwynne 1778-1806 whose pupils praised him in an *Omnia Bene* song as a kind Cambrian Host, "A Master that ne'er lived to plague us". Under Edwin Merriman 1807-21 and George Proctor 1821-29 free boys were kept at 12, and now mostly came, like the boarders, from the professional classes. Indeed the hope of free tuition lured to Lewes several genteel yet penurious widows with cherished sons to educate. Socially the bottom-line was drawn below surveyors and master printers, though Thomas Saxby was a saddler's son who left to sew leather in the family shop, despite his excellent Greek. The virtual exclusion of Trade by the 1820s doubtless satisfied the trustees, Milords Chichester, Gage and Hampden, Sir George Shiffner, and the Reverend and Honourable John Neville. However genteel parents exposed the school to Secession. When denied the headship in 1821, Merriman's deputy, Robert Airey, poached pupils for his new academy in Brighton. George Proctor (a mindless flogger) restored the boarders to 40 or more, but then departed with many of them on a steamboat to Queen Elizabeth's College Guernsey in 1829. Charles Williams 1829-33 "kept such a poor table" that the boys nearly starved. Indeed Harvey Boys Ellman left with a "low fever", and the school again eroded. After the Reform Act of 1832 the bartering of free places for tradesmen's votes was revived; commercial courses were offered;, and the school's "whole stamp" slid downmarket.

Also set up to promote sound learning was Steere's Exhibition, an assisted place tenable for three or four years at Oxford or

Cambridge. The bequest in 1662 had charged the High Constables and four nominees to choose the sons of "godly poor parents", preferably parsons, in or near Lewes. The fund-rents came from Steere's Houses, 76 High Street and adjacent cottages in St Martins Lane. Yet till 1782 this income was mostly used for "necessary repairs", sanctioned by the feoffees. Indeed Thomas Horsfield could find very few awards: £3 4s 11d in 1714 to John Bristed (the debt-ridden headmaster) whose father Ezekiel was Rector of Newhaven; £4 or so about 1724 to Robert Austen (Bristed's successor); and £13 in 1765 to Austen's pupil William Hawes (whose father presented Austen to Berwick Rectory, on the understanding he would resign when William was qualified to claim it). However in 1782 £60 went to James Hurdis, the future Oxford Professor of Poetry; the son of a customs officer at Bishopstone, he enjoyed the steady patronage of Lord Pelham. Thereafter payments were more frequent. Some went to "poor" clerical parents like genial William Gwynne (1795 and 1800) and whist-loving Archdeacon Edward Raynes (1817), some to the Lewes school proprietors John Button (1807) and James Tracy Dunn (1824), and the land surveyor William Figg (1828).

The daily grind of Classical syntax at the grammar school, so painful to Boys Ellman in the 1820s, left ample scope for Commercial academies. Cater Rand (cl687-1748) came to Lewes in 1714 as an excise officer, but by 1732 he also kept a school, which his son Charles and Charles's widow Lucy continued till Cater II (1749-1825) took over. Besides preparing his pupils for "all Manner of Business", Cater II gave LECTURES in EXPERIMENTAL PHILOSOPHY. These invited the boys (and the public at large) to rise above "the low Pursuits of sensual and tasteless Amusements". His syllabus embraced pneumatics, electricity, astronomy, geography, mechanics, optics, hydrostatics, hydraulics, magnetism and chemistry. His pupils also studied mathematics by recourse to "the Globes, Orrery, Conic Sections, Hadley's Quadrant, Theodolite, Sector, Scale, Sliding-Rule, Charts, Maps". He deployed too a formidable Philosophical Apparatus which included "Electric Machines, Air Pump, the Mechanical Powers, Microscopes, Telescopes, Hydrostatic Balance" etc.. Admirable but avant-garde, these methods speeded perhaps his bankruptcy in 1784. Thereafter he kept a smaller school, partly funded by Lord Pelham, and found a safer outlet for his Sciences as a Surveyor of Forts on the Sussex Coast, and a civil engineer on the Ouse Navigation. He also intrigued young Burwood Godlee (c1803-

82) with a scale model in granite of his projected Lewes-London railway.

When Benjamin Hearnden left Cliffe in 1771 to displace Walter Gale at Mayfield School, he too advertised liberal methods, using images tailored to parents at risk from Wealden mud:

> the old rugged and tremendous Road (by many trod with Fear and trembling) is disused, and a new one perfectly smooth and easy substituted, wherein the Duty of the School from being irksome and laborious is rendered pleasant and recreative.

Also liberal was John Button (1761-1825). Paul Dunvan praised his English Grammar School, which opened at 86 High Street in 1791, as among "the best infant seminaries in Great Britain". A product of John Ryland's Baptist academy in Northampton, Button

championed English literature as a "universal magazine" of ancient and modern wisdom. Its grammar he taught "scientifically", without recourse to any "dead or foreign" language. His pupils parsed the best English authors, "as others do the Greek and Latin", and then wrote essays on things they had "seen or heard". To achieve verbal fluency, and expunge "vulgar and provincial" diction, they declaimed Select Pieces chosen for Button by Richard Brinsley Sheridan. Each year some spoke them in public, with "ease and emphatic propriety", at the *Star* assembly room. In 1797 Master Gideon Mantell offered the parting of Hector and Andromache; but in 1802 he bypassed the Pieces to denounce the "vile" treatment of English tourists in Napoleon's Paris. In 1805 Button's principles were punchily propounded:

What though no foreign dainties we afford,
With wholesome English cheer we deck our board,
Such as our fathers relished long ago,
The genuine stock of Shakespeare, Pope and Co..

The syllabus also included Spelling, Penmanship, Arithmetic, Letter Writing, Geography, Classical and British History. The Navigation teacher was fresh from a man-of-war. Dead and foreign languages were Extra.

Button's "wholesome English cheer" reflected a wider Radicalism. As the Baptist grandson of a Presbyterian pastor at Rye, he greatly admired Charles James Fox. Indeed when politics grew tense in the 1790s, Tories boycotted his school. In 1794 an accidental fire destroyed premises being built for him near St Anne's church, and he moved to the former *Swan* inn at Cliffe Corner. London supplied him with boarders, and local Dissenting tradesmen with day-boys. Gideon Mantell absorbed there the Liberalism and the eloquence which equipped him to denounce the Peterloo Massacre in 1819. Button's son, John Viney (1785-1873), compiled some *Exercises on Elocution* (1805), culled from Cowper, Southey and Watts, or fluently penned by himself. A Steere's Exhibition then sent him to Cambridge, where he took Anglican orders. So when his father died in 1825, his brother William (1796-1883), a Radical Baptist, left a London upholsterer's and sustained through 40 years the Cliffe Academy's "high reputation". A kindly man, he rejoiced to discover that the leather thongs on his servants' shoes had been stolen by rats, not by his pupils. In 1828 they launched the largest fire-balloon seen for many years, and attended lectures at the new Mechanics Institution. Indeed among 163 old-boys who gathered at the *Bear* in 1862 to honour William, and his "excellent" father's memory, were many who pioneered and cherished it: Burwood Godlee, William Harvey, Henry Browne, Robert Crosskey and Mark Antony Lower. His last words were a toast to Mr Gladstone.

Calling themselves a Society of Schoolmasters, John Button, Victor Amadeus Raymond, James Tracy Dunn and Henry Roscorla advertised in February 1811 a common starting date for the coming quarter. Raymond was a Swiss Protestant and attended the Westgate Meeting. In 1789 he bought Dr Frewen's spacious premises on School Hill, once the *Turks Head*. Among the boys he coached "assiduously", for "public schools or the commercial line", was Henry Byng, later a Vice-Admiral. His father John endorsed Raymond's opinion of the local air: "*Le Site de Lewes est delicieux, le Ciel pur et serein*". French was "constantly" spoken; and when James Tracy Dunn took over Raymond's pupils in 1820, he enlarged the French,

Dunn's Academy (Sussex Archaeological Society)

Classical, Commercial and Mathematical Academy at Friars Walk he had opened in 1796. He sponsored lectures on Stenography; encouraged "scenic entertainment" like *The Blind Boy* and *The Sleeping Draught*; and set up "a very handy turning lathe", a slimmer investment in Philosophical Apparatus than Cater II made. By 1827 his pupils converged from "town and country", from France and America, the East and West Indies. His son, the Reverend J.C.T. Dunn, a Steere's Exhibitioner, resigned in 1837 from Cuckfield grammar school to succeed him. Henry Roscorla had started his Classical and Commercial Academy at St Thomas's Square in 1806, and dedicated to Sir Godfrey Webster at Battle Abbey a statistical table showing the distances between Sussex towns. His Academy enrolled up to 20 young gentlemen, and embodied principles "peculiar to itself". His successor, Edward Augustus Carleton 1822-33, favoured "the Eton plan". This promised "an intimate acquaintance" with Latin, Greek, bookkeeping etc., and required each pupil to bring six towels and a silver spoon.

John Dudeney (ESRO)

Strictly commercial was the school kept by John Dudeney (1782-1852), a shepherd's son born at Rottingdean. A dame school in derelict Plumpton Place taught him little, except to drive geese onto the moat (where carp were "first kept" in England). While minding sheep on Plumpton Plain in 1792 he explained to Paul Dunvan the habits of the wheatear, after another boy thought to fob the Frenchman off with a heath-chatter's eggs and a wagtail's nest. In return Dunvan gave him a *Short History of England* and a *Robinson Crusoe*. These fired a passion for knowledge. He bought primers on mathematics and astronomy at the Lewes fairs, with stray pence earned trapping moles and wheatears. The seven shillings for a dictionary to interpret *Les Aventures de Telemaque* came from a well-wisher riding by. John Cripps, a kindly Lewes Justice, lent him Solomon's *Geographical Grammar*. When under-shepherd at Kingston he stored a slate and books beneath a large flint on Newmarket Hill. While head-shepherd at Rottingdean he perused a Hebrew bible, and borrowed globes from Parson Hooker. At Michaelmas 1804 he began a day-school at Southover, then moved to the Freemasons Hall by West Gate. But the new Lancastrian School drew his pupils away. So he cast type for John Baxter, till Mr Inskip's small academy down St Johns Street fell vacant in 1814. In the end he averaged a hundred pupils, though fears that George Cheeseman had the Itch took his mind off a sermon in 1822.

Academies for Young Ladies also graced the town. Stephen and Elizabeth Philpot 1733-70 kept theirs at St Anne's Rectory, rented from debt-ridden Parson Bristed. Stephen had studied with the best London dancing-masters, and with the violinist Michael Christen Festing. In 1747 he published an *Essay* on the role of dance in women's education. Armed with a "well informed and discerning mind", they could repel "those silly artifices which are used to ensnare and deceive", and a Polite Education could reinforce this. Perfect manners and deportment ensured "gracefulness of looks, voice, words, motions and gestures". So did the "true harmony and composure...of limbs and countenance" fostered by dance. Not of course the peasant uproar of "a Cheshire Rounds, a common jigg, or a hornpipe", but those stately rhythms in vogue at Louis XIV's Versailles, the minuet, the louvre, the rigadoon. Though based at Lewes, Philpot was peripatetic. *His Essay*, dedicated to the Duchess of Somerset, was begun at Petworth House while tutoring her daughters. At Brightling he groomed John Fuller's children, and also their neighbour Sir John Lade, a parvenu brewer from Southwark whose matchless bust by Rysbrack adorns Warbleton church. Like the rigadoon-loving Philpot, Fuller was a Tory. So were Lord Mansell of Newick Park who sponsored his benefit concert at the *Star* in 1744, and the surgeon Henry Manning who bought his *Essay* in 1748. However a county-wide political truce brought him Whig patrons by the 1750s. The Poole girls from The Hooke came to board; and so perhaps did Maria Milward from Pevensey, since she popped out from a Lewes academy each Sunday evening to sing psalms with her aunt. And thanks probably to the Duke of Newcastle, Philpot became a Royal Musician in Ordinary, serenading the Court on State occasions, sumptuously clad in black velvet and scarlet damask. The appointment also promoted his textbook, *The Art of Playing on the Violin* (1766).

Stephen II became organist at the London Foundlings Hospital; and his brother Charles taught dance at Leicester. So their sister Anne Gastineaux sold the school to Charlotte and Philadelphia Lund 1772-85, the daughters of a Lewes parson. Next came Susan Royall, a member of the Lewes Library Society, and then the Misses Dodson 1793-7 who seemingly sold up very abruptly. The syllabus in 1772 included English, French, arithmetic, geography, drawing, Tambour-Work, and other Useful and Ornamental Needlework, besides music and dancing taught by "proper masters".

About 1789 the sisters Mary and Hannah Adams moved their academy from Cliffe, where Charles Adams was curate, to School Hill. There till about 1817 they shared the *Ciel, pur et serein*, with Monsieur Raymond next door, though in 1797-8 bonfires and rockets menaced their premises on the Fifth. However Miss Hannah was already acquainted with mobs. After spending three years in Paris learning the language, her grasp of Gallic idiom grew even wider in

1792-3 when the Terror and passport problems at Dieppe prolonged a return visit several months. Despite this, at least one pupil, Elizabeth Hitchener (c1781-1822), imbibed from "Miss Adams" an immense enthusiasm for Political Liberty. Indeed she became in 1811 the soul-mate of Percy Bysshe Shelley, who yearned to adopt her beloved Miss Adams as his own "moral mother", and rescue her from a hostile sister and Reactionary foes at Lewes. Probably Hannah was the younger and the Enlightened one. By an odd coincidence Shelley's fleshly mother, Elizabeth Pilford (1763-1846), before her marriage lived for 12 years at The Friars with her aunt Lady Charlotte Poole. In her poem *The Weald of Sussex* Miss Hitchener nicely blended her childhood affection for Lewes and for Freedom:

> And Town more pleasing boasts not Albion's Isle;
> Tho' raised without design to please the eye;
> Design could not more sweet effect produce;
> The lofty hill, rich valley, softest shades;
> And the meandering of thy fertile course;
> The distant Ocean's breeze, the castled tower,
> The interesting ruin ivy-wreathed,
> An emblem as of Liberty's green flag,
> Which seems o'er tyranny and gothic strength,
> Triumphantly its standard thus to rear.

Russell's Memorial (Chaplin)

6
The County Town: Sense and Sensibility

...buttresses, pillars, stone door-ways, mullions and tracery of spacious windows, arched apartments and vaults, particularly that called the Dungeon, and the cell termed the Lanthorn-house; flights of stone steps, especially those to which legend had assigned the thrilling title of the bloody steps.

THE PRIORY RUINS AT SOUTHOVER: MANTELL'S *RAMBLE* 64-5.

Nothing...appears more indicative of the progress of science...than the application of this aeriform fluid, to purposes of public convenience and private comfort...a magic flame, which darts its penetrating rays through lanes and alleys, where darkness before perpetually reigned.

THE ADVENT OF GAS LIGHT: HORSFIELD I 343.

From party feuds the Senator withdraws To Learning's humble dome and peaceful cause; Priests and preceptors seek her calm retreat, And brother tradesmen here in concord meet; Doctors their drugs forsake, and swains their fields, To cull the choicer fruits which science yields; Grocers neglect their sugar and bohea, And e'en attorneys here forget their fee.

JOHN VINEY BUTTON, *THE LEWES LIBRARY SOCIETY* (1804).

The professional men in Georgian Lewes, the doctors, lawyers, pastors and preceptors, had all received some academic training, which made them the mainstay of the town's intellectual life. Some used their leisure to ponder the antiquities of mid-Sussex, a pursuit encouraged by the Rational Enlightenment and by its troublesome twin, the Romantic Revolution. The Lewes attorney John Rowe (c1560-1639) had set a precedent by carefully transcribing manorial and Borough records. The physician John Tabor excavated a Roman villa at Sea Houses in Eastbourne, uncovering a mosaic of

St. James's Hospital (Horsfield's History)

S^T JAMES' HOSPITAL, SOUTHOVER.

brown and white tesserae, and the foundations of a bath-house. His report in the *Philosophical Transactions* of the Royal Society (1718) used classical and medieval texts to argue (erroneously) that Sea Houses was the site of Roman Anderida. At Southover the headmaster Robert Austen (c1709-86) probed the footings of the nave and side aisles of medieval St James's hospital, and of an outer northern aisle, seemingly lined with cubicles. The former chancel had been a cottage, he was told, since about 1730 when materials from "the last of the Spittal houses" were used to convert it. He also traced the precinct wall of the priory, and recorded a local tradition that the Mount there was a post-Dissolution artefact,

> raised by one of the Earls of Dorset between whom and a brother of his Living at Lewes a Difference arose on the Acct of being overlooked by each other.

These findings he sent in 1772 to Frederick Grose for inclusion in *The Antiquities of England and Wales*. Being also the Curate at St Anne's, he oversaw the repair and resetting of a Norman "circular door of entrance" in 1775.

An excess of "literary modesty" caused Austen to order that his research notes be burned after his death. Those made by the Lewes-born attorney John Elliot (1725-82) were also never written up. Being the Bloomsbury-based associate of Henry Burtenshaw, he could comb London libraries for clues about the early history of Lewes and its Rape, though his wife, "a pure, regenerated Methodist", nagged him "to relinquish the Museum for Moorfields, and profane Antiquities for the New Jerusalem", while his prosaic father, Obadiah the brewer, complained that more gold could be got from a volume of precedents than from "all the musty lore of Spelman, Camden or Usher". Undeterred, Elliot supplied useful detail for Dr Watson's *Memoirs of the Earls of Warren and Surrey*. Often though the sources lacked precision. Did Lewes, like the Hebridean island, derive its name from a Celtic phrase meaning "the hand upon the waters"? Did the Romans call the Sussex Ouse Trisanton, as Ptolemy and Richard of Cirencester both implied? Did the High Street of the Borough overlay the via principia of a Roman fort? Did the Saxons dig the trenches round St John-in-Castro church, and did these earthworks defend from the Danes a ferry below? Did King Alfred build the castle? And what of Magnus, the royal anchorite at St John's? Was he Harold Godwinson, smuggled there alive from Senlac? Geraldus Cambrensis thought the king found sanctuary in St John's church at Chester, but perhaps his sources confused "in Castro" and "in Cestria". And was the dedication stone from the priory, now at Southover church, inscribed T.A.D.E. or I.A.D.E.? Did Archbishop Theobald officiate, or John of Avignon? Elliot bequeathed his copious notes to a correspondent, William Burrell, along with a portrait of John Rowe which James Basire engraved for him from a miniature at Buxted Place.

[Sir] William Burrell (1732-96), MP for Haslemere, was a civil lawyer whose wide estates in Sussex included Upper Stoneham Farm at Malling. Intending to write a history of the shire, he examined cartularies, epitaphs and aumbries, and commissioned topographical drawings from James Lambert and Samuel Hieronymous Grimm. However after a severe stroke cut short his research, he left his portfolios (and Elliot's) to the British Museum. He paid to have the fine Romanesque memorial to Gundrada de Warenne removed to a purpose-built tabernacle in Southover church, after Parson William Clarke of Buxted (an eminent numismatist) identified it at Isfield amid the Shurley tombs. His own monument at West Grinstead was

Gundrada's memorial

designed by Flaxman, a "pretty urn on top of a bloody-minded kind of sarcophagus".

Paul Dunvan's *Ancient and Modern History of Lewes and Brighthelmstone* appeared in 1795. Though unfamiliar with Burrell's portfolios, he did scan Austen's notes, "my first and best guides through the obscure maze into which I have ventured with more zeal than ability". He too remains obscure. He was "of French extraction", and instanced Bordeaux when urging that Cliffe's West Street be widened. Also an usher at the grammar school under the genial Gwynne, he recorded the first stone of Button's academy being laid in 1794. In return for data on the wheatear, he gave ten-year-old John Dudeney a *Short History of England* and a *Robinson Crusoe*, a discerning kindness. He was also singled out as a "riotous" Radical, at a town meeting to launch a Loyal Association against Republicans and Levellers in December 1792. His politics could explain his *History* being anonymous, though its publisher William Lee alleged an Excess of Diffidence when dedicating it, "with a sponsor's adoptive care", to the Prince of Wales, a Royal Patriot who "in the brilliant Maturity of Judgment, is the most steady Advocate for the Rights of well-regulated Society". Pittite Repression however overrode the Rights of Radicals. James Drowley was also "riotous" in December 1792, and he left for America soon after. When Dunvan quitted Lewes is unclear.

So Radical was Dunvan's *History* that the Advanced Whigs, William Green and William Cooper, each ordered two copies. He applauded Reason, Liberty and Enlightenment, and denounced Popery, Feudalism and War. He credited the "immortal" King Alfred with granting Lewes its first guild merchant, and with designing (probably) its castle. The Saxon Alfred ruled by "national election, the only lawful base for kingly power". Then William I, that "atrocious" Conqueror, imposed the "intricate despotism of military infudation", just as his Norman scribes shackled "fe" on the sturdy English noun Clif. Lewes's first feudal lord, Warenne, was skilled in "human butchery". To Southover he invited those "holy despots", the Cluniac monks, so swollen with "lust, hypocrisy, gluttony and pride". Their huge pigeon-house harboured doves equally parasitic:

> To the injured husbandman they were as sacred as the divinity they typify. Conscious of security, they anticipated the sickle, and rioted from field to field, the wanton wards of feudalism and superstition.

Pigeon-house at Southover

Because the Battle of Lewes ensured "a lasting mode of national representation", every patriot's heart should be "the cenotaph of Montfort", even though he was a Frenchman. Henry VIII expelled the holy despots from Southover, yet as a libidinous epicure, he rioted "in the charms, and next in the blood of the same woman". Dunvan also denounced more topical abuses: griping landowners, lingering seigneurial imposts, English contempt for Scotsmen and Irishmen; wars waged with a cruelty unknown to "the tyger, scorpion or crocodile of Africa"; and colonial slavery, spawned by "European avarice".

Like Elliot, Dunvan found little solid evidence about pre-Norman Lewes, though under the Romanized Regni it became, presumably, the "greatest mart and thoroughfare" in Sussex. Dr William Stukely, the Druid specialist, placed it on Ermine Street between London and Newhaven (Portus Novus). Possibly King Cissa fortified it. Perhaps too the Danes blockaded it, and built the trenches visible on the "wall-lands". Domesday Book, feudal lords, murage grants and the Great Battle offered firmer ground, but "etymological conjecture" did not. Malling he derived from Mealewe "corn" and Ing "a low place"; School Hill from Cool-hill, a tribute to "the constant draught of air" blowing on it. He compiled a yearly Chronology, starting in 1542, partly from the Town Books and John Rowe's manuscripts. This included the High Constables, the Borough MPs, the Borough Fellowship, the Marian martyrs, a Poisoner Self-Poisoned, charities and trustees, fires and fire-engines, Private Oak's dissection, Henry Blackman's accolade, and the General Inoculation. His parish surveys covered the Canons at Malling, the Cliffe charters, the identity of Magnus, the grammar school, the pesthouse, the Ouse Navigation, low life at the races, antiquities and antiquarians, Richard Russell and James Lambert. He omitted Tom Paine, by 1795 the bogy man of Pittite Reaction.

Much of Dunvan's material reappeared in Thomas Horsfield's *The History and Antiquities of Lewes and its Vicinity,* published as two lavish volumes in 1824 and 1827. Horsfield was the pastor at Westgate chapel, and his Radicalism had a Unitarian edge. He saluted the Marian martyrs who died at Lewes for "free inquiry in matters of religion". They left a "dark damp cell" beneath the *Star* to confront "the faggots which blazed before it". Under Charles II "the harpies of bigotry" seized the property of Lewes Dissenters whose worship offended "the minions of a lascivious court". Like Dunvan he denounced (as though pounding a pulpit cushion) "the poison tree of Rome", the "haughty, imperious and tyrannical" Warennes, the "arbitrary, bigoted, licentious" Henry VIII. He rejoiced that goats now browsed at Southover where the Cluniac despots had trodden. He admired King Alfred, King Harold and William Wallace, but not De Montfort, promoting instead the Whig paladins of the 1680s, John Locke, Lord William Russell and Algernon Sidney. And he deplored the "empty sophistry" Tom Paine had deployed against Christianity.

His stately narrative reworked Dunvan's sources, pondered Elliot's theories, and digressed: the Druid's harp "drowned the shriek of the expiring victim on the funeral pile"; the Romano-Britons embraced "effeminate softness" by donning woollen trousers; the Saxons plastered their "buoyant skiffs" with an "impermeable unctuous composition"; the wild thyme so common on the Lewes Downs and on the Hills of Hymettus gave a "very superior relish" to Sussex mutton and Periclean honey. He waxed circumstantial about Charles II's flight after Worcester: the voyage from Brighton, the ebony bowl given to Henry Blackman's ancestor, and the pensions still granted to the descendants of the Boscobel Pendrills, one of whom now kept the *Royal Oak* in St Marys Lane. However after 1702 his History became a disjointed listing of public buildings, public addresses, coastal storms, the Volunteers, meeting-houses, "miscellaneous notes", Henry Blackman knighted, and a bullock struck by lightning.

Though its antiquarians were diligent, Lewes's medieval fabrics crumbled steadily. Even the parish churches grew unsafe. In 1698 the steeple at Southover collapsed. In 1748 "ruinous" St Michael's was remodelled (and Sir George Goring's Renaissance tomb broken up). In the 1750s St Thomas's received the "neat" interior admired by Archbishop Secker. In 1779 decaying St John's suffered a "destructive reparation": "the brasses, stain'd glass, and any thing moveable" falling "a prey to the masons and glaziers". In 1806 when "ruinous" All Saints was rebuilt except for the tower, the demolition briefly revealed "a rude painting" of two infants. Redundant medieval churches and hospitals fared even worse. In 1761 the tower of St Nicholas's, the Broken Church by Aylwards Corner, was toppled, and the debris dumped in a disused public well nearby. About 1825 the remnants of St Peter's near Rotten Row Corner, "late perpendicular" in style, were carted away. By the 1770s St James's hospital was reduced to a patched-up stable, St Nicholas's hospital to a Romanesque gable-end, and the friary to a dovehouse and the precinct wall. At Malling Deanery Serjeant Kempe (Dr Russell's son) pulled down the Canons' refectory and filled up their fish ponds.

All Saints Church (Horsfield's History)

The ruins of Southover priory also eroded. Young Gideon Mantell, "early and late", gathered encaustic tiles and carved capitals.

St Nicholas's Hospital (Horsfield's History)

The draper Thomas Woollgar (1761-1821) removed painted glass and relics of "the olden time". The "elegant water-closet", he unearthed near the churchyard wall, made a neat burial vault for the Fuller family. Meanwhile arches fell and steps crumbled. Three wings were demolished in 1804 of the "prodigious" cruciform pigeon house, roughly 80 by 80 feet, with recesses of hewn chalk for 3228 pairs of doves; the other wing came down soon after. So did an elliptical "oven", 17 feet in diameter, with "square spiracles" in its wall, popularly viewed as a cunning Cluniac device for staging "juggling tricks or miracles". In 1832 the great precinct gate, its clustered columns adorned with nail-headed quartrefoils, was shifted and shattered, to facilitate the building of Priory Crescent, during which many skeletons were found "regularly interred":

Precinct Gate in 1832, (Henwood)

The princely Priory exists no more -
So slight and fragile are all earthly ties:
And though fate's mandate we in vain deplore -
The Cross will vanish - and the Crescent rise.

Lewes castle by contrast attracted pilgrim lovers of the Picturesque, and received more care. However the archway of the Borough's west gate was removed "for a wager" in 1763, Henry Burtenshaw losing £20 as a result. Its two bastions (and the Borough's Black Hole) were replaced about 1790 by a Freemasons' Hall and Westgate House.

The West Gate (Horsfield's History)

Besides medieval masonry, local earthworks intrigued Lewes antiquarians. Elliot examined the trenches round St John's churchyard, and the conical mounds at its southern corners. Dunvan blamed Cluniac "profusion" for the Mount at Southover, and for "the excavation thereby occasioned", namely the nearby Dripping Pan (tradition blamed an Earl of Dorset, an origin favoured by students of the Early Modern landscaped garden). The pits scattered across the Lewes Downs Dunvan assigned to "early Britons" who revelled in cock-fighting and Druidic sacrifice. The long barrow above Malling, so like a ship's keel upturned, was perhaps a naval commander's tomb. The many round barrows probably began as boundary marks, but received later "the inurned ashes" of the Roman and "the uncoffined corse" of the Saxon and Dane. Horsfield credited the squarish hill-forts at Whitehawk, Hollingbury and Ditchling to Vespasian's conquering legions; the Saxons perhaps rounded the corners off others. He pondered the cultural context of the flints, spears, torques, beads and urns which crammed local show-cases by the 1820s. He puzzled too over some wedge-shaped "celts", encrusted with a "fine green aerugo", unearthed on Firle Hill; were they battle-axes, spearheads, walking staves, military standards, Roman chisels, or Druidic hooks used when snipping mistletoe?

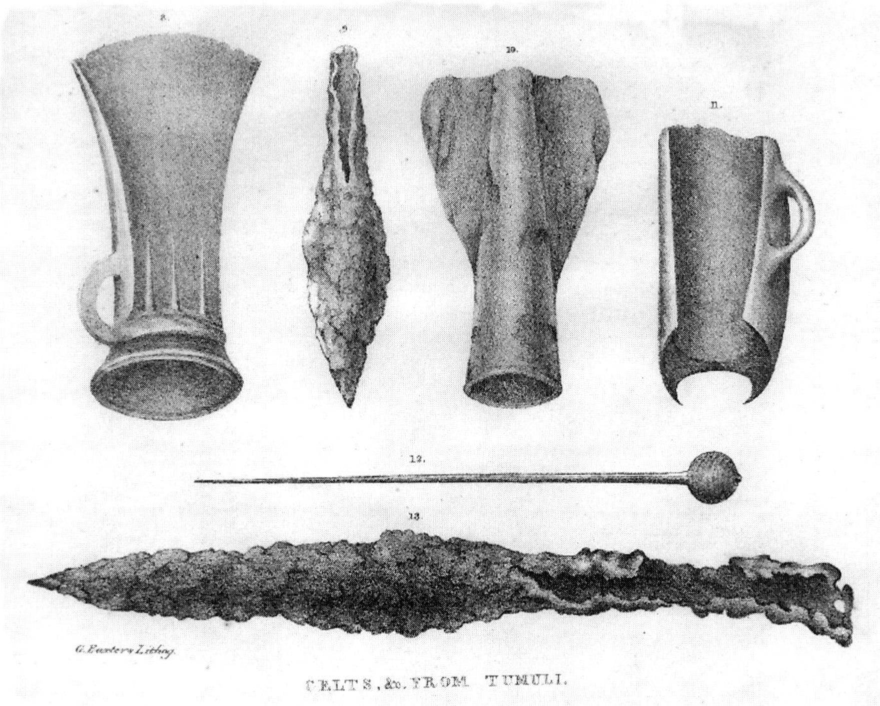

Excavated artefacts (Horsfield's History)

Human bones also intrigued. Dunvan thought some massive grave-pits near St Nicholas's hospital, cut through by the improved Lewes to Brighton road, were a burial-place for men slain during the Great Battle. When flint-diggers found infants' bones in five "Crocks" near Newmarket Hill in 1788, the *Journal* less plausibly deemed them to be "the issue of unlawful intercourse, murdered by unnatural parents". Roman remains, when chanced upon, were especially awesome, as William Hay remarked in his poem *Mount Caburn*:

> Struck with amazement doth the labouring hind
> Their arms, and their Mosaic pavements find;
> Urns, which have long their sacred ashes kept,
> And Caesars, which on coins have ages slept.

Such finds prompted systematic barrow-robbing. One Southdown shepherd took to "opening fresh tumuli" full-time, after disturbing a batch of Roman urns on Beeding Hill about 1800. More typical was Militia-Surgeon Shrapnall. While stationed at Lewes barracks he pillaged several barrows towards Mount Harry, unearthing skeletons "environed...by a greyish and rather greasy mould". In July 1810 the gentleman-farmer Thomas Beard excavated "the calcined remains of some youthful warrior of distinction" near Rottingdean.

In 1812 Beard shared further Antiquarian Research near Iford Bushes and Salt Dean Gap with John Marten Cripps (c1780-1853), whose father lent John Dudeney the *Geographical Grammar*. Between 1796 and 1802 Cripps had made an intrepid Grand Tour with his Cambridge tutor Edward Clarke (whose father, the numismatist, identified Gundrada's memorial at Isfield). To bypass Napoleon they went via Russia to Troy, Mount Ida, Jerusalem, Cairo, Parnassus and Vienna. From the Mediterranean they sent home many cargoes of purchases; and remarkably when the *Princessa* foundered off Eastbourne, Cripps senior was on hand to salvage a colossal head of Ceres from Eleusis, destined for Cambridge University Library, and now prominent in the Fitzwilliam. By 1805 trophies from the Tour were on public display at School Hill House, the residence of Cripps senior. They included paintings, drawings and medals, "a specimen of Opalized Wood, the finest ever seen", and Herbals collected by Professor Pallas of Russia and Dr Noezan of Sweden, "a favourite disciple" of Linnaeus. Later Cripps cultivated the Bread Fruit Potato, and some seeds from the Black Lilies that grew near Napoleon's tomb on St Helena.

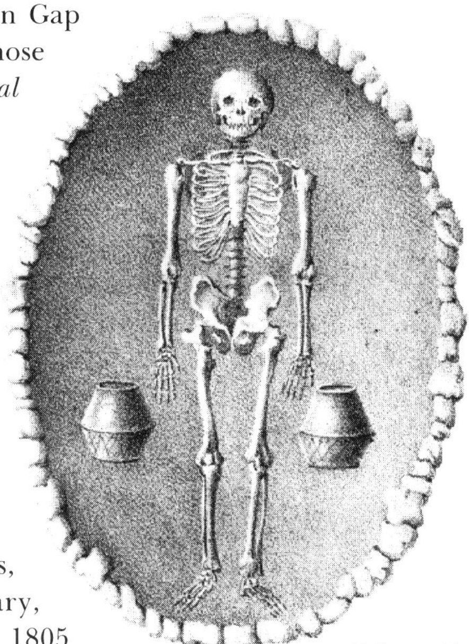

Skeleton with urns (Horsfield's History)

Besides treasure-hunting in the priory, Gideon Mantell opened barrows near Mount Caburn and Oxsettle Bottom. One urn packed with calcined bones also yielded a brass ring, a bone armilla, and beads of amber, jet and "green porcelain", all illustrated in Horsfield's *History*. While digging out an arbour in the castle mound behind his surgery he discovered an urn containing the bones of a headless cockerel, which Horsfield thought could be a Roman "augural relic". In St Michael's church Mantell opened a lead coffin beneath the mutilated brass of a knight "of the noble house of De Warren", and exposed

> a tall slender corpse, enveloped in a linen shroud...it was imbedded in moist saw-dust, apparently of cedar. The outline of the face, as seen covered by the thin wet linen envelope, was eminently beautiful.

He was more pragmatic when roadworks disturbed skeletons on Malling Hill:

> These Saxon churls must have lived on acorns, and other hard pulse, or their teeth could not have been worn down as they are.

The "shapely figured aspect" of the smoothly sculptured Lewes Downs also intrigued observers. While riding to visit Aunt Snooke and Timothy at Ringmer, Gilbert White pondered what "fermentation", what "plastic power", had caused the chalklands "to swell and heave their broad backs into the sky so much above the less animated clay of the wild below". Dunvan attributed their "Combs or narrow winding vales" to water oozing from "immense heaps of macerated matter"; and Gideon Mantell in his *Fossils of the South Downs* (1822)

Strata near Lewes (Horsfield's History)

fully explained those "subterraneous forces which, in periods incalculably remote, elevated the bottom of a deep sea above the level of the waters". Much of his research for the book was very local. In South Street quarry he found the first fossil fish ever "discovered in the chalk", publicizing it in the *Transactions* of the Linnean Society (1814). Southerham pit yielded him another "beautiful" specimen with fins and scales intact, and Malling pit produced an enormous ammonite. At Castle Hill above Newhaven the Plastic Clay proved rich in Selenite and Sub-sulphate of Alumine. From Mount Harry he sketched the Cliffe Hills, aided by a camera lucida. The *Fossils* so impressed John Marten Cripps that he persuaded George IV to subscribe; and the book's success brought many visitors to Mantell's residence at Castle Place where they politely admired the Geology displayed on the first floor. Indeed genteel fossil-hunters began to outbid him at his favourite quarries.

His researches in the Weald uncovered the steamy fresh-water origin of its "less animated" clays. In 1819 Mr Leney sold him some "superb" fossil euphorbia gathered near Cuckfield. He examined beds of Sussex marble at Plashett Park and seams of ferruginous sand at Little Horsted. In 1830 he was still collecting fossil paludinae and ferns, at Pit-wood quarry near Cross-in-Hand; and in 1833 his *Geology of South-East England* presented the evidence for what Horace Smith called "some Mississippi" traversing Haywards Heath in "all the pomp of tropical creation". Especially exciting were the fossil bones he found in 1822 at Tilgate Forest near Worth (an area once afflicted, it was said, by dragons). They belonged to a dinosaur, a lizard 25 or 30 feet in length, which he named iguanadon. His discovery brought Professor Buckland and Charles Lyell post-haste from Oxford; and clinched his election to the Council of the Geological Society. Mantell's work on this fossil flora and fauna underpinned Mark Antony Lower's vision of a Primordial Weald

> teeming with thick jungles, composed of graceful and arborescent ferns, conifers and cycadea; high sunny river-banks, where basked herbivorous Saurians, gigantic and terrible, while bat-like Pterodactyls rose on colossal pinions and fanned the sultry air.

Also fanned was the torrid imagination of John Martin whose drama-packed paintings included *The Deluge*, *Pandemonium* and *The Fall of Babylon*. Besides visiting Castle Place, he drew a frontispiece for Mantell's *Wonders of Geology* (1838) which depicted a browsing iguanadon menaced by a megalosaurus and a giant crocodile.

Though an exact scientist and surgeon, Mantell was very much a Romantic who delighted in the Wonders of Geology. The relics of Time Past and the beauties of Nature thrilled his catholic sensibility: a slender corpse in a linen shroud or an echoing undercroft at Battle Abbey; a bed of the bee orchid, early primroses near Glynde, or a mass of flowering water-lilies on the Ouse near Barcombe mill, savoured after seeing a smallpox patient at Isfield. He loved the Wealden Picturesque: a lake beneath high rocks near Uckfield; a cottage at Sheffield Park, "most enchantingly placed in a little recess of the sandstone, overhung by majestic beech, oak and ash". The Sublime also touched him. As twilight fell near Coombe Place, the scene grew

> calm and still as death; the sun had sunk below the horizon yet its lustre threw a warm glow over the sky...the scene was indeed a Claude Lorraine in perfection.

At Brighton "the tempestuous foaming of the billows" drew him to the very end of the storm-damaged chain pier. And the downfall of Napoleon saddened him. He honoured the Emperor's natal day, collected his medals, and deplored his exile on St Helena. The Corsican outsider's fate troubled the Lewes cordwainer's son, as he wrested fame (but not fortune) from Southdown pits and Wealden quarries during the sterile Tory Reaction after Waterloo:

> ...whatso'er my fate I'll not complain
> If that my humble name enroll'd shall be
> Among the glorious intellectual train
> Whose fame shall live thro' all futurity,
> If that the wreath be mine which science twines
> For those who court her smiles and worship at her shrines.

The Creation of the wide watermeadows below Lewes also beguiled Parson James Hurdis (1763-1801), the Steere's Exhibitioner who became a friend of William Cowper and Oxford Professor of Poetry:

> Where is the car that bore the hills away
> To make yon ample basin, bowl immense,
> Vast amphitheatre of sky-crown'd downs,
> Where oft the hurried waters lose the way,
> And spreading wide become an inland sea?

Hurdis tutored Lord Pelham's son, and was made Rector of Bishopstone, his native parish, which he celebrated in the *Favourite*

Village. Its neat Arcadian verse also depicted the seasons on the Lewes Downs. John Betjeman much admired this panegyric and fondly pictured the Painter Poet, "isolated among windy miles of sheep-nibbled downs", scattering sand on ink "made of oak-gall". Hurdis compared the "frothy globes" of the guelder shrub to the foam

> Of new milk bubbling in the cow-herd's pail;

and a grasshopper's chirp to

> the silvery chink
> Of wages told into the ploughman's palm.

He noted the lark ascending to make an "exquisite anthem...sweeter still"; the mushrooms "rosy-gill'd and cloth'd in snow"; and the ancient hill fort that

> ...with haughty grace
> Its wither'd turban wears of perish'd heath.

Sadly Hurdis died young. He "fell lamented in life's early noon", as John Viney Button, another Steere's Exhibitioner, put it. His epitaph was penned by Blake's prosaic patron, William Hayley:

> Hurdis! ingenious poet and divine!
> A tender sanctity of thought was thine.

Lewesians strove to mould, not merely admire the Picturesque. An obvious challenge was the castle. Its mighty Gothic barbican

Lewes Castle (Horsfield's History)

flanked a turreted shell-keep on a steep mound which commanded a wide prospect. On the eastern slopes the ironmonger Benjamin Court created a "hanging garden". Then the draper Thomas Friend rented the barbican, the southern slopes, and the keep which he made into a summerhouse, adorned with a Mannerist doorway and Chippendale Gothick casements. His embellishments attracted many visitors, among them John Wilkes, Prince Ernest of Mecklenburg-Strelitz, and John Byng who also studied some ancient masonry on Brack Mount (a name Dunvan derived from "braecan", to break or moulder). Friend's great-nephew Thomas Kemp encouraged functions in the keep. During a subscription dinner in 1803 a meteor passed by, like "a flaming sword, beautifully radiated at its head". Soon after Mr Mortram the Aeronaut rose a prodigious height in his balloon, descending safely at Newhaven. By 1805 the South Saxon Lodge of Lewes Freemasons held what Horsfield called its "Eleusinian mysteries" in the barbican tower (the Great Architect of which, many believed, was King Alfred). After 1811 Thomas Read Kemp spent £600 on repairs to the castle, and fitted out one turret

Baldy's Garden in 1785 (Grimm: British Library Addit. Ms. 5672, fo.7)

for a Guardian who tended the shrubs in 1838.

In May 1771 Prince Ernest also admired the prospect from Baldy's Garden above Cliffe Corner, after regally tipping the "strewers" along his route from the *White Hart*. Thomas Baldy (c1711-82) adorned the "delectable eminence" on the chalk bluff above his china-shop with shrubs and trees, beehives and winding walks. Watercolours of Sussex castles hung in the summerhouse, and seats in sheltered alcoves commanded vistas of the High Street, the Lewes Downs, the Weald, and the watermeadows along the Ouse, peopled in due season with haymakers, duck shooters and skaters. Other visitors pursuing the Picturesque included Samuel Hieronymous Grimm, the topographical artist used by William Burrell, and Miss Lund the school mistress, whose rapture overflowed into verse:

The beauteous scenes that all around it smile
Delight our eye and all our care beguile.

Though portrayed by Dunvan as a "besotted" mismanager of the Church Estate at Cliffe, Baldy was undoubtedly "a virtuoso in various researches". Besides his Garden and schemes for a Grotto beneath, he secured two angels to crown a new organ in Cliffe church, from the dismantled instrument formerly played by Handel at Canons House. Baldy was left 100 guineas by another landscape enthusiast, the banker Samuel Durrant, who laid out Durrants Folly, 15 acres of pleasure-ground by the Juggs Road above Winterbourne Hollow, an easy carriage-drive from his manor house at Southover.

James Lambert Senior

Also devoted to the Picturesque was James Lambert (1725-88). Though born at Willingdon, he was brought up at Cliffe Corner where his father, a flaxdresser, preceded Abraham Curtis. James kept a bookshop nearby, the *Golden Heal*. But he worked too as a coach and sign painter, a writer and gilder. He embellished a Constable's stave for Bishopstone Hundred, the church clock at East Hoathly, a Chinese bridge at The Hooke, a golden ball above the stables at Glynde Place, a weathercock and pleasure-boats at Coombe Place. He was much in demand for inn-signs and for a "likeness", of a bullock curiously scorched by lightning, or a hare whose strange colouring nonplussed Parson Wenham's hounds at Hamsey. Yet although self-taught, his artistic range grew wider. William Burrell chose him, along with Grimm, to record Sussex antiquities in watercolour. Dunvan admired his "faithful" studies of Nature, from "the moss to the oak, from the shell to the promontory", praising the perspective and richly tinted skies. His work was shown at the Royal Academy in 1775-76, and one landscape gained a premium from the Society of Arts and Sciences. But he remained diffidently provincial, a close friend of the Smith brothers at Chichester. At Goodwood House his *View of Portsmouth Harbour* hangs a discreet distance from canvases by Canaletto and Guardi.

Lambert's trade card (ESRO)

Lambert's brother John was Baldy's partner and legatee, so probably James advised on the Garden, the winding walks, beehives and alcove-seats, and painted the watercolours in the summerhouse. John was a caged-bird fancier. He owned books on Geography and six prints of ruins at Rome. He bequeathed the Garden to his nephew James (c1761-99) who also inherited from uncle James a barometer, a "pentagraft" and his commercial goodwill. James senior had taught him to draw, while recording Sussex antiquities for Burrell. A sketch of window tracery at Robertsbridge Abbey suggests he reworked his nephew's effort. James junior proved the weaker artist, though he painted a competent Royal Arms for Eastbourne church. His heir was the plumber George Hoey, who kept up the

Garden. The summerhouse glowed with coloured lights in 1805 to celebrate Trafalgar; and in 1846 a "moderate gratuity" still admitted admirers of the Picturesque.

BALLOON ASCENT.
FROM THE GAS WORKS, LEWES.
MONDAY, SEPT. 22, 1828.

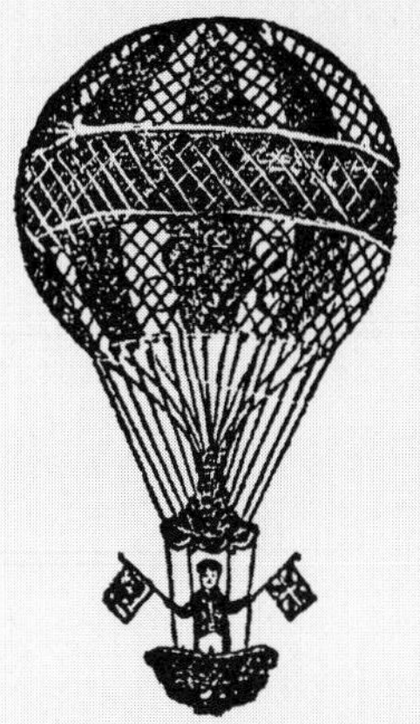

MR. GREEN respectfully announces to the Nobility, Gentry, and Inhabitants of the Town of LEWES and its Vicinity, that he intends making an ASCENT with his MAGNIFICENT BALLOON, on MONDAY, the 22d of September, 1828, at Three o'clock precisely,(being Lewes Great Sheep Fair Day) from a commodious Situation, near the GAS WORKS. A Band of Music will be in Attendance.

Tickets of Admission at One Shilling and Two Shillings each, may be had at Lee's, Lower's, and Baxter's Libraries, and of Mr. GREEN, at Mr. Jones's, Linen Draper, bottom of School Hill, Lewes. Full particulars in the Hand Bills.

The artist-engraver George Baxter (1804-67) also depicted local scenes. A pupil at Button's academy and the grammar school, he drew the priory ruins for volume one of Horsfield's *History*, which his father John printed in 1823 on a new lithographic press. For volume two he engraved the twin Norman fonts at St Anne's church and Denton. He then settled in London where he evolved a new technique of colour printing, first used for his plate *Butterflies* in 1829. Patented in 1835, his Baxter Prints became hugely successful. At Lewes his niche was filled by Brighton-born Thomas Henwood (1797-1861), a competent painter in watercolour who lived at Waterloo Place by 1825. Besides stately homes for Horsfield's *History of Sussex* (1835), he drew Aeronaut Green ascending from the gasworks (1828), and William Davies, the scorer at the Priory cricket ground, complete with claret bottle and hobnob.

Fortunately the Picturesque often yielded to Satire and Politics in the endless verse of Thomas "Clio" Rickman (1761-1834). His father John was the Cliffe brewer, and his uncle Thomas the corn merchant; hence the vapid lines,

Who'er the flow'ry fields delight,
Or softly purling rill;
Him the kind dryads all invite,
To visit Barcombe Mill.

As vapid was a tribute to Parson Davies at Glynde:

How oft, when sinking Sol, o'er yonder down,
Left the pale moon to mark her steady course,
Hast thou, the heavenly scenery to crown etc. etc.

Worse still was his salute, while struck by gout, to the joys of "unfettered mind":

Exclusive, bold, and free;
No downy flannel wraps it round.

Yet his epitaph for the Newhaven brewer, Thomas Tipper, showed the wit of his best political satire:

Honest he was, ingenious, blunt and kind,
And dared do, what few dare do, speak his mind.
PHILOSOPHY and HISTORY well he knew,
Was versed in PHYSICK and in SURGERY too;
The best old STINGO he both brewed and sold,
Nor did one knavish act to get his Gold.
He played through life a varied part,
And knew immortal HUDIBRAS by heart.
Reader, in real truth, such was the Man,
Be better, wiser, laugh more if you can.

Little local colour informed the literary labours of Dr John Delap (1725-1812), for nearly 50 years Vicar of Kingston-with-Iford, though as a resident of Cliffe at South Street he did salute its 45 freeholders sallying to Chichester in 1774. His *Marcellus a Monody* (1751) mourned the demise of Frederick Prince of Wales, but unsuccessful stage-tragedies dominated his output. *Hecuba* (1761) flopped at Drury Lane, despite an epilogue composed and spoken by Garrick. *The Royal Suppliants* (1781) lasted ten nights, and *The Captives* (1786) only three, being "set at liberty amidst roars of laughter", as Kemble unkindly put it. His personality perhaps was over-intense. Through the Thrales he met Dr Johnson who deplored the hypochondria in his verse: "do not be like the spider...and spin conversation thus incessantly out of thy own bowels". He also encountered Fanny Burney at a Brighton library in 1779, and dwelt obsessively on his latest tragedy:

> he returned to the same thing a million of times, asked the same questions, exacted the same compliments...till I almost fell asleep with the sound of the same words: and at last, with what little animation was left me, I contrived to make Mrs Thrale propose a walk on the Steyne, and crawling out of the shop, I sought - and found - revival from the breezes.

Nonetheless she breakfasted with him at South Street. In 1803 with undimmed enthusiasm he unleashed his *Dramatic Poems:* Gunilda, Usurper, Matilda, and Abdalla. Though ignored elsewhere, Lewesians rallied to them. The *Journal* reported that Abdalla depicted "in lively colours the inquity of the Slave Trade"; the Lewes theatre loyally staged it. Subscribers to the *Poems* included the Shelleys on St Annes Hill, and their friends the Miss Thrales who visited them; indeed in September 1789 Henry Shelley and the eldest Miss were rumoured to be engaged. Presumably because of the Thrales the Shelleys had earlier entertained Dr Johnson. It is said he marooned a small but talkative Miss Shelley in a cherry tree, and then forgot her till dinner time.

Tradition also has it that the seaside banditti and their swooning captives, so often depicted by John Hamilton Mortimer (1740-79), owed much to his childhood among smugglers at Eastbourne, though not to his schooling at Lewes. Horsfield credited him with an altarpiece at Southover, a *Last Supper*; but his less talented uncle Roger probably painted it. Southover also displayed a *Baptism of Christ* which Horsfield thought "indifferent". In other Lewes churches hung more canvases showing tenebrous scenes from Holy Scripture in a High Renaissance or Baroque Manner. St Thomas's boasted a "very superior" *Ascension* of Netherlandish provenance, given in 1779 by a London art dealer Bernard Van Der Gutcht, who married locally. Lord Chichester gave to All Saints a *John the Baptist in Prison*, bought in Italy and "long appreciated" at Stanmer Park. Parson Crofts adorned St John's with a *Presentation of Children to the Saviour*, Venetian in style, which Captain Pawlet of Halnaker House received as a naval prize. The Grand Manner also lurked in local mansions. At Firle Place in 1735 a tourist admired what he believed to be Annibale Caracci's *Saint Jerome*, Nicholas Poussin's *Ishmael and Agar*, Caravaggio's *Abraham and Isaac*, and *Apollo Flaying Marsyas* by Rubens. At Stanmer Park the same tourist overlooked a fine portrait of a Persian Lady because (so a Tory annotator of his manuscript Tour surmised) "his Gutts and his Brains were so full of Venison and Whiggism". During raceweek in 1762 Lewesians savoured a mobile display of High Art. Mr Motet exhibited "six curious Pieces of Marble Sculpture" designed for the King of France and "taken during the last War". They showed "the Sufferings of our Saviour, in upwards of 400 fine Figures in Relievo". With them were several paintings by "the celebrated Raphael".

Quite apart from professional men and Mr Motet, the town's booksellers and printers sustained local intellectual life. Thomas Norman supplied the Borough in 1708 with Mr Nelson's manual for High Constables. In 1709 he bound the Town Book of Records, and in the 1720s he supplied Acts of Parliament to the Clerk of the Peace. The Borough paid the bookseller Edward Verrall (1707-67) to print notices during an outbreak of smallpox in 1731. William Lee (1713-86), a native of Chichester, published and printed the *Lewes Journal* from 1745, and was joined for a few years by Verrall. Their newsmen trudged across the county laden with *Journals*, stationery, Blanks (for bureaucratic use), spectacles, fiddle strings, elixirs, cordials, tinctures and pamphlets, including a sermon Parson Bristed preached in St Michael's urging Repentance as a prudent response to local earthquake tremours. Wearing his bookseller's hat James Lambert in the late 1750s stocked *The History of an English Seraglio*, *Select Psalms* chosen by himself, engraved portraits of Mr Henry Pelham and Frederick of Prussia, and a large map of Germany for connoisseurs of his campaigns. In 1774 Lambert and John Vine of Heathfield also promoted "Letter Paper with Lines to write by".

In 1772 William Lee moved his press to 64 High Street, where his sons William (1747-1830) and Arthur (1759-1824) succeeded him. Before 1800 its varied output included almanacks and assize sermons; Cater Rand's *Philosophical Lectures*, and his *Tables* for calculating the value of gold; manuals on reviving the drowned and, when invasion threatened, on swordsmanship; John Smeaton's *Report* on the Lewes and Laughton Levels; and the *Proceedings* of the Sussex Agricultural Society, with the prize cattle engraved after "actual admeasurement". Sprightlier in tone were Richard Sicklemore's musical dramas, *Saltinbanco* and *Aboukir Bay* (alias *The Glorious First of August*). More highbrow *Poems* and *Fugitive Pieces* were supplied by William Dine, a parish clerk at Chiddingly, by Parson Joseph Wise of

Penhurst, and by Richard Michell, curate of East Dean, alias the Man of the Rocks, a grammar school pupil of Robert Austen. Utterly serious in tone was an *Essay on the Seduction of Women* by a Lewes saddler Edward Relfe, which deplored the swelling tide of London prostitutes, "sliding from Corner to Corner, outwardly covered with Rags, and inwardly infected with a destructive scandalous Disease." Yet as the *Journal* cannily commented,

> despite many just Observations...the Misfortune is, that those whom he wishes to reclaim, will not easily be prevailed upon to read his arguments.

Perhaps Relfe also wrote the letter to the *Journal* in 1769 which revealed that many "soberly inclined" youths were enticed into Hovels and Hay-lofts by prostitutes infesting Lewes High Street, "as abandoned as any the great metropolis can produce".

Though it serialized *Roderick Random* in 1749, the *Journal* was not intellectually demanding. Indeed the gullibility of William Lee junior attracted "fibbing" correspondents. Hence the sheep at Northease weighing over 18 stone; the wild ducks nesting in the Shelleys' rookery; the mushroom on Plumpton Plain 13 inches wide; the extreme examples of "maternal soliticide" in rats and domestic fowl; the letters describing MERMAIDS OR SEA-WOMEN; and the single bullet that

> killed a partridge, shot a man, a hog and a hogsty, broke 14 panes of glass, and knocked down six gingerbread kings and queens on a mantle piece opposite the window.

Gideon Mantell regretted this weakness, but still commended Lee as the "beau-ideal of a country editor of the old school". Optimistic and original, he ballooned and fossil-hunted into his eighties, his grey hair streaked mahogany by careless use of Atkin's Tyrian Dye.

Lee's newsmen still carried elixirs and hair colouring as they trudged towards Chichester, Petworth, Horsham, Tunbridge Wells, Robertsbridge and Rye. In January 1834 their New Year broadsheet bemoaned this toilsome trade by punning reference to Lewes's new public utility:

> Unblest by Intellect's bright ray,
> No Science helps us on our way;
> (Tho' often in the driving storm
> A Water Company we form).

The versifier perhaps was the prolific Arthur Lee junior (c1787-1850). In his *Pryor's Dream* (c1848) a railway engine is foretold, roaring through the hallowed precincts at Southover:

Like a dragon in ire, it vomited fire,
And its scales were brassye brighte.
A fiende, who stoode on the creature's back,
To manage its onwarde course,
Thro' the Chapter-house spedde o'er the bones of the deade,
With fierce and ruthlesse force.

In 1789 the *Lewes and Brighthelmstone Pacquet*, a weekly newspaper, was launched at 51 High Street by Thomas Budgen (1765-1832), a surveyor, printer and bookseller from Frant. Its news coverage was thin, its type often eccentric, and Number 26 (Thursday 21 January 1790) proved the last, though Budgen blamed his mounting workload as a surveyor. More successful was John Baxter (1781-1858) from Rickhurst in Surrey, who set up a press on School Hill in 1802, after training in London near the Strand. He began his annual *Sussex Pocket Books* in 1804, and printed Button's *Directory of Lewes and Brighton* in 1805. His list later included a Library of Agricultural Knowledge, the collected works of Luther, and Lambert's *Cricketers' Guide* which sold 300,000 copies. On the technical side he adapted a leather inking roller to replace the felt ball, but abandoned efforts to make paper from nettles. He also lavished care on illustrations. For the woodcuts in a quarto Bible (1811) he employed Clennell and White, pupils of Thomas Bewick. The lithographs and copperplates for Horsfield's *History* involved his son George who produced the Baxter Prints. His own career peaked in 1837 with the launch of the *Sussex Agricultural Express* which sold 160,000 copies by 1847.

The bookseller Edward Verrall feared commercial ruin in 1758, after John Woodgate, a versatile linen draper, opened a circulating library at Cliffe. By 1805, because of growing demand for the three-volume novel, John Baxter, William Bennett (from the tailoring dynasty) and Elizabeth Budgen, Thomas's sister, could each offer this genteel service. When R.W. Lower succeeded Miss Budgen in 1823, prominent among her 2000 volumes were the novels of the Northern Unknown (Walter Scott). In 1836 he promoted *Tom Cladpole's Jurney to Lunnon*, "written in pure Sussex doggerel" by a village schoolmaster at Chiddingly, Richard Lower, the father of Mark Antony.

The Northern Unknown's popularity caused Horsfield to complain in 1824 that "works of mere imagination" had invaded the shelves of the Lewes Library Society. This was formed in January 1786 by nine townsfolk who resented the "trash" so prevalent in circulating libraries. Each paid 2s 6d down and a shilling monthly. By 1794 there were 60 members, and by April 1801 the 1342 volumes included "almost every estimable work in the English language", bought at a cost of £546. In 1814 premises were purchased on School Hill; and in 1824 92 subscribers browsed among 3400 books. New members now paid six guineas down, and 25 shillings a year. This evident vigour inspired the *Lewes Library Society; A Poem* (1804) by John Viney Button. It saluted the founder-chairman Dr Joseph Ridge, the treasurer Cater Rand, and the secretary Thomas Woollgar, a botanist and antiquarian:

> He knows each laughing flow'r that gilds the mead,
> Unfolds the silky texture of a grass,
> Proclaims its genus, and defines its class.

It praised the devoted librarian, "obliging" Adams:

> His rolling eye at one short glance surveys,
> Law, sermons, poems, histories and plays,
> Whether Divines for CAMPBELL'S Lectures ask,
> Or Miss demands the Shipwreck, or the Task.

Eleven ladies filled "with beauty's rays the hallow'd shrine", while "manly vot'ries" converged from Brighton, Ditchling, Iford, Litlington, Buxted, and even Westfield, much as the siege of Troy drew Greek paladins

> From fair Boetia, and the Locrian plain,
> Thebes, and the islands of th'Egean main.

A black japanned ballot-box sifted aspiring members:

Unbrib'd, unbiassed, the iv'ry counters fall;
The draw'rs inverted their decrees reveal.
And a puchases committee vetoed
The scholiast's learning, and the bigot's cant.

Between 1815 and 1822 Gideon Mantell, Horsfield and John Dudeney supported a short-lived Lewes Philosophical Society. Henry Browne junior lectured on horology, and Mantell's brother Joshua (1795-1865), a promising chemist, on the properties of Silver. He also isolated Silicius and Barium with an "oxi-hidrogen blow pipe", and did other experiments before appreciative audiences at the *Star*. Himself a devotee of Science, Horsfield warmly welcomed the gas-works which opened at Cliffe in 1822 with "full masonic honours". He foresaw the new "aeriform fluid" darting its "magic flame" down the darkest back-alley, though the Gas Company's minutes reveal how slowly the pipes progressed, even along the High Street.

Members of the defunct Philosophical Society were prominent in the Lewes Mechanics' Institution, founded in November 1825 to disseminate Useful Knowledge. Within 12 months it recruited over 200 members, mostly tradesmen, and housed 500 books and an extensive Philosophical Apparatus in purpose-built premises by the theatre (itself renamed the Public Temple). Packed audiences heard Dudeney lecture on Astronomy, John Webb Woollgar on Mechanics and Horsfield on Pneumatics. Burwood Godlee, the coal merchant who superintended the gasworks, spoke on Electricity and on Steam Power, putting "in full play an ingeniously constructed engine". Dr Mantell explained the properties of arsenic, and the blunders by Surgeon Evans that sent Daniel Leney to the gallows. Henry Browne junior tested the Radiation of Heat, with phosphorus, charcoal and two mirrors. Like the Baxters' concern for printing techniques, these lectures embodied the High Seriousness which enabled Lewesians to expand and diversify their town's manufacturing base in the 1830s and 1840s.

7

The County Town: Sport and Amusement

The provincial amateurs of the fancy perceiving Tom Oliver, Bob Purcell, Harris and Aby. Belasco on the course, well known heroes of the P. R., gave a hint that a bit of milling would be a treat to the country folk. The Opponent of Spring, in consultation with his pals, said, "it should be done, if the blunt was forthcoming, as how he had got under his care a sheeny from the East End of the Metropolis who was anxious for a shy, and also a kid from Brighton, who wanted a character to send him up to Town, with a bit of the Steeven into the bargain". A purse was soon collected; and the Jew threw his beaver into the ring with good pluck. He said his name was Jacobs, and he had defeated Gadger, at Hampton Races; and he only weighed 8 st. 4 lb.. His adversary Wren weighed 10 st.. Jacobs was handled by Bob (the Wheeler) and Roberts; and Wren by Cooling and Grevett. Fifteen rounds were well contested, occupying 31 minutes. The Jew was over-weighted, but he fought with great courage, till it was Mount Harry to a mole-hill, and no chance. The Sheeny had one of his ogles closed, his conque damaged, and his upper-works in Chancery... it was a capital turn-up; the yokels were quite delighted; and the swells were also pleased.

A PRIZE-FIGHT AT LEWES RACES DESCRIBED BY PIERCE EGAN (LJ 11 AUG 1823).

As well as Antiquities, High Art and the Picturesque, Georgian Lewes offered boisterous amusements. By 1714 the summer races were well established. Their centre-piece was a King's Plate worth 100 guineas, open to six-year-olds carrying 12 stone; the distance was four miles. Other Plate Races were staged at Newmarket, Guildford, Winchester, Norwich, Lincoln, Nottingham, York and Black Hambledon near Burnley. They appealed to all ranks of society. At Lewes rustic Will Marchant watched in May 1718, genteel Lucy Pelham in May 1720. Indeed because the Lewes Plate Race was so popular with "all the Gentlemen" of Sussex, it was moved forward from May by 1724 to dovetail with the Midsummer Assizes, which also drew the shire elite to the county town. It also allowed the Race Steward, the Duke of Newcastle (1693-1768), to display his political grip on the county, by arriving "on the hill" with a bevy of client MPs, docile peers and pliant Justices. The crowds exceeded even those at Cliffe sheep fair, so much real estate in mid-Sussex was auctioned at Lewes the same week.

In August 1729 the races lasted three days. *Thunderbolt* walked over for the King's Plate; *Sweetlips* won a £20 plate for galloways (a robust breed from the Scottish Lowlands); and *Fair Play* won a 50 guinea plate, with Sir Robert Fagge's *Alexander* second, and Sir William Gage's *Plowman* third. Sir Robert, "a famous Racer on the Lewes Turf", was remembered as a "Fat, Greasy Old Butcher" whose dung-coated carriage was harnessed with ropes and contained "a kept lady or two". Sir William was also "very lecirous". He seduced glamorous Miss Parnel Baldy, a grocer's daughter at Cliffe, though she married well and snubbed him later. And Bel Norton "tumbled over" in his coach, so an inscribed window-pane at Antioch House recorded. On the racecourse itself raffishness, gaming-tables, pick-pockets and heavy betting abounded. In 1760 the Duke of Richmond won 200 guineas, matching his *Muley Ishmael* against Sir Matthew Fetherston's *Sally*. A victim of race-fever was John Osbaldeston, Henry Burtenshaw's clerk. He entered two horses in August 1763 and nearly starved his family to keep them.

By then the races were consolidating. Lewes publicans pleaded for "a third Day's Plate", to spread the meeting securely over Thursday, Friday and Saturday; and William Plumer, a Borough MP, stumped up half the £50 needed. In 1768 Richmond succeeded Newcastle as the event's ducal patron and gave a £50 plate open to horses bred in Sussex. At Goodwood House Sir William Chambers built him a majestic stable-block, and George Stubbs portrayed his hunters. In October 1769 John Woodgate collected subscriptions for a race-stand at his circulating library. The Stewards in 1770 were Thomas Hay of Glyndebourne (Eastern) and Lord George Lennox (Western). They arranged dinners and dances at the *White Hart*, the *Star* and Verrall's assembly-room; and a hairdresser came down from Grosvenor Square. Sir Ferdinando Poole of Lewes and Sir John Shelley of Michelgrove stewarded a packed three-day event in 1774, which included a King's Plate, a Lewes Plate, a Members' Plate, Richmond's Plate, and a Brighthelmstone Plate, funded from that burgeoning resort.

One visitor there was the Duke of Cumberland, the hero of Culloden. In September 1782 he watched some sweepstakes run at Lewes, and soon after he welcomed to The Steine his nephew, the Prince of Wales, who quickly became a steady patron of the Lewes meeting. In 1784 the Prince came with the Duc de Chartres and dined with Richmond at the *Star;* such a confluence of Royal Blood almost dumbfounding the *Journal*. In 1787 he dined with Colonel Pelham, and his party included the Princess de L'Ombelle, the Dukes of Bedford, Queensberry and Ancaster, Charles James Fox and Mrs Fitzherbert. Other years the Prince hobnobbed with Sir Ferdinando at The Friars and Colonel Newton at Southover. In 1803 he combined the races with the Agricultural Show, his birthday celebrations, and a grand military review on Newmarket Hill. His stables at Brighton rivalled those at Goodwood; at Lewes his horses, *Pegasus* and *Knowsley*, won a King's Plate. On "the hill" his equipage was always faultless, though his cronies were not. Lord Barrymore so incensed Mr Beeby from Ringmer that a duel was only just averted; and in 1792 a Lewes Grand Jury indicted "Hellgate" for assaulting a harmless linen draper on The Steine. Though the Prince did not attend the race balls, their splendour increased. In 1789 Miss Anne North's suavely performed minuets enchanted a "grand and brilliant" gathering. Yet the Prince's patronage ended abruptly after 1807. Perhaps he took umbrage when a Town Meeting in 1809 deplored the Corrupt Practices of the Duke of York while Commander-in-Chief. In 1816 the *Journal* blamed Lewesians for a lack of "cordiality", and noted in 1817 that none, except the Miss Shelleys, were invited to Princess Charlotte's birthday ball at The Pavilion.

Sir Ferdinando Poole (1731-1804) proved a popular Race Steward; and his roomy family coach, The Tub, regularly conveyed infirm Lewesians up to "the hill". He also owned a fine stud in the meadows behind The Friars. In 1793 his prize stallion *Waxy* won the Derby at 12-1, by half a length from Lord Egremont's *Gohanna*, the odds-on favourite. In all *Waxy* sired 190 winners, including the Derby winners *Pope*, *Whalebone*, *Blucher* and *Whisker*. From The Friars in 1801 *Miscreant* and *Duchess of Limbs* were stolen by two Gentlemen-Thieves, who demanded a post-chaise to the gallows when condemned to hang on Horsham Common. None the worse for the ordeal, *Miscreant* (*by Dragon, out of Glumdalea, covered by Waxy*) fetched £126 when Mr Tattersall auctioned Poole's bloodstock on 1 August 1804, the day between Brighton and Lewes races. The East India Company paid 800 guineas for the stallion *Worthy*. The Duke of Grafton bought *Waxy*, who was ultimately laid to well-earned rest beside All Saints church at Newmarket. Poole also presided over a club of racing enthusiasts at the *Pelham Arms*, who celebrated his birthday on 6 November with fireworks. In August 1802 they raised money to enter *Taper* for the Ladies' Plate and *Tawney* for the Town Plate.

Being the public house nearest the course, the *Pelham Arms* attracted racing men (and perhaps harriers too, since its sign was the *Dog* till 1784). The landlord John Scott 1747-68 rode for the raffish Sir Robert Fagge of Glynleigh, and in his stables the itinerant stallions *Fearnought* and *Stump* serviced local mares. His stepson, Thomas Dowlen, was remarkable for "lowness of stature". Richard Williams 1787-1807 hosted Poole's club of turf-men and became clerk of the Lewes course. The *Running Horse* with its extensive stables opened nearby in 1789, with Richard Goddard, Henry Shelley's ex-coachman, as landlord. Its sign depicted the famous mare *Eclipse* whose foal *Pot-8-os* sired *Waxy*. Her owner was Captain O'Kelly, "a Huge Square shouldered coarse Irishman", whose residence was rumoured to be "little better than a Bawdy House". He visited the course with Sir Charles Bunbury in 1780. Goddard moved in 1809 to the newly built *Black Horse*, only a few yards away.

Also nearby, at Spital Corner, were the racing stables erected about 1780 on two acres of pasture by Sir John Lade. A great-nephew of the Southwark brewer whom Stephen Philpot groomed and Michael Rysbrack sculptured, he was also, like Barrymore, a volatile racing crony of the Prince of Wales. His wife Laetitia, reputedly an ex-courtesan, was portrayed by Stubbs as an assured equestrienne. Till 1798 John and Charles Rider ran the stables. Then came Thomas Brown (c1753-1842), a native of Royston. As a twelve-year-old groom he conducted *Sharp Shins* to Poole's stud at The Friars, and stayed on to train *Waxy*, *Mentor*, *Jemima* and *Kerenhappuch*. At his Spital stables in August 1823 *Little John*, a stallion of "great bone and power", tarried to cover. 36 horses exercised there in July 1829 before the races at Lewes, Brighton and Goodwood. He also broke in colts and trained hunters. His success prompted a Lewes drawing-master, Mr Osmont, to propose in 1833 a celebratory MEZZOTINTO,

1830.

TO COVER THIS SEASON,

Until the First of August, at Mr. THOS. BROWN'S Racing Stables, LEWES, at Five Guineas thorough-bred Mares; all others at Two Guineas and a half; the money to be paid at the time of covering.

ROBIN HOOD, a bay Horse, 15 hands 2 in. high, with great bone and power, bred by the Earl of EGREMONT, got by Octavius, out of an own sister to Wanderer; her dam Catherine, sister to Colibri, by Woodpecker, out of Camilla, by Trentham.

Robin Hood won one King's Plate, besides Plates, Matches, and Sweepstakes.

Good accommodations for Mares, and Mares and Foals, where every possible care will be taken of them.—Grass and hay at the usual prices; corn, if ordered.

engraved by Mr Lupton after a portrait by Mr Archer. Also equestrian was the Riding School in Fisher Street on Black Lion Field, opened before 1760 and demolished in the 1820s. Possibly the jockey William Lawrence used it. In 1724 he took care of the horses belonging to the assize judges and their retinue. Later on Newcastle made him clerk of the course, with a base at Verrall's coffee-house.

The whalebacked downs above Lewes also attracted cricketers from a wide radius. In 1694 a Pelham betted on a local match. In 1735 Lord Middlesex and sportive Sir William Gage fielded "11 Gentlemen of Kent, and 11 of Sussex", to the delight of a passing tourist:

> Thus gloriously do British Noblemen employ themselves, while neither the Council, nor the Camp [nor Bel Norton] demand their Presence. Hence may they learn to ward off the Blows of their Enemies, & to send such Balls against France as never a Batt in the Kingdom can turn.

(At Portslade in 1741 a mid-Sussex team did fight off the other eleven with "heavy blows" from their bats.) On Cliffe Hill in August 1756 Mayfield challenged the rest of Sussex; and on Spital Hill in June 1763 Lewes met Isfield-cum-Uckfield. Possibly at The Friars, the Prince of Wales watched the town play Sir Ferdinando and his javelin men; and at sheltered Houndean Bottom Lewes challenged Seaford in July 1815. Other teams converged from Newhaven, Poynings and Waldron. But at the papermill the "steady women" preferred stool-ball in 1828.

William Davies, scorer to the Lewes Priory Cricket Club, (Henwood)

The cricket swelled the flood of wagers buoying up Georgian sport. Gentlemen from East and West of Lewes played for a "considerable sum" in June 1763. Heavy betting also spiced the games on the Lewes bowling green in the Castle Yard. In 1639 John Rowe the Antiquarian and William Thomas the Clerk of the Peace had recommended John Standing to manage the green and sell liquid refreshment. In May 1753 Charles Boore, who kept the *Castle* nearby, reorganized the club. His widow, and then James Markwick 1771-2, also kept the tavern and the green. One talented player they watched was Tom

Paine, who "observed much more exactness with the measuring-stick, than he was accustomed to do at the beer-barrel with his dipping-rule". In the 1790s soldiers practised sword drill on the green, and the Horse Artillery paraded there to hear the Articles of War. This usage could explain why the *Journal* praised the turf in 1803 as among "the best in the Kingdom for variety of ground". By August 1827, when club-members dined "on the sward under awnings", they tackled this "variety" by employing woods with a bias heavier than those rolled on flat greens, and capable, if cast wide, of approaching the jack from behind.

At the *Castle* in 1773 cock-fighting mingled betting with bloodshed, a potent combination. Two guineas a Battle and five guineas the Odd were offered in 1778 when Lewes met Newhaven at the *Swan* in Cliffe. The prize money doubled for an up-market two-day match at the *Star* between East and West, at which Messrs Vinal and Gladwish were the accredited Feeders of 42 combatants. At a Wealden contest in 1762 Lewes owners challenged the Gentlemen of East Hoathly ("if any such there be", queried Thomas Turner). In 1830 the sport was staged behind the *Fountain* tavern, though the merriment of stoning cockerels at Eastertide was in decline. Bull-baiting took place in 1781 at Coombe Bottom, a natural arena behind the *Wheatsheaf*, also used for shooting matches and prize-fights. The first dog to pin the bull gained its master 20 shillings.

Prize-fights gave fullest vent to betting and blood lust. In 1722 the Marchant boys tramped in from Hurstpierpoint to savour a bout. 200 people watched a building labourer and a negro exchange hard but "awkward" blows for 20 minutes in 1788. At Coombe Bottom a Lewes blacksmith fought an armourer from the Light Horse. During an "agreed" bout in 1805 Thomas Dykes killed John Jordan. Contests were much in demand during race-week. In 1790 the "amiable" Duke of York let 30 spectators climb onto his phaeton, and 2000 more scuffled to form a ring, before a gypsy (one of the "Black Legged society") vanquished a local youth. In 1792 Joe Ward won a "severe" battle with a river-cutter on the Ouse Navigation. Such was the pugilism observed by Pierce Egan (1772-1849) while a compositor on the *Journal*. After returning to the metropolis, he wrote best-sellers like *Boxiana*, and *Life in London*, "the Day and Night Scenes of Jerry Hawthorn, Esq., and his elegant friend, Corinthian Tom". The "glitter and dissipation" on the course sometimes prompted unstructured violence. A bloody affray in 1763 pitted the Infantry against the Cavalry; and local horse-thieves tried to lynch a deviant colleague, Jigg of Jevington.

Hunting the hare and the fox near Lewes was also popular. By 1714 "several" gentlemen kept packs of hounds, though one tourist complained:

> you must follow the Dogs up Hill and down Hill, at the hazard of your neck... the Horses run down a Precipice naturally without Harm, except your Fear or Ignorance makes you stop them, and then you endanger the loss of both your own Life and that of your Horses.

Despite these hazards, a pack of harriers with Irish blood in their pedigree was brought from Parham about 1750 to hunt along the Brookside (the watermeadows towards Newhaven), and on the Downs above. In 1763 they pursued a doe across Northease Hill. Six were maliciously poisoned in 1791 at the kennels near Greenwall kept by the Master, tanner John Chatfield. Harrison Carr housed them at Iford by 1823. The East Sussex Fox Hounds was formed at Ringmer in 1821, to hunt the Downs and Weald between Eastbourne and the Adur, with Major Cator (Royal Artillery) in command. The AGM and the hunt-ball took place at the *Star*, and when hunt-races at Lewes were first staged in March 1829, Milords Gage and Chichester were Stewards, and nearly 5000 people watched. One year Princess Victoria attended, and John Ellman II coaxed her to present a cup.

The varied environs of Lewes fostered other sports. The wild fowl in the watermeadows down to Newhaven were "the best Winter Game for a Gun" imaginable. Abundant woodcock, snipe and geese allowed the gunsmith Thomas Lloyd (c1737-1830) to bag 130 birds in a week, despite the shooting-pieces then available. John Byng noted the many pointer-dogs being trained on the Lewes Downs near Falmer, a village well situated for

> a shooter, a walker, or a harehunter, who might here during a long autumn enjoy these sports rationally, with the comforts of a sea view, and a breeze; or if frisky, and eager to be unhappy and expensive, step down to Shergolds [at Brighton] for his claret and all the wicked etceteras!

Along the Ouse the fishing was excellent. The *Journal* reported (perhaps unreliably) the presence of salmon in 1800, and also a string of memorable catches: a jack taken near Malling Deanery, weighing over 31 lbs, and upwards of four feet long; a trout from Isfield millstream, nearly 11 lbs in weight, and 21 inches "from eye to fork". At Malling a letter-carrier drowned while treading eels out of the river-mud into a basket, a "simple and precarious" local pastime.

The passion to pursue, trap or shoot, endangered some species of quarry, such as the wheatears served "fresh or potted" at the *White Hart,* the otters hunted along Glynde Reach in 1762, the polecat itemized in the church accounts of St Anne's in 1741, and the bustard last seen on the Lewes Downs at Four Lords Dool about 1750. The Ouse Navigation, by draining away their sheet-water, displaced the bald coots from Ranscombe Brooks.

This enviable choice of sport (and perhaps Brighton's "wicked etceteras") encouraged the gentlemen of mid-Sussex to patronize at Lewes a winter season of assemblies, concerts and plays, which rescued their womenfolk from sodden fields and dripping coppices. Miss Dobell at Streat Place (the last of her line), and Mrs Medley at mud-girt Coneysborough Park, both insisted on a house at Lewes being hired in 1746. Before the roads were turnpiked other local gentry, the Pelhams, the Bridgers, the Gages, the Trevors and the Hays, must sometimes have stayed overnight; and even in the 1790s the Pelhams of Catsfield and the Fullers of Brightling retained spacious town-houses. Despite owning rural acres, a few gentry families chose to live permanently in Lewes, though Sir Ferdinando Poole (1804), Colonel Newton (1808) and Henry Shelley (1812) died with no sons to succeed them. After William Green eloped with wealthy Miss Collier, they settled in the High Street. John Marten Cripps displayed trophies from his Grand Tour in School Hill House. As Justices of the Peace these gentlemen dominated the Lewes Petty Sessions, whereas in chartered Boroughs shopkeeping Aldermen tended to rule the roost. Other residents with claims to gentility helped cherish the winter season: the physicians and half-pay officers; the up-market surgeons and attorneys; the wealthy widows and spinsters whose Sedan chairs negotiated the steep twittens; and the black-coated parsons who left their Lewes "Rookery" each Sabbath to preach in their neglected parishes. Typical were the occupiers of Antioch House: Dr Edward Poole and his heiress from the West Indies; Captain James Cranston to whom Admiral De Langara surrendered; and whist-loving Archdeacon Raynes.

Yet from 1733 onwards the developing Lewes season was damaged by strife between Whig and Tory in the Borough and Shire. Because John Cripps, the landlord of the *Star*, and John Lidgitter who kept the coffee-house opposite, were both Tories, the Duke of Newcastle leased ironmonger Court's showrooms facing the *White Hart*, and installed Richard Verrall junior to run a Whig coffee-house, and Mrs Trower to regulate a Whig assembly-room. A leading county Tory, Thomas Sergison, then improved the Great Room at

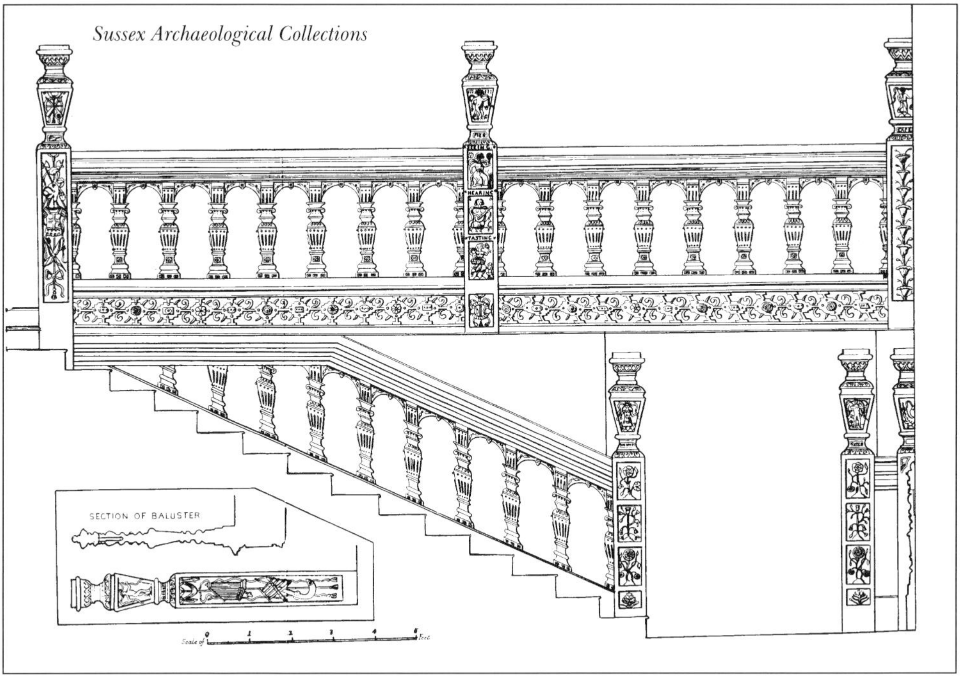

Sussex Archaeological Collections

the Star, and put in a fine Renaissance staircase from his disused mansion at Slaugham. However a political truce in the late 1740s closed this social chasm. The assemblies reunited, and Lewes became "a very gay Place". Nearly 20 couples celebrated the King's Birthday in October 1751, reinforced by "pretty gentlemen" from Sir Richard Rick's dragoons, whose next review promised another ball. Herbert's regiment of foot was also eagerly awaited. In the winter of 1763-4 on the Wednesday near the full moon Mrs Virgoe marshalled the monthly assemblies at Newcastle House. In January Mrs Green counted 82 "Gentry" (the "Common Sort" being excluded); by March the endless "Routs" threatened to exhaust even her flighty nature.

Lidgitter's coffee-house opposite the *Star* shut down in the mid-

1740s. But another then opened near the bridge at 224 High Street, owned by the Lewes merchants trading to Barbados. After it closed in 1770, the *Bear* offered similar refreshment. At Newcastle House Henry Verrall, Richard's brother, managed the coffee-house with "respectability and profit" from 1742 till 1779, and the assembly room from 1764. He witnessed Tom Paine's marriage at St Michael's, and probably made the remark (over a glass of punch after a game of bowls) that Frederick of Prussia was an excellent king, having "so much of the devil in him", which caused Paine to decide that kings "might very well be dispensed with". After Verrall died Thomas Harben turned Newcastle House into a bank, stamp-office and hardware store. So the winter assemblies moved to the *Star* where John Jenner was landlord; and a new coffee-house was opened next door on Fisher Street Corner, kept till 1809 by his wife Jane, and then by her cousin Jane Harrison (c1761-1835).

Like the race-balls, the winter assemblies held at the *Star* grew in splendour. Mrs Fitzherbert came over from Brighton in October 1790, and mingled with many "persons of fashion". Another glittering throng admired the white satin robe worn by Lady Sheffield in January 1795. Perhaps Miss Jane Austen also attended. The opening scenes of her unfinished novel *The Watsons*, begun in 1804, describe an October assembly at L. in Sussex, four hours by post-chaise from London. Miss Emma Watson's party arrive very early, amid "the bustle, noise, and draughts of air of the broad entrance-passage of an inn" (but not the *White Hart* which offers only "a whist club"). They ascend a wide staircase (Sergison's), where no sound "but the first scrape of one violin, blessed the ears", and cross a short gallery to the assembly room "brilliant in lights". Around the fireplace another family party is stiffly seated, and several officers lounge together or pass in and out from the card-room. Then is heard the "inspiriting" sound of carriages. "Portly chaperons" appear, "and strings of smartly-dressed girls...with now and then a fresh gentleman straggler". During the second dance "several minutes of extraordinary bustle without, and watchful curiosity within" herald the carefully timed arrival of the Osbornes from Osborne Castle, "preceded by the attentive master of the inn [Mr Dunn] to open a door which was never shut". (Lord Francis Godolphin Osborne, a Lewes MP in 1802-07, was related by marriage to the Pelhams of Stanmer Park.) As the ball continues, Emma observes a young boy's distress when casually denied a dance promised him earlier by Miss Osborne. Impulsively she partners him, and all eyes turn upon them, even those of Lord Osborne, aloof, single and thirty. Afterwards Miss Austen changed L. in Sussex to D. in Surrey, possibly because she needed Emma's father, a local parson, to attend an Archdeacon's visitation, but not in the town where the assembly was held.

Though the Renaissance staircase was wide, the Great Room at the *Star* was a mere 45 by 26 by 14 feet. However from 1812 a chicly Neo-Classical assembly-room in the new Shire Hall was available, 60 by 30 by 27 feet. The walls and hangings were fawn, the Grecian sofas scarlet. Six chandeliers illumined a portrait of the Prince Regent donated by Himself, also a Sublimer study of *Richard III and the Princes in the Tower* painted by Northcote, and four plaster-of-Paris Muses fashioned by Humphrey Hopper.

Itinerant musicians often beguiled the Fashionables gathered at Lewes. At Verrall's assembly-room in August 1768 Mrs March and Signor Fidele ("lately arrived from Italy") sang selections from Piccini, Carafelli, Traetta and Buranello; and Herr Georg Noelly plucked his pantaleone, a huge dulcimer-like instrument 11 feet long, equipped with 260 strings. There too Celtic melodies were coaxed from his celebrated pedal-harp by Edward Jones, later to become Official Bard to the Prince of Wales. Delights elsewhere included harmonious Musical Glasses at the *Swan* in Cliffe; an Italian cymbal struck while John Pallany worked his Camera Obscura at the *Dorset Arms*; and a World in Miniature showing the nine Muses "playing in concert". Lewes's own music-masters often performed at the *Star*. There Lord Mansell sponsored the violinist Stephen Philpot; Mrs Fitzherbert patronized John Thring; and in 1818 William Page offered works by Borghi, Davaux, Stamitz, Pleyel and the ever-popular Piccini. Thomas Nicholson studied under Mr Noverre, the famous ballet-master at Drury Lane. After deserting his wife and children in 1820, he was advertised as genteel in appearance, but "rather stooping" in his walk.

In 1801-4 Nicholson was organist at Cliffe church, a celebrated fount of sacred harmony. So was James Lambert 1745-1788, who stocked at his nearby bookshop his own *Select Psalms for the Use of Cliffe Church* and his *Hymns on Religious Subjects*. The first organ, installed about 1740, received a trumpet-stop in 1752, and two angels from Handel's instrument at Canons. In 1802 stooping Thomas merely watched when Mr Cooke from St George's Bloomsbury inaugurated a fine-toned replacement, built by Mr

Lincoln of London; however a choir from St Michael's did sing the anthems in a "masterly and scientific" manner. A later organist, the music-seller George Peckham, supplied eight reeds to Ticehurst church. Not till 1829 were organs installed at St Anne's, All Saints and Southover, the last two being of the "Psalmodic barrel" kind, made by Mr Walker in Holborn. Sacred melody also flowed from Southover belfry, though Dunvan deemed it "stunning monotony". After appreciative townsfolk and "Country gentlemen" raised more than £200 in 1738, Captain Headley shipped its four bells to London, where Samuel Knight recast them, and supplied two more. When another two were added in 1778, teams from Horsham and Bolney rang Holt's Grandsire Triples (5040 changes) in three hours nine minutes. But when teams from Brighton and Cuckfield came to ring them in 1822, the tenor bell crashed down after 3800 changes. By then four others were cracked, a result presumably of the "almost daily" practice Dunvan so deplored. Not till 1839 was the battered peal recast; the cost being largely met by the parvenu Verralls, soon to be Lords of the Manor.

To entertain the Fashionables, troupes of actors also came to Lewes, brought mostly till the 1770s by "Kentish" managers. At St John's church a "drumbeater to the players" was buried in September 1725, and Mrs Margaret Steward, "belonging to the Puppet Show", in June 1750. Members of Mr Linnett's Company married there in December 1739. His players probably staged *A Fair Penitent* and *A Miss in Her Teens*, which were performed at the Sessions House in February 1752, and encored perhaps by "pretty gentlemen" from Rick's dragoons. Between October and December 1758 they staged *Othello*, *Romeo and Juliet*, *Henry IV* (alias "the humours of Sir John Falstaff"), *Oroonoko*, *A Bold Stroke for a Wife* and *The Careless Husband*. Before Mr Williams's Company could perform *The Funeral*, with Mrs Jefferson as Lady Charlotte, Lewesians had to persuade her father to cancel a £500 penalty, payable by her husband if she acted in public. Renowned for "symmetry of form", she died, laughing heartily, in Mr Moody's arms during rehearsals at Plymouth in 1766. Lewes race-week was enlivened in 1769 by a pantomime, a comic opera and Lofty Tumbling at the Riding School. This the actor-manager Samuel Johnson (1691-1773) then converted into a "proper" theatre, the Histrionic Academy Fish Street. His Comedians came fresh from "repeated applause" at Exeter, Salisbury and Brighton. They presented *Hamlet*, *King Charles I* and *The School for Lovers* between October and December 1770, plus two comic operas, *Love in a Village* and *The Sailor's Return*. Struck by illness in January, Johnson was helped from his chaise and tottered on stage to declaim, as advertised, select passages from Beaumont and Fletcher. In March 1773 the seasoned thespian returned with Seven Comic Lectures.

In August 1774 a purpose-built theatre opened at Brighton, managed by Roger Johnstone, a property-maker from Covent Garden. The summer season at the resort was from early June to late September, so his Company could visit Lewes during race-week, and transfer there in October to enliven its winter season. This also prompted Johnstone, and his successors at Brighton, to manage a new theatre at Lewes, built in Castleyard with entrances into Castle Ditch Lane. Its stout oak uprights supported a spacious gallery at the rear of the pit, and boxes along each side. It could seat 600 playgoers, and Charles Carver came from Covent Garden to paint the scenery. Johnstone's first season in January-March 1775 included *Romeo and Juliet*, *Jane Shore*, *The Earl of Warwick*, *The Clandestine Marriage*, and a recent smash-hit, *She Stoops to Conquer*. His successor, Joseph Fox 1777-81, was an ex-London victualler. Relying on the support of "a candid English audience", he staged at Lewes in June and July "new favourite pieces" popular in London the previous winter. But the build-up of Fashionables before race-week proved too "thin". Enduring success also eluded Mr Buckle 1782-87. His Company left Lewes for Shoreham and Arundel "with credit" in November 1786, after three months of glowing reviews which singled out Mrs Salway as Malvina and Miss Burnet as Polly Peachum. But in August 1787, two weeks after the races, he disbanded "his little force, penniless and hungry", because their "chaste and celebrated" pieces from British Drama had met "almost total neglect".

In 1789 Joseph Fox re-emerged to fund and manage new theatres at Brighton and Lewes. John Macdonnell, a pupil of Soane, exhibited at the Royal Academy a design for the latter, but whether it prefigured the "neat" structure, with flanking refreshment parlours, built in West Street is unclear. The theatre opened on 10 August, the Monday of race-week, with a visit from His Majesty's Players. Though the Lewes Band proved unequal to "Theatrical business", and two Cliffites assaulted his box-keeper, Fox managed three seasons from August to December till he died of dropsy in December 1791, heavily in debt, despite offering prospective shareholders free admission to the theatre for 21 years. Mr Palmer fared no better in 1792, and then war with France, heavy taxation and dear bread depressed further the receipts of Mr Wild in 1793, William Powell in 1794 and Mr Bernard in 1795. The town's growing "religious tendency" (see chapter 8) also made it a "bad resort" for players. Yet there were theatrical feasts. Edmund Kean played to a packed house. Miss Fontenelle conquered every heart. Mr Palmer triumphed in *Wild Oats*, in *Inkle and Yarico*, and as Don Juan in *The Libertine Destroyed.* Little Edwin in *The Romp* much amused Charles James Fox and Mrs Armstead, while Mrs Warrel's rendering of the hunting song *When Ruddy Aurora* delighted Poole and his javelin men. Dramatic too, if off-stage, were six white-clad running footmen heralding the approach of Lord Eardley, a Jewish play-goer related to Lord Gage.

Lewes's new theatre

Lady Gage helped the actor-managers John Jonas and Sampson Penley to salvage the 1795 season after Mr Bernard gave up. And indeed they returned each year till 1815, though their circuit of Eastbourne, Bexhill, Hastings and Rye, excluded Brighton. In 1799 they even leased the theatre from Widow Fox's creditors. At first they came for race-week and a fortnight either side. But in 1804-05 the Lewes Volunteers and the soldiers in the new barracks sponsored a short winter season, aided by Lord Craven who married an actress. It included *The Wonder*, *The Turnpike Gate*, Dr Delap's *Abdalla*, and a Benefit for Mrs Dwyer, a local parson's daughter who some years before made her stage debut at Lewes in *The Child of Nature,* despite her family's opposition. Presumably the new season paid, since the partners bought the theatre in 1806. They added a tier of boxes; made the auditorium circular; and brought Messrs Smith and Greenwood from Drury Lane to renew the scenery. The Nottinghamshire Militia, the 16th Hussars, the Prince of Wales's Dragoon Guards and Lady Hampden helped to patronize short autumn seasons in 1807-09 and 1812.

In 1795 a performing dog drew Lovers of "Mirth and Curiositys" to the disused playhouse in Castleyard. Arthur Lee junior was renting it in 1807, perhaps to rehearse the stage-struck amateurs who formed a Lewes Pic-Nic Society on 23 September 1806 at the *Bear*. Their efforts raised £64 for English sailors imprisoned in France:

> When last, by kind beneficence engag'd,
> We droll'd as Skirmish, or as Zonga rag'd,
> Old Ocean's Sons, Britannia's Hearts of Oak,
> From loathsome Jails a benefit bespoke.

Later they aided the families of soldiers serving in Spain, the widows and orphans of Waterloo, the distressed manufacturing districts, the County Hospital, and Spanish refugees. Arthur Lee shone as Pierce Egan's character Jerry Sneak, and also wrote verse for Christmas plays at the grammar school:

> Unstring the classic bow a little while.
> With temper'd play relieve the scholar's toil.

Besides musicians and thespians, other Novelties visited Georgian Lewes. Typical were those advertised by handbill between 1768 and 1777. The Monmouthshire Fairy, Margaret Morgan, was only 31 inches high but "strait and well shaped in every respect"; she lodged at the *King and Queen*. A Lilliputian Dwarf was 38 inches high yet the "best proportioned man ever seen"; he tarried at the *Dorset Arms*. There too from Lambeth came Mr and Mrs Astley who rode three horses at once, and their Balance Master, Mr Hawtin, who steadied a step-ladder on his thumb, and a coach-wheel on his chin. Mr Hawtin's armless sister, a "surprising" young lady from

Warwickshire, threaded a needle and cut with scissors, using her toes and feet. At the *Crown* stayed Herr Barnard Abraham and his Dog of Knowledge, a beast quite able (it was claimed) to read, cast accounts, and tell the day, the month, and the number of people in the audience. A Learned Horse arrived from Courland, to play cards and dice, and drink the company's health. While at the *Bear* Mr Wildman charmed bees from a hive into a hat, and tamed a swarm in 15 minutes: indeed as Dr Evans wrote,

> Such was the spell which, round a Wildman's arm,
> Twined in dark wreaths the fascinated swarm;
> Bright o'er his breast the glittering legions led
> Or with a living garland bound his head;
> His dextrous hand, with firm but hurtless hold,
> Could seize the chief, known by her scales of gold,
> Prune, mid the wandering train, her filmy wing,
> Or o'er her folds the silken fetter fling.

More humdrum was a sea-dog, caught sleeping on the rocks near Beachy Head, and caged at the *Bear*. Also trapped in Sussex were an osprey and golden eagle exhibited by Charles Harben, who charged "common persons" twopence, but left the others "to their honour".

Novelties remained popular. In 1786 John Burgess paid twopence to view an ox at the *Crown*, with "one horn growed strait out of its Paul, near 4 feet round". In 1795 Mr O'Brien was advertised as a celebrated Irish giant near 9 feet high. At the theatre in 1800 Mr Saxoni (the original Little Devil) performed on the tight rope, and in 1821 an Indian Juggler, Ramo Samee, delighted Gideon Mantell:

> he whirled brass balls and carving knives round him in a variety of figures...swallowed stones and eggs, and again brought them out of his mouth; placed a steel heavy blunt sword two feet long down his throat in to the stomach.

In a caravan at Cliffe Fair Place Mantell later admired two live alligators, two albinos and "an enormous fat young man". In September 1826 the climax of a Grand Mechanical and Picturesque Exhibition of Art revealed Vesuvius erupting by moonlight, with the RUNNING LAVA OF REAL FIRE. And Mr Wombwell's Wild Beasts caused an unrehearsed sensation when the van containing Nero the lion overturned on Malling Hill.

A local prodigy however was the memorist and calculator George Watson, a near-illiterate labourer born at Buxted in 1785. Mark

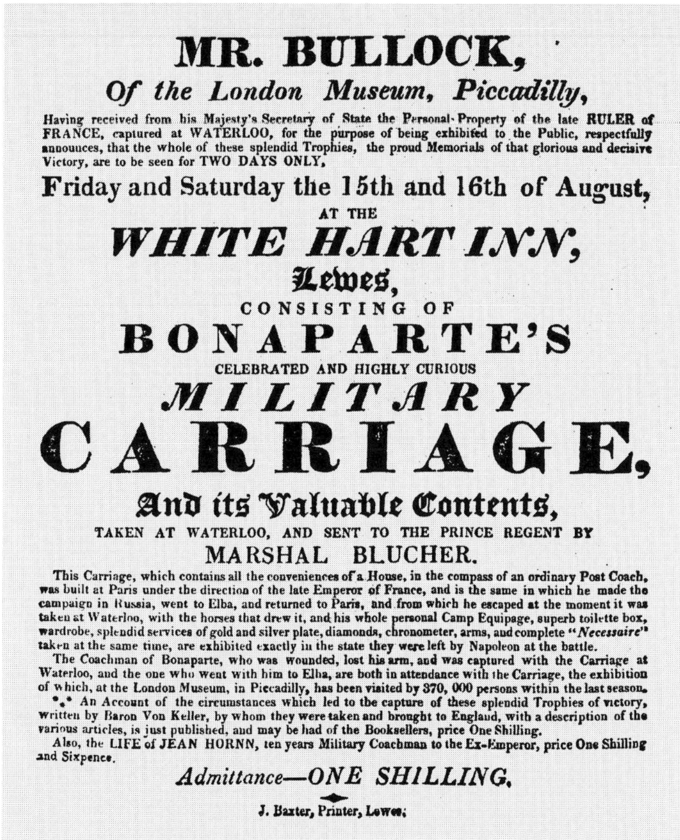

MR. BULLOCK,

Of the London Museum, Piccadilly,

Having received from his Majesty's Secretary of State the Personal Property of the late RULER of FRANCE, captured at WATERLOO, for the purpose of being exhibited to the Public, respectfully annouuces, that the whole of these splendid Trophies, the proud Memorials of that glorious and decisive Victory, are to be seen for TWO DAYS ONLY,

Friday and Saturday the 15th and 16th of August,

AT THE

WHITE HART INN,

Lewes,

CONSISTING OF

BONAPARTE'S

CELEBRATED AND HIGHLY CURIOUS

MILITARY

CARRIAGE,

And its Valuable Contents,

TAKEN AT WATERLOO, AND SENT TO THE PRINCE REGENT BY

MARSHAL BLUCHER.

This Carriage, which contains all the conveniences of a House, in the compass of an ordinary Post Coach, was built at Paris under the direction of the late Emperor of France, and is the same in which he made the campaign in Russia, went to Elba, and returned to Paris, and from which he escaped at the moment it was taken at Waterloo, with the horses that drew it, and his whole personal Camp Equipage, superb toilette box, wardrobe, splendid services of gold and silver plate, diamonds, chronometer, arms, and complete "*Necessaire*" taken at the same time, are exhibited exactly in the state they were left by Napoleon at the battle.

The Coachman of Bonaparte, who was wounded, lost his arm, and was captured with the Carriage at Waterloo, and the one who went with him to Elba, are both in attendance with the Carriage, the exhibition of which, at the London Museum, in Piccadilly, has been visited by 370, 000 persons within the last season.

*** An Account of the circumstances which led to the capture of these splendid Trophies of victory, written by Baron Von Keller, by whom they were taken and brought to England, with a description of the various articles, is just published, and may be had of the Booksellers, price One Shilling.

Also, the LIFE of JEAN HORNN, ten years Military Coachman to the Ex-Emperor, price One Shilling and Sixpence.

Admittance—ONE SHILLING.

J. Baxter, Printer, Lewes;

Napoleon's carriage (ESRO)

Antony Lower once saw him trudging out of Cliffe, his hat chalked over with figures. His strange facility stirred Mantell to ask,

> Unmixed with any other quality,
> How can thy thick and clumsy head,
> The magic maze of numbers thread?

Even more local was the town crier's son, John Phipps Townshend, who far outshone his father as a Pedestrian. On six consecutive days in 1829 he walked four times between Lewes and Brighton (64 miles), and then stood on one leg for an hour. At Bristol he walked 72 miles backwards in 24 hours.

The Wonders of Electricity also intrigued Lewesians. In 1761 Mr Silk lectured at the *White Hart* on its galvanic powers. Mr Rose advertised it as a cure for Paralytics, Agues, and all Rheumatical Cases. At the Sessions House in 1805 Mr Hardie showed its effect on the nervous system, by causing a deceased frog to skip and a dead sheep to roll its eyes. In 1774 a local bullock was struck by lightning, and sparked a keen debate on hair colour and conductivity. Dunvan attributed to lightning the downland circles known as fairy-rings, foxy brown on the outside, a vivid green within, and decorated in autumn with fungi; the electric "fluid" scorched

> the grass where it falls first; but its gentler influence tends to invigorate vegetation immediately within the circle; and if the primordial seeds of the fungus order, happen to be beneath the line of its orbit, it loosens the soil, and calls them forth by its fructifying energy.

The booths of itinerant entertainers also fringed the livestock fair held on Whitsun Tuesday; indeed they made it a summer festival popular for miles around. Already in 1614 a Brighton fishwife and an Uckfield tailor attended; and in 1694 the "shewmen" there were seized by a press-gang, herded to the *White Horse*, and marched to Shoreham. As agriculture prospered the well-stocked stalls of milliners like Mrs Pierpoint and Eve Bunting did a roaring trade in the gloves, ribbons, stockings and other Fairings bought by rustics for their sweethearts, "the virgin-bloom of the surrounding country-side" as the *Journal* perhaps imprecisely called them. Showmen and pedlars also attended the autumn sheep fair, and they remained at the Fair Place in Cliffe after the livestock dealing migrated. Ribbons, spring-locks and clasp-knives were sold, amid the swing-boats and acrobats. At a Pleasure Fair held in Southover on Easter Tuesday fourpence worth of Verrall's strong beer (the local brew) guaranteed inebriation in the 1770s. And during race-week the approaches to the course were lined with giants, Approved Tumblers, wild beasts, dancing bears, fat Pigs and musicians, among them Old Kinlock a blind clarinettist.

This rustic merrymaking withered during the long Agricultural Depression after the defeat of Napoleon. The holiday folk stayed away, or spent very sparingly. By 1816 the admission charge to the depleted booths pitched during race-week was pegged at a penny. Hopefully this encouraged a visit to the *Crown and Anchor* Tavern and Ball Room where patrons could waltz under canvas till late into the night. One free spectacle, which drew a thousand people, was the funeral at St Anne's of Charles Lee, the King of the Gipsies, who died at the course during race-week in 1832. At the Whitsun fair in 1820 the few stalls set up sold only gingerbread and baby toys. In 1828 Captain Green managed to enliven Cliffe fair with a balloon ascent from the gasworks. Some "caravan exhibitions" visited Southover fair in 1830, but the "cracked and crazy" church bells remained silent.

The Agricultural Depression also impoverished many Fashionables, while the onset of Peace saw the dispersal of the Military from mid-Sussex. So attendance fell at the four winter Lewes assemblies. Fewer than 60 couples danced in November 1826 to music by Michau, Colinet and Musard, a trio from Almack's, and only 200 Fashionables rallied to a supper ball in January 1830. The summer races also declined, even though Lord Egremont gave two 50-guinea prizes in 1816, and Lewes brewers, publicans and saddlers busied with subscriptions. In 1828 the three-day event still offered the King's Plate, a County Plate, a Ladies' Plate, a Members' Plate, a South Down Stakes, a Town Plate and a Handicap Plate. Yet as well as the Depression, the races were now overshadowed by a new, very smart August meeting at Goodwood. So "the gig and pedestrian classes" still came, but the county elite did not. In 1830 hardly "an equipage of any consequence" appeared, hardly indeed a post-horse from Brighton. Lord Egremont stayed but an hour or two; and only 160 Fashionables graced the supper ball, where Mantell's roving eye lingered on Mrs Bayly, "a very tempting syren". In 1837 the ball was abandoned; and the races dwindled to one day, plumbing "the depth of wretchedness".

The Agricultural Depression and the loss of the Military, plus a continuing Calvinistic resurgence in the town, also overshadowed the Lewes theatre. Doggedly during race-week the Race Stewards and High Sheriff patronized performances: and in August 1834 Pierce Egan himself played Logic in an adaptation of his *Tom and Jerry*. But as early as 1814 the partners Jonas and Penley forfeited their ownership of the theatre, and despite support from the Borough's MPs, from Lady Hampden, Lord Chichester, the Freemasons and Mr Dunn's Academy, its winter season now flopped badly. In 1817 *Macbeth*, *The Iron Chest* and *Venice Preserved* echoed across empty benches. In 1819 Gideon Mantell paid only half-price to relish delicious Miss Penley

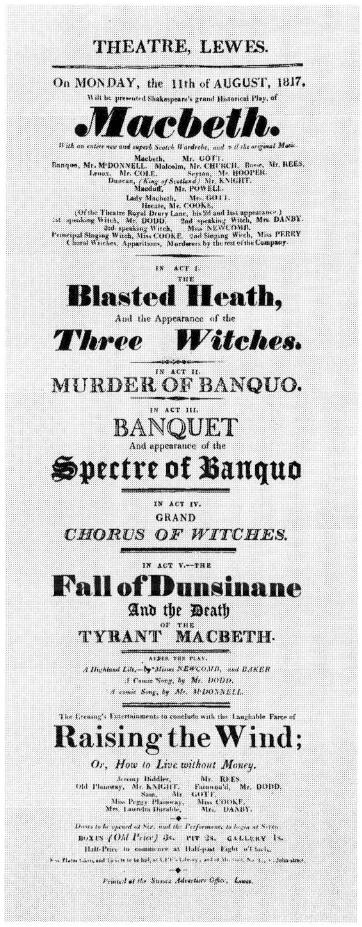

THEATRE, LEWES.

On MONDAY, the 11th of AUGUST, 1817,

Will be presented Shakespeare's grand Historical Play, of

Macbeth.

With an entire new and superb Scotch Wardrobe, and all the original Music.

Macbeth, Mr. GOTT.
Banquo, Mr. M'DONNELL. Malcolm, Mr. CHURCH. Rosse, Mr. REES.
Lenox, Mr. COLE. Seyton, Mr. HOOPER.
Duncan, *(King of Scotland)* Mr. KNIGHT.
Macduff, Mr. POWELL.
Lady Macbeth, Mrs. GOTT.
Hecate, Mr. COOKE,
(Of the Theatre Royal Drury Lane, his 2d and last appearance.)
1st speaking Witch, Mr. DODD. 2nd speaking Witch, Mrs. DANBY.
3rd speaking Witch, Miss NEWCOMB.
Principal Singing Witch, Miss COOKE. 2nd Singing Witch, Miss PERRY
Choral Witches, Apparitions, Murderers by the rest of the Company.

IN ACT I.
THE
Blasted Heath,
And the Appearance of the
Three Witches.

IN ACT II.
MURDER OF BANQUO.

IN ACT III.
BANQUET
And appearance of the
Spectre of Banquo

IN ACT IV.
GRAND
CHORUS OF WITCHES.

IN ACT V.—THE
Fall of Dunsinane
And the Death
OF THE
TYRANT MACBETH.

AFTER THE PLAY,
A Highland Lilt,—by Misses NEWCOMB, and BAKER
A Comic Song, by Mr. DODD.
A comic Song, by Mr. M'DONNELL.

The Evening's Entertainments to conclude with the Laughable Farce of

Raising the Wind;

Or, How to Live without Money.

Jeremy Diddler, Mr. REES.
Old Plainway, Mr. KNIGHT. Fainwou'd, Mr. DODD.
Sam, Mr. GOTT.
Miss Peggy Plainway, Miss COOKE.
Mrs. Laurelia Durable, Mrs. DANBY.

Doors to be opened at Six, and the Performance to begin at Seven.
BOXES *(Old Price)* 3s. PIT 2s. GALLERY 1s.
Half-Price to commence at Half-past Eight o'Clock.
[illegible]

Printed at the Sussex Advertiser Office, Lewes.

playing Ella Rosenberg. In 1822 Frederick Brooke's company from Hastings netted £40 with *The Battle of Lewes,* an "historical morceau" penned by an Eastbourne Lady. Yet though extended from three to five acts, it failed to save his 1823-24 season. Horsfield's *History* belittled the actors who "occasionally assume the buskin, and strut their brief hour" upon its stage. New owners, the coachmaker John Ade and gunsmith Edward Weston, renamed it The Public Temple in November 1825. They also installed gas lamps and a skylight to encourage its use by the Mechanics' Institution. Mr Russell and his Company came over from Brighton in 1825-6 and 1826-7, when he shone as Jerry Sneak, a part he played for over 200 nights at Drury Lane. But his next season collapsed. Edmund Kean as Shylock could still bring record receipts on 1 January 1829; yet Mr Palmer's players from London lost £100 and more the following winter, despite Miss Penley starring in *Jane Shore* and *Black-eyed Susan.*

The theatre closed for good in the 1830s, and though the races revived in the 1850s, Lewes never became, as some fondly hoped, "a second Epsom". Nor did the town retain the wider cultural importance in the shire it enjoyed in the decades before Waterloo. From the 1830s a series of Reforms ended county elections and Peculiar jurisdictions; they restructured county courts, introduced civil registration and probate, and transferred control of the Poor Law from Quarter Sessions to Boards of Guardians. This weakened Lewes as a focus of Bureaucracy, though the House of Correction did become the County Prison and a Militia barracks was built at Southover. Moreover, like its retailers, the town's professional men, its lawyers, doctors and school-proprietors, faced damaging competition as the new railway network consolidated Brighton, Eastbourne and Tunbridge Wells. The Dispensary gave only a very local service; Gideon Mantell moved to Brighton; the Grammar School languished, then expired. Brewers, iron-founders and lime-burners now dominated its economy, and they preferred Politics and Religion to Antiquities and the Picturesque, a trend reflected in the *Sussex Agricultural Express* (1837) and the *East Sussex News* (1854). And though the Sussex Archaeological Society (1846) made its headquarters at Lewes, no historian of note resided after Mark Antony Lower left for Seaford in 1867.

8

The Zion of Mid-Sussex: Anglicanism, Dissent and Resurgent Calvinism

...the blessing of God the Father in predestinating and choosing before time, and the blessing of God the Son, who gave his life to ransom all the elect from the sword of justice, and from going down to the pit of Hell...and God the Holy Spirit who in the ancient councils of eternity, where all was settled, agreed to preserve till called, and at the appointed time, to convince all that should be born heirs of salvation.

THE CALVINIST THEORY OF REDEMPTION, AS PREACHED BY SHOEMAKER JOHN GIBBS (1769-1838), PASTOR OF BETHESDA CHAPEL LEWES.

We have traitors, and evil workers within - we have sneaking and contemptuous Socinians; impudent Antinomians; artful Universalists; and half-hearted Christians to deal with.

ANNUAL REPORT OF THE LEWES CALVINISTIC BAPTISTS (1803).

My brother N. at Glynde. Mr T. Berry in Malling Street... Mr. Wimble and many others. I defy any man to impose on them in the way of business, but they will sit very patiently in a Chapel by the half hour to be lectured by a Shoemaker or a Tailor.

WILLIAM WISDOM'S MEMORANDA 1827.

Though the Archdeacon's Spiritual Court met in Georgian Lewes, the town's Anglicanism was never dynamic. In 1718 Bishop Manningham of Chichester bemoaned the Church's "little reputation" there; its Rectors, Sacred Officers and Sacraments received scant respect. And in the 1820s a "dreadful deadness" prevailed. Parson Boys Ellman recalled arid Erastian services and dry-as-dust sermons; Holy Communion doled out once a quarter; padlocked pews and cramping galleries, massive pulpits and mean altars. For a Confirmation at St Anne's in 1829 rustic cartloads of sportive teenagers jolted in, as though to the Whitsun fair. The town was also a nest of absentee clergy; each Sabbath a posse of parsons in coal-black coats rode out from their Lewes "Rookery" to croak a sermon in their neglected rural parishes. These absentees included whist-loving Archdeacon Raynes (Firle and Beddingham) who sanctified a dinner-party on Ash Wednesday by adding pancakes to the menu, and pint-sized Harry West (Berwick and Laughton) who refused to pay his Lewes landlord for broken decanters till taken to Court. Ellman also glimpsed Parson Harrison (Alfriston) limping back to Lewes after a heavy fall in the hunting field, his scarlet coat soaked with mud.

Lewes's own parish clergy in the 1820s showed little pastoral zeal. George Proctor (St Michael's) was kept busy flogging Ellman daily at the grammar school. Immediately after their ordination family patronage snugly installed George Shiffner at St Anne's with Hamsey, and Peter Guerin Crofts at St John's with Malling. Like Harrison, Crofts was a devout hunter, but he found time to decree that Gideon Mantell remove the shrubs planted on his father's grave at St John's. Mantell duly derided this sacerdotalism on a second memorial he set up inside St Michael's:

> What though no sculpture mark thy lowly grave,
> Nor yew, nor cypress, o'er thy relics wave.
> The virtuous will respect the hallow'd spot,
> When prouder names than thine shall be forgot.

Their private affluence allowed Shiffner and Crofts to lead genteel Laodicean lives, despite the meagre stipends attached to all Lewes's Rectories. Earlier, at All Saints with Cliffe, their inadequacy had sapped the evangelical zeal of incumbents dependent on them. Edmund Lund 1725-76 was a worthy "guide and Teacher". The sermons of Richard Cecil 1777-98 drew many hearers away from Lady Huntingdon's new chapel at Cliffe. Those of Thomas Aquila Dale 1798-1807 much impressed Gideon Mantell, and postponed John Dudeney's move to Methodism. Yet poverty stalked all three. When Lund's smallpox-stricken family removed to an isolated house in Friars Walk, its owner, the Duke of Newcastle, was asked to let them stay on, rent-free. Cecil was carrying home a bag of much-needed Queen Anne's Bounty when he encountered a highwayman near East Grinstead, who had heard him preach and waved him affably onward. He then removed to London, to compile a *Life* of the sculptor John Bacon. Dale had his "ruinous" parsonage at Cliffe converted into tenements, and left his widow and children dependent on public benevolence. Insolvency also dogged John Bristed 1725-83 (St Anne's and St Michael's). Besieged by creditors in 1733, he leased his parsonage to Philpot the dancing-master. Then he deserted the Duke of Newcastle's Whigs because the Tory Thomas Sergison promised him a plump benefice at Slaugham. And when the "ruinous" chancel at St Anne's collapsed in 1750 (though not during Divine Service), his continuing "Distress" caused the parish to repair it for him.

Though chancels were the Rector's concern, lay feoffees used revenue from the Cliffe Estate to keep the entire fabric of St Thomas's "neat" and "decent". But at All Saints the parsons and laity allowed the building to become so "ruinous" (except the tower) that it was rebuilt in 1807 as a galleried preaching-box, and without a chancel. The cost was met by life annuities and a loan, serviced by a parish rate. Bitter disputes arose over the rights of former pew-holders; and only 650 seats were provided, though the parish registered 1169 inhabitants in 1801 and 2112 in 1831. At Southover, St Michael's and St John's, where no chancel existed, the laity were also slow to act. The steeple at Southover collapsed in 1698, and in 1714 the Tory Lord of the Manor, Nathaniel Trayton, partly funded the renewal of the first floor, where his carved initials survive. But the three bells rehung there were then removed till the tower was completed in 1738. At "ruinous" St Michael's the Bishop and the Pelhams contributed when the south aisle and north arcade were rebuilt in 1748. At St John's, where Parson Crofts policed the graveyard, the patched and

St John sub Castro

poky nave of a once cruciform structure served a parish housing over 2300 people in 1831. Galleries, purpose-built at All Saints, multiplied elsewhere. One at St Michael's, intruded in 1829, was deplored 30 years later for its "bad air".

Though Lewes Anglicans made no impact outside the town, its Dissenting meeting-houses attracted many rustic hearers, who doubtless viewed Lewes, set upon its hill, as a second Mount Zion, prefiguring the Celestial City. Bishop Manningham thought it "miserably overrun" by Dissent in 1718, when perhaps 700 Presbyterians, Independents, General Baptists and Quakers worshipped there, the biggest build-up of Nonconformity in Eastern Sussex. The Presbyterians, the largest sect, had split asunder in 1701. Their co-pastors, Thomas Barnard (1644-1724) and Edward Newton (c1630-1712), fell out over plans to adapt the new Westgate meeting-house. Newton, so Barnard claimed, "invaded" his turn in the pulpit, sealed the Schism "with an opposite Sacrament", and departed with "a few Adherents" to a disused tabernacle in Watergate Lane, where in 1717 Newton's successor, Thomas Force 1709-42, preached to perhaps 170 hearers; among them were "16 gentlemen, 19 tradesmen, ten yeomen and 15 labourers". Meanwhile in 1711 the Westgate meeting absorbed Pastor John Olive c1708-42 and his Independents who worshipped before at School Hill. In 1717 this combined congregation of perhaps 425 hearers was credited with 33 gentlemen, 50 tradesmen, 18 yeomen and 19 labourers. The Lewesians helping to buy the freehold in 1719 included a maltster, corn-chandler, distiller, butcher, tallow-chandler, grocer, hatter, draper, upholsterer, currier, dyer, bricklayer, carpenter, blacksmith and clockmaker, an apothecary Thomas Fissenden , a schoolmaster Richard Button and a bookseller Thomas Norman. Hearers converged from as far as Steyning, Lindfield, Hailsham and Westham.

At Westgate and at Watergate Lane the awesome doctrine of Predestination still formed the bedrock of belief. Before time began, "in the ancient councils of eternity", God had chosen which souls Christ would ransom on the cross from the eternal pains of Hell. Like Paul on the Damascus road, these Elect souls were made Finally Assured in this life that they were indeed "born heirs of salvation". This doctrine left no space for the exercise of Free Will, and demanded the vigorous vetting of those wishing to join a Calvinistic meeting. Yet by 1723 disputes were racking Westgate, dividing pastor from pastor. The trust deed merely required that Protestant

Dissenters used the building "for the worshipping of Almighty God". As an Independent, Pastor Olive still adhered presumably to Predestination. But his new co-pastor, Joseph Beach 1716-42, perhaps favoured a less rigid approach to Redemption, involving gentler spiritual tests. The Olivites considered padlocking the pulpit, and withdrawing temporarily to Pastor Force in Watergate Lane where "Deaths and Removes" had eroded the hearers. But what if the Beachites proved obdurate, or formed a new Church with disgruntled sheep from Mr Force's fold? In the end they waited on the Providence of "Him who walketh in the midst of the Golden Candlesticks", and He endorsed the status-quo. The cracks were still papered over in January 1740 when a four-hour service and a Fast greeted the war with Spain: Pastor Olive expounded Jeremiah 14:8, Pastor Beach Revelation 3:2, and Pastor Force, by invitation, Jonah 3:5.

A more flexible theology did take root at Westgate after Ebenezer Johnston (c1719-91) from Dumfries became sole pastor in 1742. Among his 11 ordaining ministers was Dr Philip Doddridge, Johnston's tutor at Northampton Academy, who trained his pupils to be "liberal in theology" and "catholic in churchmanship". Johnston duly rejected "absolute, arbitrary Election and Reprobation"; and in 1749 he loyally purchased Doddridge's *Invitation to Thirsty Souls*. His flirting with Free Will did not deter prominent Lewesians paying to repair Westgate in 1756: they included the rentier Richard Barnard, the surgeons John Snashall, John Chambers and Thomas Davey, ironmonger Joseph Attersoll, tanner John Snashall, the hatters Richard Read and Richard Palmer, draper James Campbell, dyer Samuel Jones, tobacconist Samuel Olive, mason John Morris and clockmaker James Weston. Two itinerant Scotsmen also contributed, as did William Boys at Ashcombe House, and six Ridges farming at Kingston, Iford, Stanmer and Hamsey. Nor did Johnston's liberal theology deter the hearers at Watergate Lane from removing to Westgate after Pastor Joseph Watkins 1742-56 retired. A Scottish peer, Lord Napier, also attended, and his funeral hatchment was hung there in April 1773; earlier his son accidentally shot dead a tutor at Corsica Hall.

However some hearers nurtured at Westgate, among them Johnston's brothers-in-law, John and William Ridge, did become trustees of the Methodist chapel at Cliffe which Lady Huntingdon opened in 1775 to preach full-blooded Predestination. And tensions

Westgate Chapel (E.H.New)

over Free Will may have encouraged the rather rapid turnover of pastors between 1783 and 1803 when Richard Shiells preceded William Evan Bishop, John Langdon and Evan Davies. Certainly Samuel Parker 1803-11 expounded a full-blooded liberal theology in his books on the Lord's Supper (1796) and the Old Testament (1805); and at Westgate "Young Persons" in particular enjoyed his probing lectures on Balaam's ass, Jonah in the whale, and the fossil evidence for the Flood. Also fiercely liberal, indeed "Socinian", was Thomas Horsfield (1792-1837), a "strong-minded Yorkshireman" who arrived in 1817 "fresh from the heady atmosphere of the Unitarian Academy at Hackney". To promote the "undivided worship" of "the one true God", he persuaded the meeting to replace Isaac Watts's hymn book (1708) with one more universal in tone. His Rational Optimism, like Parker's, attracted "inquiring young men", and overflowed into his *History* of Lewes, into the Philosophical Society and the Mechanics' Institution, into Radical politics and support for Catholic Emancipation. Yet despite the applause of Young Persons, his "undivided" God was a very minority taste, and numbers at Westgate dwindled. In 1823 half the 18 subscribers to the repair fund were Ridges, and three were Johnstons. In 1829 the hearers numbered "about 150", compared with "425" in 1717, plus "170" at Watergate Lane.

Moreover these 150 hearers included a contingent of General Baptists who migrated to Westgate in 1825-6 from Eastport Lane in Southover. Horsfield fostered the move by starting a joint Fellowship Fund, and his successor at Westgate, Charles Porteous Valentine 1828-40, trained at the General Baptist Academy. In 1714 the 50 or so hearers at Southover were linked to a more vigorous Baptist cause at Ditchling; indeed when a new meeting-house was opened at Eastport Lane in 1741, with a burial ground attached, only four trustees were Lewesians, Stephen Juden maltster, Matthew Hunter grocer, Thomas Hunter weaver

Eastport Lane Chapel (E.H.New)

and John Harman pipemaker; the rest resided at Ditchling, Plumpton, Clayton, Patcham, Isfield and Firle. Thereafter, as at Westgate, the hearers embraced an ever more liberal theology. In 1798 they were in contact with the Southern Unitarian Association, and in 1803 they were perhaps the "sneaking and contemptuous Socinians" identified within the Christian fold at Lewes. In 1811 they hosted religious conferences, emphatically non-sectarian in character. In 1822 their large library found room for Locke's *Second Vindication* and Hazlitt's *Essays*. Prominent subscribers were Henry Browne who championed the Mechanics' Institution, and his partner William Crosskey, whose son Henry became a Unitarian minister in Birmingham, and preached a gospel of civic enterprise which inspired the Gas-and-Water Socialism of Joseph Chamberlain. Their pastors were briefly listed in Horsfield's *History:* Drowley 1790, R Snelgrove 1808, W Davies 1809, JH Morris 1810, W Dobell 1814, R Martin 1816, James Taplin 1822. James Drowley preached at Southover and Ditchling between 1786 and 1792. As a draper at Cliffe Corner he sold second-hand clothes to John Burgess, a loyal hearer. Being also a political Radical he emigrated to New York before 1795 to escape the rigours of Pittite Repression.

Though long established, the Quakers also failed to recruit heavily. In 1717 perhaps a dozen families from Lewes, Kingston and Rottingdean worshipped at Puddle Wharf in Friars Walk. In 1829 "about 36" Friends gathered at a meeting-house built in 1784 some 100 yards to the south-west. Recruitment was not encouraged by their plain apparel and use of the singular pronoun, their refusal "to take off the hat by way of compliment", their resolute pacifism and ultra-scrupulous trading. One prominent Friend, Ambrose Galloway, transported his cargoes (cannon included) in Newhaven-based ships called the *Plain Dealing* and the *Owner's Goodwill*. Ambrose II left £1000 to Quaker charities in 1738, though the Dresden china and silver sauce pans, bequeathed to Widow Short, suggest a sybarite lurked beneath the plain apparel. Later the Rickmans and Godlees, large scale millers, brewers and traders in corn and coal, dominated the sect, but Thomas "Clio" the Radical publicist, and Thomas the architect, broke away. Besides Plain Dealing some Friends were committed to Humanity. The corn-factor Daniel Burns defended a soldier in 1788 from his officer's "persevering malignity". The furniture-seller John Marten (1767-1832) condemned the regime Lord Sheffield imposed on Fletching workhouse. He failed to win a reprieve for a burglar John Piper, who nonetheless thanked him from the scaffold at Horsham. When eight years old his brother William (1764-1823) stopped frolicking on the Sabbath because a thunderclap signalled Divine Displeasure. As a young man, in "a seeking state", William savoured the General Baptists, Lady Huntingdon's Methodists and Parson Aquila Dale, before locating his Redeemer at Friars Walk. He promoted Infant Education and targeted Lewes theatre-goers, handing them pamphlets on the "right Employment of Time", and sticking up playbills which previewed the rigours of the Last Judgement. When he refused to illuminate his draper's shop after the King was restored to health, three window panes were smashed.

However from the 1760s the Erastian calm of the Established Church at Lewes, and the growing theological liberalism of its Old Dissenters, were both confounded by new-style Calvinists urgently preaching Predestinate Grace and Final Assurance. In September 1760 the *Journal* (ever a foe of Enthusiasm in religion) professed alarm that George Whitefield, the leading Calvinistic Methodist missioner, might come over from Brighton. Instead came preachers sent by his disciple, Selina Countess of Huntingdon (1707-91). In 1761 she sold her jewels to build a chapel at Brighton, and being a peeress, she appointed chaplains to kindle "a living faith" there, and throughout mid-Sussex. At Lewes their efforts were ill-received. "Great umbrage" was taken when William Romaine occupied an Anglican pulpit; so he preached in the open fields where "many poor sinners were cut to the heart". Martin Madan and William Fletcher also found the churches barred against them. Moreover such fervid evangelism provoked the mob (as the Salvation Army discovered over a century later). On Bonfire Night in 1769 a crowd menaced the School Hill residence of genteel Widow Norton, who had let the house next door to a Methodist Preacher. A missioner was pelted with eggs at Uckfield for disturbing "the peace of the Church". This the *Journal* approved; likewise a journeyman carpenter, turned preacher, being burned in effigy at Cliffe. It also reported that a Beeding man, who ran stark naked down Lewes High Street at noon, had been unhinged by Enthusiasm.

Undaunted, on 13 August 1775 Lady Huntingdon opened a chapel at East Street in Cliffe (thenceforth Chapel Hill); her missioners Thomas Pentycross and Henry Peckwell preached. Thereafter services were disturbed by a rabble flinging stones and "lighted

Combustibles". Mary Wimble (1769-1831) remembered fire-brands being thrown at her muslin frock as she walked there. Yet 59 "serious people" formed a Society in April 1776, to worship there as "Dissenters from the National established church", and to preach a gospel "commonly called Calvinistical". Among them were Westgate hearers at odds with Pastor Johnston's liberal theology. But Chaplain Peckwell was soon warning Selina that "serious" people were also "pick-some", and would expect a "constant" pastor, not itinerants from London or from her training college at Trevecca in North Wales. And indeed many hearers did transfer to charismatic Parson Cecil (the highwayman's choice). So in 1781 the "distracted" remnant at Chapel Hill engaged from Brighton the Trevecca-trained Joseph Middleton (c1754-1805) at £50 a year, despite his opinion that an Adult Believer was "the only proper subject" of Baptism, and Total Immersion "the only proper mode". The Society seemed happy with this caveat. Indeed when adopting the Westminster Assembly's Shorter Catechism, it also affirmed "the right of private judgment as the result of free enquiry", which provoked debate over whether God was the creator of sin, and whether sin was "a body". Yet in July 1784 committed Paedo-Baptists staged a coup: by demanding the chapel key from Middleton, they provoked the First Secession.

Foundry Lane Chapel (Pastor Middleton)

He withdrew to the disused Quaker meeting-house at Puddle Wharf, where Abraham Larwill and 25 other adherents promised him £7 a quarter. His first sermon expounded Exodus 20:24: "In all places where I record my name, I will come unto thee, and I will bless thee". Though the new Church explicitly endorsed Believers' Baptism, its Communion table lay open to all Christians. In May 1785 it joined the Associated Baptist Churches of Kent and Sussex, and in August, aided by London well-wishers, it moved to a new wooden tabernacle at Cliffe, in what became Foundry Lane. Middleton also fostered a mid-Sussex Connexion. In 1785 he sponsored an exodus from Selina's chapel at Five Ash Down which established a Baptist meeting at Uckfield. At Handcross and Brighton he ordained new pastors in 1797. His Lewes hearers also evangelized. The banker Thomas Dicker preached at Hailsham, and the shoemaker John Atterall at Eastbourne. (William Hattrell, a relative perhaps, was registered as "a Gospel Preacher and a rogue", when buried at St Michael's in 1796.)

Despite this evangelical outreach, Middleton's Baptists fell on hard times. Apart from Thomas Dicker and John Button, the hearers were mostly artisans, and though the membership reached 117 in 1793, thereafter it dwindled as war-taxes, dear bread, disease and migration to America took their toll. The remnant saw themselves as a "barren fig-tree" blasted by Divine Wrath. "Suns are turning into darkness and moons into blood", they lamented. By 1803 Heresy and Backsliding also menaced them, being rampant among local cohorts of "sneaking and contemptuous Socinians, impudent Antimonians, artful Universalists and half-hearted Christians". "May the Lord appear for Britain as he appeared for Judah", was their plea in 1804. However under Pastor Moses Fisher 1805-13 they did proselytize a nearby village, possibly Barcombe, and support missions to the equally "dark" East Indies. After Fisher left for Liverpool the Church endured a prolonged "widowed state", and members sank to 54, though in 1817 they broke new ground by drinking "a social Cup of Tea together in the Vestry". Pastor JB Pewtress 1818-22 encouraged them to quit Foundry Lane for Eastgate in January 1819. But a large and lingering debt on the new meeting-house reduced the stipend of Josiah Denham 1822-27, who departed for America bemoaning how deeply the spiritual condition of the hearers had wounded his Heart. Yet they mustered "350" in 1829; and under Pastor Israel Soule 1829-37, John Button's son-in-law, the Church stabilized.

Quite other trials had beset Selina's chapel at Cliffe. Trevecca-trained Jenkin Jenkins (c1749-1810), Middleton's Paedo-Baptist successor, persuaded his well-heeled hearers to raise £70 in 1798 for the war against the Satanic French Republic. He worried however about the authenticity of his own Election, retreating now and then to Wales; and his preaching dwelt much on Divine Reprobation. Probably his were the "censorious, ill-matured and condemning" sermons which, local Baptists complained, caused many Lewesians to despair of Salvation and wallow in Worldliness. When John Gibbs, a committed hearer, claimed an encounter with Christ, Jenkins acidly dismissed it as "hyprocrisy sent from the Devil". Only after Jenkins met the evangelist William Huntington (1745-1813) at Maresfield in 1792 did his Assurance become Final.

Pastor Jenkin Jenkins (ESRO)

William Huntington

Alias the Redeemed Coalheaver, alias Parson Sack, Huntington was the bastard of a brutal Cranbrook farmer. After getting a girl pregnant, he fled into Surrey and turned his thoughts to Redemption. While pruning a pear tree near Sunbury, he beheld Christ "in a most glorious manner...all stained with blood"; and knew himself brought thereby "under the covenant love of God's elect". At Thames Ditton, where he mingled coalheaving, cobbling and fervent field-preaching, a hostile crowd was pacified (he claimed) by a command from George III, Providentially passing by. His mission prospered, and in 1783 his London disciples built him Providence chapel, Great Titchfield Street, where a thousand hearers sometime included Princess Amelia and Lord Liverpool. The rugged religious tracts he penned were also popular: indeed sales of *The Kingdom of*

Heaven Taken By Prayer matched those of *The Pilgrim's Progress*. With the proceeds he bought a neat villa and 54 acres at Cricklewood; and in 1808 he married a devotee, Lady Sanderson, the widow of a London Lord Mayor.

After they met at Maresfield, the Coalheaver buoyed up Pastor Jenkins. He dubbed him a "Welsh Ambassador of God's Truth", and sent him letters of spiritual comfort, later published as *Contemplations on the God of Israel*. He also counselled the pastor's flock at Chapel Hill. Indeed his rapturous exchange of soul-experience with Mrs Mary Hooper passed into print as *Correspondence between Noctua Aurita of the Desert and Philomela of the King's Dale*. When Joseph Morris contracted typhus, Huntington and his Lady came post-haste to School Hill and prayed at his bedside; the butcher duly recovered. But Selina's other missioners disliked the Coalheaver. So in 1805 Pastor Jenkins, butcher Morris and Philomela headed a Second Secession from Cliffe Hill. They migrated to Jireh chapel, a "neat and convenient" tabernacle funded by "the Citizens of Zion", as the Huntingtonians called themselves. In July 1805 the Coalheaver preached there to a thousand hearers, and launched his own Sussex Connexion. Providence chapels were opened at Brighton and Chichester for William Brook, a former curate at St Nicholas's in Brighton, whose austere sermons had disconcerted the Prince of Wales. In 1813 Huntingdon chose to be buried beside Jenkins in the garden behind Jireh chapel which received Philomela in 1833. Vast crowds watched the mile-long cortege arrive from Tunbridge Wells: many carriages came from London, making its streets "strangely quiet". The massive tomb still bears the pugnacious epitaph Huntington composed:

> Here lies the Coalheaver...beloved of his God, but abhorred of men: the omniscient Judge, at the grand assize, shall ratify and confirm this to the confusion of many thousands; for England and its metropolis shall know that there hath been a prophet among them. W.H. S.S.

Sinner Saved was his cherished, and only qualification.

Finally Assured as to the Next World, and with a carriage and pair in this, Jenkins died in 1810, followed by Brook in 1811. Their mantles passed to John Vinall (1782-1860) who ministered at Lewes and Brighton till 1857, and at Chichester till 1831. He extended the Connexion to Lower Dicker in 1812, and to Cavendish Place Chapel

Pastor John Vinall (ESRO)

at Eastbourne by 1826. Jireh was enlarged in 1824, and drew a "1000" hearers in 1829, the largest congregation in Lewes. The son of a miller's grinder at Henfield, Vinall became an apprentice boot-maker, revelling in bell-ringing and song. Then his master moved to Lewes, where a soberer Vinall savoured the sermons of Parson Aquila Dale and Pastor Jenkins, but it was Huntington who set him "at sweet and happy liberty" in 1805 from any fear of Hell. A further "rich anointing" by the Holy Spirit equipped him to bring Final Assurance to many: James Lewis felt

> the burden of sin removed - guilt, wrath, fear, misery, and bondage taken out of and from off my conscience...peace flowed into my soul...and love, praise, gratitude, and thanksgiving ascended up to the throne of grace.

Lewis believed Vinall was as fitted to preach as Saint Paul who also lacked education, which outraged Canon Walker at Chichester:

> Paul and...the apostles were inspired, but inspiration ceased in the apostolic age; there is no such thing nowadays.

John Gibbs (1769-1838) too was a Lewes shoemaker "steadied" by Huntington while seeking Assurance. Because of God's "gracious dealings" he overcame early trials: his mother dying of smallpox on Ditchling Common; his drunken father; profane and dishonest employers. When a hearer of Pastor Jenkins, he saw in a Vision "a glorious person" who

> drew near and came up to me; he came from the east and passed toward the west; he stopped a little while, and smiled on me, which smile I shall never forget, or the rapture of joy that it communicated.

Jenkins dismissed this as "hypocrisy sent from the Devil", but Gibbs rallied by reading Huntington whose own Vision had been at Sunbury. He began house-preaching, and in 1811 his little flock leased Refuge chapel, newly and "neatly" built in Lancaster Street by Amon Wilds. They invited Pastor Vigors McCulla from Brighton to officiate monthly. But unknown to Gibbs, McCulla detested Huntington, and penned a pamphlet to prove it, *The Coalheaver In The Balance*. He managed to lock the Gibbsites out and close down the chapel, which became Brown's Commercial Day School. Gibbs then rented a warehouse in St Johns Street from Thomas Mantell's widow. He fitted out his new Bethesda chapel with battered seats from the barracks and a pulpit of unplaned boards. There his witness bore fruit. The chapel was rebuilt in 1827, and sheltered "250" Calvinistic Dissenters in 1829.

After Pastor Jenkins, butcher Morris and Philomela led the second exodus, Cliffe chapel was reopened in July 1805 by Pastor White from Cheshunt College (which had replaced Trevecca). The Lewes trustees were George Adams broker, Thomas Hill baker, Joseph Simes draper and George Wille timber-merchant. They lacked a "constant" pastor, but heeded a sermon in May 1806 from the Reverend Rowland Hill, a baronet's son whose London chapel co-ordinated 3000 children in 13 Sunday Schools. By April 1808 200 scholars were enrolled at Chapel Hill from "the poor of all denominations". After singing hymns at Charles Wille's house, each received a cake and a glass of wine. However in 1816 Wille, his father George and Nehemiah Wimble spearheaded a Third Secession. They funded a proprietary chapel, Tabernacle, on the former Friars estate. Its foundation trench yielded a coin comfortingly inscribed *Verbum*

Dominus manet in eternum. The Church's members included broker Adams, seedsman James Stronach, builder Thomas Smith, gunmaker Thomas Lloyd and wine-merchant John Harvey. Like the Protestant Dissenters at Cliffe chapel, they professed "the doctrines of the Church of England...as explained by Calvinists and contained in the [Westminster] assembly's catechism"; indeed Matthew Wilks, their first preacher, succeeded George Whitefield at Moorfield Tabernacle. They soon enrolled almost 300 children in a Fragment School, inviting down Rowland Hill, and taking as a text, "Gather up the fragments that remain that nothing may be lost". Nor was "darkness" among the heathen neglected; in 1830 the Juvenile Missionary Society admired an array of idols discarded in Africa and the South Seas. Yet unlike most Huntingdonians (and the Coalheaver), the Willes and Wimble were Whigs, keen to repeal the Test and Corporation Acts; so perhaps politics fuelled their exodus. With almost 60 members and "over 500" hearers, Tabernacle ceased to be proprietory in 1829, and Evan Jones 1829-62 became their full-time pastor. In 1832 the chapel was enlarged and given a proud Ionic portico (though a Chastening duly followed).

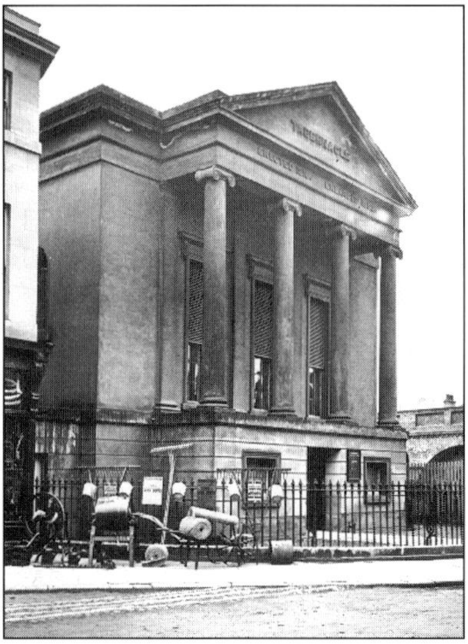

Tabernacle Chapel (Reeves)

At Cliffe chapel Pastor John Kerby rode out the Third Secession, publishing a commentary on Luther's theology, and a tribute to the late Princess Charlotte. In 1829 Pastor Harris mustered "400" hearers. But in 1839 disruptive refugees flooded in from Tabernacle, after signing "charges" against Pastor Jones. Charles Wille, who remained loyal, chronicled God's Vengeance on them: James Weller died deranged; George Adams expired "in a state of stupor" with £50 of Tabernacle funds unaccounted for; Nehemiah Wimble passed away bleeding from the mouth, his affairs in Chancery; Thomas Berry went bankrupt, owing £17,000; Thomas Dicker's son was packed off to America with an "indecent disease"; a flint-digger in Coombe Bottom glimpsed Dicker's daughter carnally consorting with a clergyman; other apostates watched their children sicken and wives miscarry.

This resurgence of fierce, if fissiparous, Calvinism weakened the

Established Church and Old Dissent, and also impeded the local growth of Arminian Methodism which allowed Free Will a role in Redemption. Its founder, John Wesley, crossed mid-Sussex only once, in October 1758, pausing to sleep at Rottingdean. So Rye became the focus of a Sussex Circuit in 1765. At Eastbourne and Brighton the seed was belatedly planted about 1800 by soldier-evangelists stationed at the new coastal barracks. At Lewes they were reinforced by immigrant papermill workers, first at Dolphin Lane in 1806, and then from April 1807 at a warehouse in St Marys Lane which they bought soon after. (Thomas Mantell had built it in 1788, apparently for Lady Huntingdon's missioners who left before 1796). The local trustees were all outsiders, William Baxter barrack-sergeant, Joseph Purcess papermaker, George Morley farmer and John Dudeney, newly arrived from shepherding at Rottingdean. However two full-time preachers, Robert Pilter and William Homer, quickly consolidated a Lewes and Brighton Circuit. By 1816 300 members attended "preaching places" as distant as Worthing, Cuckfield, Withyham, Heathfield and Bexhill. After Brighton and Worthing were hived off in 1825, Dudeney and 13 other lay-preachers served Eastbourne, Hellingly, Waldron, Framfield and Duddleswell, arriving on foot or on the Circuit's "preaching horse". By 1829 "300" hearers gathered at St Mary's Lane.

By then "50" Arminian Bible Christians worshipped at the abandoned Baptist meeting-house in Eastport Lane. Earlier the Quaker John Marten had found them a room over shoemaker Huggett's on School Hill. These "Ranters", as the *Journal* called them, began in the West Country in 1816, when William O'Bryan (1778-1868) broke with Wesleyan Methodism. In 1823 they reached Brighton; and in May 1824 a female missioner, perhaps Sarah Willis, preached near Lewes theatre to 500 hearers, which provoked the *Journal* to query whether her "fascinating features" unsettled the Love Feasts held by the sect. In April 1827 "Sister Sarah" was burlesqued at the theatre; and applause drowned a performance there of *The Miller and his Men*, when the mill was seen to be a pair of sweeps attached to the rostrum she usually preached from.

Very different was the sect begun in 1816 by the banker George Baring and his brother-in-law Thomas Read Kemp, who gave up his Lewes parliamentary seat to become a Dissenting minister. He delivered "persuasive, mild, energetic and unassuming" sermons in a former fire-engine house by the castle barbican. At Brighton he built

Trinity Chapel in Ship Street, and also an ambitious residence replicating King Solomon's Temple at Jerusalem (now the Girls' High School). But by 1823 the sect had disintegrated amid "awful extremes of error", and Kemp returned to the Established Church and Parliament. His Lewes chapel became a charity school, the fire-engine having been handsomely housed elsewhere.

The new Connexions and Circuits pioneered across mid-Sussex by Lewes Baptists, Huntingtonians and Arminian Methodists, and the rustic hearers at Tabernacle, Bethesda and Chapel Hill, made good the failing outreach of Old Dissent, and revived the town as a focus of evangelical endeavour. In Victorian Lewes this potent spiritual mix was further strengthened by new vigour among Anglicans, Unitarians and Quakers, and by the worship of Roman Catholics, Primitive Methodists and Presbyterians. This integrated with the political divide between Liberal and Conservative to create tensions which moulded the town's cultural life.

Westgate Vestry (E.H.New)

9
Political Nerve-Centre: The Duke of Newcastle and his Legacy 1714-82

At Bishopstone Near to the Sea,
Upon the Sussex Coast,
As good a Duke as Duke can be
Lives there - the County's Toast.

His Home and he both open are
To all that come both near and far.
He has no Private Selfish Ends,
Esteems his honest Steady Friends.

You ne're can want while he's your Head,
He gives you Freedom, Meat and Bread.
Your credit nor your Stocks can't fall
While Pelham represents you all.

Then fill your Glass. Full let it be.
Newcastle drink while you can see;
With Heart and Voice, all Voters Sing,
Long live Great Holles - Sussex's King.

A Sussex Toast (Michaelmas 1741) composed by Timothy Goose, a farm servant near Lewes (BL 32,698 80-2).

The Duke promised a tailor named Kidger the making of his Grace's liveries. he heard no more. at Christmas he made out the Bill and carried it to his Grace's audit at Halland. "to T. Kidger, for not making Your Grace's liveries £10.0.0.". The Steward took it to his Grace. Smiling, he told them to pay it.

Nursing a Lewes elector: William Wisdom's Memoranda.

Till Ideology reared its hydra-head in the late 1780s, the local landowners dominated parliamentary elections in Georgian Sussex. They influenced the 40 shilling freeholders who chose the county's two MPs, and in the Eastern Division they competed to control the borough seats at Rye, Winchelsea, Hastings, Seaford and East Grinstead, all stagnant towns with small electorates wide open to bribery and intimidation. And though Lewes Borough enjoyed a vigorous commerce and culture, and all its male householders assessed for the poor rate were entitled to vote, nonetheless its politics were moulded for over 50 years by a landed oligarch, Thomas Pelham-Holles (1693-1768), Duke of Newcastle, whose coming-of-age coincided with the new Hanoverian dynasty.

Earlier, in Stuart times, bitter national disputes about the Constitution and the Established Church had weakened the grip of landowners on local electorates. These disputes were largely resolved by the Glorious Revolution (1688) and the Hanoverian accession, which satisfied the Dissenters and Whig grandees, and marginalized High Anglican Tories. At Lewes passions had been intense. During the Civil War and Commonwealth Presbyterian and Independent tradesmen had controlled the Borough. But after the Restoration of an Anglican monarch in 1660 they were ousted as civic leaders by Tory loyalists, branded as religious Dissenters, and forced to worship in back-alleys under threat of fine or imprisonment. Yet they remained numerous, coherent and affluent, being aided by Anglican Whigs among the local gentry, especially by Newcastle's father, Sir Thomas Pelham (c1653-1712), who owned wide estates at Laughton, Halland and Bishopstone, and sat for the Borough between 1679 and 1702.

Halland House (Horsfield's History)

The Glorious Revolution restored Lewes Dissenters to civic influence and gave them freedom of worship. Their gratitude to Sir Thomas ensured the election of his uncle, Sir Nicholas Pelham from Catsfield, as a Borough MP in 1702, and in 1705 of Nicholas's son Thomas (1678-1760). But in 1705 the Independents and Presbyterians also fielded Thomas Fagge, a worshipper at Westgate, with a mansion in St Michael's (later Newcastle House) and an estate at Glynleigh near Hailsham (where in 1717 his widow hosted Pastor John Smith and "110" Presbyterian hearers). As a Radical Puritan Fagge presumably opposed the Test and Corporation Acts, relics of the Clarendon Code which excluded Dissenters from Public Office and the Universities. Fagge's bid for the second Borough seat challenged Thomas Pelham's running-mate Richard Paine, an Anglican Whig. 107 out of 215 voters polled for Fagge, including Pastor Newton, Pastor Barnard's brother, Pastor Olive's father, and many other Dissenters. But only 32 electors plumped for Fagge; the others also polled for Pelham or Paine, who emerged with 147 and 125 votes. Compared with the Dissenters, the Lewes Tories performed weakly. Their candidate Nathaniel Trayton (1663-1715), a lawyer resident on School Hill, tactically retired with four votes. In 1709 he bought Southover manor, and his initials were carved on the church tower in 1714, so presumably he gave generously to its rebuilding.

Fagge's was the last serious challenge at Lewes by Radical Dissent. The general election in 1714 comfortably returned Thomas Pelham and John Morley Trevor (1681-1719) of Glynde Place, a Whig great-grandson of John Hampden. The promotion by George I of Whig ministers and Erastian bishops caused Toryism to lose coherence, and Dissent to drop its guard. Fagge the Radical Puritan and Trayton the Ultra-Churchman left few successors. This blander political climate suited Thomas Pelham-Holles. Besides his father's Sussex estates, he inherited much of Nottinghamshire through his mother. His wealth and pedigree ensured his rapid rise as a Whig oligarch. He became Duke of Newcastle in 1715, Lord Chamberlain in 1717, and a Secretary of State in 1724, when his cherished brother Henry (1695-1754), already a Sussex MP, was made Secretary at War. Under Walpole their influence increased, and in 1743 Henry became First Lord of the Treasury, followed by Thomas in 1754. Being powerful ministers for several decades they controlled much official patronage in the Treasury, the Customs and Excise, the Post Office, the Colonies, the Judiciary, the Armed Services, the Royal

The Duke of Newcastle

Dockyards, the Victualling Office, the Universities and the Established Church. And because ideology had drained away from politics Newcastle, who loved election management, used this patronage lavishly to reward his Sussex supporters, in the shire and in Rye, Hastings, Seaford and Lewes, whether peers, gentry, parsons, freeholders or burgesses.

The Duke greatly valued Lewes, both as his father's former seat and as the Eastern Division's cultural focus, and realizing its large, alert electorate needed tactful handling, he sustained in public the polite fiction that an Independent Borough was giving him a spontaneous allegiance. However he favoured Lewesians with pickings from his ministerial patronage, and with a steady stream of orders for groceries, fabrics, wines, medicine and plumbing, dispatched from his households at Halland and Bishopstone, and from those of an extended Pelham "Family" rapidly taking local root and itself steadily enriched by Newcastle's patronage. Uncle Henry (cl656-1721), who prospered as Clerk of the Pells, bought Stanmer Park in 1713, and his sons, Henry (1694-1725) and Thomas (1705-37), sat for Lewes in 1722-5 and 1727-37. Formerly a merchant in Constantinople, Thomas received the alias "Turk". Thomas Pelham

Stanmer Park (Horsfield's History)

from Catsfield, a Borough MP since 1705, acquired in 1725 the Elizabethan mansion in St Andrews Lane, known thereafter as Pelham House. His daughters, too, loyally cemented the Family's local influence. Elizabeth wedded William Hay (1695-1755) of Glyndebourne, who served Newcastle as Chairman of Quarter Sessions and MP for Seaford, and became a Commissioner in the Victualling Office and Keeper of Records in the Tower of London. Her sister Margaret married Sir William Ashburnham, a baronet in Holy Orders, swiftly elevated by Family influence to the see of Chichester. Turk Pelham's sisters also pulled their weight. Frances wedded the Cheshire baronet, Sir Francis Poole (1682-1763), who leased The Friars estate at Lewes in 1734 and became Deputy Paymaster of Minorca, a sinecure requiring no contact with that fortress isle. Turk's sister Grace married Francis's brother William (1696-1779) who bought The Hooke at Chailey in 1732. He was useful to Newcastle as a local Justice, and was made Receiver General at the Stamp Office. Besides this extended Pelham Family, the Duke cultivated the households at Firle Park and Glynde Place. The sportive Sir William Gage (1695-1744), who renounced Popery and embraced Protestantism (along with Bel Norton), became a Knight of the Bath. John Trevor (1716-43) was made an Admiralty Commissioner, and his clerical kinsman Dr Richard Trevor soon blossomed as Bishop of St Davids, and then of Durham.

At the 1722 Borough election Thomas and Henry Pelham faced John Spence, a Malling landowner linked with the Westgate Presbyterians, whose Baptist great-uncle had sat in the Barebones Parliament. But by then Lewes Dissenters had little use for a champion. The Whig ministers of George I had repealed the Schism and the Occasional Conformity Acts, which the Tories passed under Queen Anne to hamper Dissenting academies and municipal office-holders. So Pastor Olive and most prominent Westgate hearers polled for the Pelhams, only a few voted for a Pelham and Spence; and the 20 electors plumping for Spence were mostly veteran Tories out to harass the Pelhams. He received 62 votes, Thomas 109 and Henry 116.

Pelham House
(James Lambert: British Library Addit. Ms. 5677 fo. 4)

In 1727 Thomas and Turk Pelham were returned unopposed. But by 1733 they faced a coalition of malcontents which tested the Duke's influence to its utmost. Walpole's government was accused of flooding Parliament with Sinecurists and Placemen, needlessly expanding the Army and the National Debt, levying new duties on wine and tobacco, and forcing excisemen into every shop and home. The Lewes victualler Edward Whiskey and the grocer John Wilbar also denounced the extra packaging and paperwork. Protests against the Excise Scheme were sometimes passionate. In "all the weald of Kent", Newcastle was informed, "the Middle Sort are as mad as in the Time of Sacheveral". Walpole's effigy was burned to ashes at Hailsham, and torn to pieces at Selmeston. During Cliffe sheep fair in October 1733 Galloway the Quaker protested by firing cannon from a raft near the bridge. As the Duke's brother Henry bleakly put it:

> The whole country almost is poison'd; very little regard in the common people for the King and the Royal Family, less for the Ministry; in short it is personal interest must carry this election.

Indeed amid the uproar Thomas and Turk almost lost their seats in April 1734. Apart from Edward Trayton, the leading Tories were new-comers to the Borough; the rentiers John Bromfield and John Holford, the lawyers Richard Newdigate and William Kempe, the physician Benjamin Comber, the surgeon Henry Manning, the mercer William Durrant, and their chief fixer, the merchant John Whitfeld (though he resided in Cliffe). Their candidate Thomas Sergison (1701-67), who owned Cuckfield Park, was aided by other local landowners, by John Bridger at Coombe Place, Edward Medley at Coneysborough near Barcombe, Walter Dobell at Streat Place, Christopher Mansell at Newick Park, and Henry Campion at Danny Park. Campion in his youth had favoured the Old Pretender, but doubtless the Toryism of some others fed on their being outside the patronage network Newcastle had built up.

Long before the election these well-heeled malcontents co-ordinated their custom to win support among Borough tradesmen. Draper John Michelbourne was seduced from the Pelhams by an order for liveries from Danny Park. Upholsterer Abraham Edwards and plumber George Brooke, "uncertain" at first, received contracts to renovate Cuckfield Park. Clockmaker Isaac Guepin was reminded how much he "owed his bread" to John Whitfeld. Saddler Joseph Mosely was "promised more". Shoemaker Oliver Willard deserted Newcastle even though his father was the Duke's copyhold tenant at Laughton. Tailor Andrew Lawrence was clinched when "Mr Pelham" failed to get him chosen as the next Crier to the Court of Quarter Sessions. More general inducements were a new Charity School taught by John Head, and a stream of Meetings, Treats, Clubs and Balls at the *Star* and Lidgitter's coffee-house, where voters and their wives were made much of by affable Tory grandees and their ladies.

The Tories also linked up with a few malcontent Borough Dissenters, once John Spence persuaded Nathaniel Garland, a "Rigid Dissenter", to stand against the Pelhams. Though a wealthy London merchant, his forbears had been Lewes Independents. Quite how he coalesced with "so high a churchman" as Sergison is unclear. Yet in August 1733 their supporters united to make a "heat" at the *Star*. Posters at the market-house proclaimed them both to be "zealously affected" to the Protestant Succession, and "directly opposed" to the Excise Scheme. However most Dissenters, including Pastor Force at Market Lane, stayed loyal to the Pelhams. Indeed Pastor Jones, a guest preacher at Westgate, denounced the Coalition as "wicked", even though Garland was present. And the Pelhamites menaced his image as "a Patriot and a Saint" by alleging he offered a sawyer William Shelton £20 for his vote. Among the few Dissenters joining the Coalition was Friend Galloway, whose sect had complex links with Ultra-Toryism dating back to James II. A few others, led by Pastor Olive, polled for Garland and a Pelham.

Neither Thomas nor Turk could outface the Coalition. Both were Placemen; both voted for the Excise Scheme; and both were inept electioneers. Depressed by his own inertia, Thomas suffered a nervous collapse. Turk rode in from Stanmer, but only to booze, brag and brawl: the years at Constantinople had clearly taken their toll. Belatedly they launched Clubs to rally support. Tradesmen met at the *White Hart*, "inferior voters" at the *Black Lion* and *White Lion*, where the jockey William Lawrence led the subsidized carousing. The campaign was rescued by William Hay and by Thomas's son Thomas (c1705-43), an ex-diplomat and MP for Hastings. They worked closely with Coroner Michell and Headmaster Welby whose careers the Duke had furthered. Other key lieutenants were promised official patronage: apothecary Brett was to become a Distributor of Stamped Paper; the brother-in-law of Justice John Apsley, a Commissioner of Bankrupts; and apothecary Wheatley's son, an ensign. Loyal tradesmen enjoyed a flood of orders from Stanmer, Glynde, Glyndebourne, Firle, Bishopstone and Halland. Richard Verrall at the *White Hart* and William Batchelor at the Post Office were also rewarded. And Mr Springett of Plumpton offered to posthumously fund any Charity School the Pelhams might open in the Borough.

William Hay and Thomas then tackled the floating voters. Club meetings at the *Red Lion* "encouraged" its landlord Erasmus Rowe. A wavering perukemaker was promised the stitching of Pelham election cockades; a wavering sheriff's bailiff was "spoken to" by Coroner Michell. Nicholas Browne, a "drummer" open to the highest bidder, was taken on as a gardener. Vacillating butchers and carpenters received lucrative contracts. Parson Bristed was rescued from his creditors, and agreed to prevent the Tory dancing master Stephen Philpot moving into St Anne's Rectory till after polling day. Where possible apostate electors, like Isaac Guepin, were evicted from their homes. The Coalition turned the same screw. Parson Charles Dixon pressured shoemaker Thomas Morris, his tenant at St John's Church House, into attending a Club at the *White Horse*. When "warned out" by the Coalition, William Ashby feared he would "lye in the street", but the Duke found him a home in St Marys Lane, and built him a malt house nextdoor. Both sides also ousted widows and other non-electors to make space for supporters.

Because the county election also promised to be hard-fought, William Hay fed the Duke a stream of data on 40 shilling freeholders at Cliffe. One was carpenter to John Spence; another hired a malt house from Friend Galloway; a third repaired ships for John Whitfeld. Smith wanted a loan at four per cent. Heaver was grieved that the Duke had failed to find an eventide home at Trinity House for a sailor's widow he knew. Attorney Hammond complained that £40-worth of "good services", rendered to the Whig cause 20 years before, were still unpaid for. And Sharp was inclined to go wrong, though "his mother-in-law says he shall go right".

Quite apart from clubs and carousing, bribes and custom, cajoling and eviction, both sides strove to rig the election of High Constables at the Borough Court Leet in October 1733, because as Borough Returning Officers they would decide "the Validity of disputable Votes" on polling day. They were chosen at the Court by the Steward, from a list of four "Senior" jurors, drawn up by a jury chosen by the Steward from the customary manorial tenants of Lewes Burgus. No firm rules governed the selection of the jury, the Senior jurors, or the High Constables. So the Steward could manipulate the procedure, provided his seigneurial master, the Lord of the Leet, agreed. This Honour rotated between Lord Abergavenny and the Duke of Dorset, both allies of Newcastle, and the Duke of Norfolk, a neutral grandee, whose turn it was. He gave his Steward, Mr Gratwick, a free hand, into which John Whitfeld slipped 50 guineas, to ensure Coalitionist Constables. But after Thomas Pelham slipped him more, the Town Book, the official record of the Leet, was wrestled from the Senior Constable, tanner Richard Puxty, a cantankerous Tory, and a plausible jury with a safe Pelhamite majority was concocted. From its partisan short-list Gratwick duly selected Thomas Friend and James Reeves. "The whole town attended", Thomas Pelham informed the Duke; "the jury did their business...with all the quietness that could be"; and the thwarted

Coalitionists retreated to the *Star* for a "drunken meeting". In 1705 and 1722 the Pelhamites had also managed this manoeuvre, though now the stakes were higher.

Battle was then joined at the New Year parish vestry meetings, where householders assessed for the poor-rate were reviewed and doubtful cases voted on. In theory only residents of "known ability", or renting property worth at least £10 a year, were included, so that the less affluent were denied any grounds to claim a legal settlement. But now, amid much "noise and turmoil", each side competed to include partisans and exclude opponents. The Pelhamites carried the day in St Michael's, and Justice John Apsley from St Annes Hill happily signed the new rate book. In All Saints, St Anne's and St John's the Coalitionists prevailed, and Tory Justices from Cuckfield, Brightling and Willingdon duly signed. Each side then appealed to the Easter Quarter Sessions at Lewes to quash the votes they lost as "partial and illegal". On 26 April (the day before the poll) the Pelhamites mustered a majority on the Bench which allowed only the St Michael's book, arguing that "foreign" Justices were not competent to sanction Lewes rates. This caused much confusion at the hustings, and gave the High Constables, Friend and Reeves, great scope for partisanship.

Before the poll Newcastle himself arrived. Being adept at "Burgessing", he toured the Borough and attended the hustings. Despite this the "wicked" Coalition cohered very well. 78 electors voted for Thomas and Turk, and 67 for Garland and Sergison. And the Borough was now so polarized that no elector plumped, and only 11 cross-voted, eight for a Pelham and Garland, three for a Pelham and Sergison. Turk received 84 votes, Thomas 83, Garland 75 and Sergison 70. This narrow victory moreover had depended on the Constables rejecting 24 "disputable" Coalitionists and allowing 24 "disputable" Pelhamites, which provoked an angry exchange of pamphlets, the third some 93 pages long. Did ironmonger Court vacate his showrooms before polling day? Was John Bristed rated for his parsonage? Did he lock out his lawful tenant Stephen Philpot? Did Thomas Hollibone (the Duke's busy letter-carrier) depend on Mrs Hollibone for his Borough settlement? Were the premises rented by Lawrence the jockey worth £10 a year? Did John Peckham, a fuller from Fletching, merely lodge in the Borough on Saturday night, and worship at Westgate on the Sabbath? Such technicalities were bitterly debated.

CASES of the twenty four Perſons, as ſet forth in the Pamphlet.	ANSWERS thereto, and Reaſons for admitting them to Poll.
BEN. COURT, Ironmonger, *That he had lett his Houſe to the Duke of* Newcaſtle *from* Chriſtmas *laſt, and that his Grace was then in poſſeſſion of the Houſe and Houſhold Goods*, Mr. Court *being there only on Sufferance, to ſell his Shop Goods, but Mr.* Friend *ſaid he thought in his Conſcience he had a Right to vote.* Obſerve, *Mr.* Court *often ſaid his Houſe and Vote ſhould go together.*	AS to Mr. *Court*'s having any Agreement with the Duke of *Newcaſtle*, or not, 'tis no way material, in regard to his Vote, for he ſtill continues in his Houſe, having never given Poſſeſſion of it to any other Perſon, and muſt himſelf be charged to the Poor Rates, and other Taxes, till he removes from thence.
2. JOHN BRISTED, Clerk, *That he was never taxed for his Houſe, only for his glebe Land, that lay without the Borough, and was ſo poor, that the Pariſh excuſed his Taxes in* 1732, *but Mr.* Friend *ſaid he was taxed for Lands lying in the ſame Pariſh, and he ſhould poll him.*	2. JOHN BRISTED has always been tax'd to the Poor Rates, for his Tythes and glebe Land, a Part of which is his Parſonage-Houſe, within the Borough where he has reſided for ſome Years paſt, and by a Receipt now in his Hands, it appears he paid as much, or more Taxes in 1732, than in any Year before or ſince.

So dubious a victory caused Newcastle to reorganize the flow of Pelham cash, custom and patronage. No detail proved too minute: the arrival of a gingerbread maker, also trading in oranges and lemons, and of a pastry cook, able to supply Halland with hams, tongues and sturgeon; the appointment of a hop-duty collector, of two extra customs-officers in the Borough, of Mr Friend's crony as a land-carriage waiter at Southwark, of Mr Wheatley's assistant as a naval surgeon's mate, of Mr Turner as a window-tax surveyor. Turner made the clock Newcastle bestowed on the market-house in 1734, and later pleaded that his son, dismissed "crippled and naked" from his regiment, be admitted to Chelsea Hospital: "let me once more upon my knees, and my family too, in tears, beg of you this time to be his friend". Aided by Thomas and Turk, the Duke also began buying up, or leasing, any available house, workshop or croft in the Borough. These he crammed with pliable tenants whose annual rent, nominally £10 or more, he often remitted and whose parish rates he often paid. Lavish house repairs moreover allowed him to oblige many masons, carpenters and plumbers. By 1741 he already controlled most of the 70 tenements which housed 55 loyal electors in 1767. And to counter Tory junketing at the *Star* and Lidgitter's, he turned ironmonger Court's premises into a coffee-house and assembly-room.

Sergison too bought up houses: indeed on occasion he and the Duke grabbed a moiety each. By 1767 his 51 tenements sheltered 45 voters. In 1739 he rebuilt the *Star* to better entertain local Tories. He launched the *Dolphin* which displayed his coat-of-arms. He seduced poor Parson Bristed with promises of a plump benefice at Slaugham. Yet Newcastle outreached him, winning over two key lieutenants, John Whitfeld and William Kempe. The Duke's efforts bore fruit in February 1738, after Turk died of drink. 133 "determined" voters were mustered at the *White Hart*, to ensure John Trevor (1716-43) of Glynde, a trusty Pelhamite, was elected unopposed.

The Star Coffee House and Inn (Reeves)

The Duke then employed Kempe to manage his houses, and funded Whitfeld to build up a Club among "inferior voters". Some 50 were drawn in by strong drink and a shilling or two. This reliance on erstwhile foes nettled long-serving lieutenants ensconced at the *White Hart*; and after a querulous conclave at Claremont, they obliged him to disown Whitfeld in December 1740. "The Town of Lewes is our Plague", he plausibly complained, "but I think it safe". Yet the Club stayed loyal to the wily Whitfeld, so the Duke had to reinstate him, with a large sum for future expenses. To double-check their loyalty Sir William Gage marched Club members to the hustings in May 1741, and Newcastle watched them poll. 271 householders voted, compared with 156 in 1734, many more having been crammed into the rate books. Thomas Pelham replaced his neurasthenic father and received 156 votes, John Trevor 154, and Sergison 117, including 107 plumpers. Whitfeld's Club had indeed tipped the balance. In March 1742, after Trevor became an Admiralty Commissioner, Whitfeld's "diligence and prudent management" ensured his unopposed re-election.

Yet the Duke's respite proved brief. In August 1743 Thomas

Pelham died of consumption; a few weeks later Trevor died deranged, after attempting suicide with scissors. The vacancies were difficult to fill. Dr Richard Trevor, the new squire of Glynde, was soon to be Bishop of St Davids. No Catsfield Pelham was available; Turk's sons at Stanmer were minors; Newcastle himself was childless; and his brother Henry's sons had died young. The Duke made do with Turk's brother-in-law at The Friars, "Good-humoured, down-right, Hearty" Sir Francis Poole. He sometimes joined "the Towne people on a Moonlight evening for a Game of Foot Ball", and sprained himself leaping the bowling-green fence. The Duke also toyed with Garland, now a political ally, and approved by the Dissenters, but Whitfeld objected. So he chose a "stranger" to the Borough, his brother-in-law Sir John Shelley, to "stand only once" as a stop-gap.

Seemingly the by-elections were uncontested; and Sergison began to hint at an "honourable peace", if the Duke endorsed him as Shelley's successor, which would give Newcastle some relief from rent and rate subsidies, "inferior" Clubs and brawling lieutenants. Moreover in 1744 Sir William Gage died; and though Firle Place was not overrun (as rumour insisted) with Catholic priests, "Jackabits" and "Irish French", the new Viscount Gage did challenge the Duke's electoral grip on Seaford, and threaten trouble at Lewes. Moreover the Invasion Scare of 1744-6, which sparked the Great Panic at Chichester and rumours of Papist plotters at Firle, helped reconcile the county gentry. Whig or Tory, they served in the shire Militia and socialized at the *Star* and the *White Hart*. So Newcastle endorsed the "peace". In June 1747 Poole and Sergison were returned unopposed, and party strife no longer marred the summer races at Lewes or fragmented its winter assemblies.

Thereafter for 15 years the Duke's respite was real. In April 1754 Poole and Sergison were again elected unopposed; and in March 1761 they overwhelmed a challenge from John Fuller, a Wealden landowner living on School Hill, remotely related to the Brightling clan, and previously sponsored by Newcastle as MP for Tregony. Only about 40 "malcontents" joined his Independent Club. Poole polled 165 votes, Sergison 154 and Fuller a mere 36. To reinforce the "peace" the Duke showered Places and Favours on local gentry and Lewesians: a Lieutenancy in the Dragoons for Thomas Hay of Glyndebourne; armament contracts for the Fullers at Brightling; a place in the Band of Pensioners for John Bridger junior; a "law faculty place" at Oxford for Dr Russell's son; a free passage to Lisbon on a man-of-war for Henry Campion's grandson. Less choppy was Dr Trevor's mitred progress from St Davids to Durham. At Lewes attorney William Michell was made Treasurer of the Salt Office; Henry Shelley a Searcher of the Customs; and William Kempe (after 16 years of cajoling) Attorney General of New York State. Smaller fry also importuned: Robert Chester and Manfield Verrall wanted to be tide-waiters; William Attree a joiner in the royal dockyards; William Lee a Messenger to the Printing Presses in the Stamp Office. Pleas poured in to release impressed seamen, to reprieve convicted smugglers, to remove billeted soldiers. At Glynde the husbandmen took to "ringing their Plowshares" when the generous Duke rode by. His local apogee came in race week 1759, when "crowds of joyful and loyal friends" on the Lewes course celebrated with him the victory at Minden. At Halland, ten cooks (four of them French) fed a second throng; and 500 feasted at Bishopstone Place, causing Parson Hurdis years later to elegize its

> rich possessor, whose warm heart
> Peopled the vale with his unnumber'd guests;
> Who spread profusion round the hall within,
> And to the border of the lawn without.

However the accession of George III heralded the Duke's dismissal as Prime Minister, and the expulsion of many "South Saxons" from their Places and Emoluments. Soon after in February 1763 Sir Francis Poole died, and Newcastle still lacked a "Relation or local man" to succeed him. So he chose William Plumer (1736-1822), a rich "stranger" related to the Duke of Devonshire, who was cavalcaded into the Borough

> by Lord Abergavenny, Lord John Cavendish, Thomas Pelham of Stanmer, Thomas Sergison Esq., Rose and Stephen Fuller Esq., J. Shelley Esq., to espouse his interest...the same evening the Constables went through the Borough with the Gentleman's Compliments, and invited the inhabitants to dine with them the next day at the White Hart or Star, who in general did, and unanimously approved the Choice made by their noble Duke, to whom they showed their utmost Gratitude and Respect by often drinking his Health, with repeated and unlimited Huzzas.

No Treasury money (now in hostile hands) aided John Fuller to stand, and Plumer was chosen "without the least stir against him".

He funded a Plate at the summer races, and weekly doles of beef in winter, distributed by the "5 Burrugh Butchers".

When Sergison died in 1766, Newcastle replaced him pro tem with Lord Edward Bentinck, the Duke of Portland's brother, just back from the Grand Tour. But for the general election in March 1768 he groomed Thomas Hampden (1747-1824), whose uncle Bishop Trevor considered buying Sergison's houses, till their new owner Mr Nott upped the price. Then William Plumer withdrew to contest Hertfordshire, causing the Duke seemingly to endorse Thomas Hay (1733-86) of Glyndebourne, whose father William, married to a Catsfield Pelham, had served him well. But though Thomas was a "modest, virtuous, sensible" graduate of Gottingen, and a former aide-de-camp to Lord Granby, Newcastle then ditched him for Sir Thomas Miller (1731-1816), a "stranger" from Lavant in West Sussex. The Duke, now ailing and prone to panic, feared Hay might buy Sergison's houses and form an alliance with Hampden, to "the perpetual exclusion" of mainstream Pelhams. The Stanmer branch, moreover, detested both Hay and his sponsor, Sir Francis Poole's son Ferdinando, whose mother was also a Pelham. "Family" unity, the bedrock of Newcastle's influence, was clearly crumbling.

Feeling their Honour was at stake, Poole persuaded Hay to stand as an "independent". Support came from John Fuller and his Clubmen, and from Lord Abergavenny and Henry Shelley, now at odds with Newcastle. Mr Nott also warned his tenants in Sergison's houses to vote for Hay, or face "immediate severities"; perhaps he hoped to up their price by making the Borough marginal. Much depended on the Duke's client voters, his tenants, tradesmen and cronies. But some were already pledged to Hay, or still believed he had the Duke's support. The Stanmer Pelhams offered little help; and Hampden, Miller's running-mate, developed scruples about bribery. On the eve of poll Hay's friends felt able to roast a celebratory runt at The Friars. 184 electors cast 115 votes for Hampden, 110 for Hay, and 92 for Miller. The 73 polling for Miller and Hampden included the Grammar School Master, the Clerk of the Peace, the Archdeacon's Registrar, the King's Musician and the Postmaster, but by no means all the clients Newcastle had so painfully amassed. 19 electors voted for Miller and Hay; 50 plumped for Hay; 41 polled for Hay and Hampden; and Samuel Durrant plumped for Hampden. Amid the confusion, the High Constables chose to abstain.

Outraged by what he deemed base ingratitude, the Duke

demanded abject apologies from his erring tenants. Still shaken, he died in November 1768, being buried near his brother Henry in the chancel at Laughton, where their graves are unmarked. His Sussex estates, his Lewes houses and the Pelham barony passed to Turk's son Thomas (1725-1805) at Stanmer. The new Lord Pelham drew close to the Court Party. He loyally supported George III and Lord North against John Wilkes and the American colonists; in return he became Keeper of the Great Wardrobe and Surveyor-General of the London Customs. At Lewes he used Newcastle's client voters to regain control of one seat. In 1774 the Duke's rejected candidate, Sir Thomas Miller, came top of the poll with 120 votes, 33 of them plumpers; and in 1780 the Baron's second son Henry (1759-97), a consumptive Captain in the Foot Guards, won with 95 votes, 18 of them plumpers. Being a pro-Court candidate, Treasury money flowed on Henry's behalf at the *White Hart*, the *Dog* and the *Brewers Arms*, and rewarded musicians, bell-ringers and cockade-makers.

Though the other candidates in 1774 and 1780 were anti-Court, Lord Pelham did not covet the second Lewes seat, or require his clients to plump for Miller and Captain Henry. In 1774 Thomas Hay stood in alliance with John Trevor, Hampden's younger brother; Glyndebourne leagued with Glynde Place, as Newcastle had feared. A third anti-Court candidate also emerged, the barrister William Kempe, Dr Russell's son at Malling. The intricate cross-voting gave Miller 120, Hay 102, Trevor 82 and Kempe 40. 72 electors boycotted Miller, including Sir Ferdinando, Henry Shelley, John Fuller, William Green and ten attorneys, physicians and surgeons. In 1780 Thomas Hay polled 75 votes, but a new anti-Court candidate, the wealthy Lewes wool merchant, Thomas Kemp (c1746-1811), polled 91. In the bitter winter of 1775-6 Kemp had donated beef, bread and beer to deserving townsfolk; and before the poll his largesse probably flowed as freely as the Treasury's did for Captain Henry. Most labourers and shoemakers polled for Kemp and Pelham, whereas Hay, who was averse to "treating", scored more heavily among the affluent.

Because he displaced the "virtuous" Colonel Hay, Kemp was much derided, as a parvenu tradesman, as the tongue-tied tool of an ambitious wife from wettest Romney Marsh, as a trafficker in bribes who won over Henry Shelley with "a small share of the wool business", as Captain Kemp using the Borough Volunteers to drum up votes:

> The company of Asses I will make over to my Friend Mr Comber, and honour Mr Blackman with a Lieutenancy in that respectible Corps - I will promote Mr Whitfield from a Sergeant to an Ensign - provided he quits that vulgar business of a Grocer.

Yet Kemp was himself party to some scandalous verses by Thomas "Clio" Rickman, penned despite his Quaker father at Bear Yard. They alleged that Elizabeth Plumer cajoled her husband to switch his vote from Kemp to Captain Henry: that she

> Made poor Jacky sneak (to gain her own ends),
> Kiss a Lord's breech and forsake his old friends;

that she also persuaded her brother, "Puritanical Drew",

> Who silent and prim, she sent to look big.
> In coat likewise turn'd and white flowing wig;

and that by finding favour at Stanmer, she hoped to further a liaison with Captain Cranston nextdoor at Antioch House, "at the End of the Town":

> For Pelhams, she cry'd, in hopes of attention
> From the young Captain, and what I won't mention.

This trash landed Rickman in the Court of King's Bench.

Whether the up-market electors who boycotted Miller and Captain Henry viewed them as foes of the Borough's Independence, as agents of a quasi-feudal Interest at Stanmer, or as spokesmen for an arbitrary government, is unknown. Anti-government feeling certainly ran high. In August 1770 applauding crowds and pealing bells greeted the "great patriot" John Wilkes, who stayed overnight at the *Star* and visited the castle. The slogan "Wilkes and Liberty" became "all the cry" locally; and he returned several times to the *Star*. In 1774 a rapturous reception greeted Sir Thomas Wilson, the Independent local candidate for Sussex, who triumphed at Chichester over a pro-Court Westerner. In 1779 emotion surged afresh when Admiral Keppel, widely regarded as a scapegoat, was acquitted of incompetence. An effigy of his state prosecutor was dragged through the High Street, beaten, mangled, shot and burned.

Thomas Paine (1737-1809), while at Lewes as an excise officer, was also no friend of England's Ancien Regime. Arriving in 1768, he lodged at Bull House with a Westgate Presbyterian, the grocer Samuel Olive, who as Senior High Constable abstained at the March election. At St Michael's church in March 1771, after Olive's death,

Tom Paine (Sussex Archaeological Society)

Paine married his daughter Elizabeth, a school mistress, and took over his shop, busying with home-made bacon and a horse-driven mill which ground snuff and tobacco. In the 1790s he was remembered as "the hero of our Bowling-green", as "the Commodore" skating intrepidly on local ponds, and as a keen debater at the Headstrong Club in the *White Hart*, where he so often won an old Greek Homer, awarded to the "most obstinate haranguer", that it was inscribed,

> The Headstrong Book, or Original Book of Obstinacy,
> Written by **** **** of Lewes in Sussex, and Revised and
> Corrected by THOMAS PAINE.

Being for the first time a householder, he could savour the government of the Borough. With the coffee-house keeper Henry Verrall he assiduously attended Vestry and Town Meetings, to approve a rate or the Constables' accounts, to banish from the pavements any "Wheelbarrow...Sledge or Single Wheel". Verrall witnessed his marriage, and was presumably the bowling companion whose assessment of Frederick the Great caused Paine to question the usefulness of Monarchy. And surely it was Paine who penned a letter to the *Journal* in October 1773, signed HUMANUS, which denounced the deportation in an open cart from Yorkshire to Lewes of William Weston, an ailing whitesmith aged 35:

> If to endanger a sick man's life (which I fear is but too often the case, to save a trifling expence) in removing him a distance from the parish in which he sickened, though he had not gained a legal settlement there, is consistent with the laws of this Realm, I am sure it is acting in direct opposition to the laws of God and Nature; and shall ever insist upon it, that when such an instance happens, and the removed object dies on his journey, or immediately after, the person instrumental to his removal, is guilty of Murder, and ought not to escape with impunity, even though it were the act of an unfeeling, CIVIL TYRANT. Sometimes in a case of this kind, it may justly be alleged, that the greatest care imaginable was taken of the deceased, during the course of his journey. What then? It may extenuate, but cannot exculpate. The above may appear presumptuous from an individual, but the assertion is hazarded.
>
> I was led to this Reflection, Mr. Printer, by seeing a poor, dying man (whose name I shall forbear mentioning) brought to your parish on Wednesday evening last, in a small, open cart, having nothing to shelter him from the inclement weather, but a little straw, lightly strewed over him, and in which shameful manner it appeared, he had been passed, on the Vagrant Act, from a parish in Yorkshire, where he was taken ill, to the parish of St. Michael, Lewes, Sussex; an act of cruelty, at the bare thought of which, human nature shudders with Abhorrence! Such an act can admit of no palliation; then to the eternal disgrace of the Authors of such barbarous cruelty be it published, how every person present at the removal of the straw, was struck with horror and amazement, when the shocking spectacle was displayed to their view, emaciated, and unable to move himself, with little other covering than what nature had given him, except

(if I may be allowed the expression) a coat of Vermin, which were eagerly devouring him alive. 'Tis horrid to relate, and a melancholy fact that cannot be controverted. In such a state of torment had this poor miserable creature lain for thirty-six days, as appears by the date of his DEATH-WARRANT. Good God! How could he survive it? 'Twas sure a peculiar act of thy all-ruling providence, to bring him, in his last hour, to excite compassion in his friends, that they might raise the Iron Hand of JUSTICE to avenge the untimely blow; for he had not been long conveyed to a comfortable apartment, when death snatched him from his miseries and the world; and he was on Friday last interred, without the Coroner's Inquest setting on his body: But I hope the relation of so melancholy a fact, will stimulate some humane person, in whose power it is, to make Inquisition into this more than brutal transaction; when I fear it will appear too plain to admit a doubt, that the inexpressible sufferings of the above unfortunate young man. was the consequence of timely assistance being denied him by - What name can we find suitable to them? Or what do they deserve? - Hanging of Men I was ever averse to, but could exult in seeing that punishment hourly inflicted in ridding the world of MONSTERS.

The passionate precision, the phrasing and sentiment are surely Paine's. They anticipate the political tracts he was soon to write in America, and almost 20 years later in London at Clio Rickman's. Paine separated from Elizabeth in June 1774 (local rumour later hinted at non-consummation). The bacon and snuff business had failed; and the *Case* that he drafted, to increase the pay of excise officers, got him dismissed from the service. So he headed for London, and shortly after emigrated.

Bull House (E.H.New)

10

Political Nerve-Centre: The Battle for Reform 1782-1830

We have seen, Sire, a war of the most lavish expenditure, succeeded by a peace of deep and various evils, and for all the sacrifices of liberty and property which under the alleged necessities of that war were required at our hands, we have received in return only hollow professions of economy and solid proofs of oppression. Increased military establishments, arbitrary penal exactments, the employment and justification of spies, the recurrence to loans, the extension of patronage, and open or secret persecution of all opponents, the rejection and derision of petitions, a constant jealousy of liberty at home, mysterious connections abroad, and above all an earnest vindication of every exposed abuse, have been chosen by Your Majesty's Ministers as the preferable means of conducting the affairs of this great and enlightened nation to prosperity and happiness, and if, as might have been expected these means have ultimately produced a train of consequences, which in the acknowledged increase of poverty and of crime, of public burden and general discontent, and in the admitted decline of every source of industry and every branch of revenue, seem to threaten the public tranquillity, we humbly presume to submit, Your Majesty, that it deeply concerns the future happiness of Your Majesty's reign... to have these grievances, while yet there be time, cautiously enquired into, and effectually relieved.

A LOYAL ADDRESS TO GEORGE IV FROM LEWES BOROUGH, 3 JANUARY 1821 (*TOWN BOOK* 237).

When in 1782 Lord Rockingham's Whigs replaced Lord North's Tory ministry, hopes were raised of Peace with America, a Reform of Parliament, an erosion of Places and Sinecures, an end to discrimination against Catholics and Dissenters. At Lewes a group of Whigs, among them William Green, Dr Frewen, Francis Whitfeld and Thomas Harben, formally thanked their MP Thomas Kemp for opposing North, and drafted a Loyal Address applauding Rockingham's Constitutional Principles. Captain Henry Pelham, being a supporter of North, disowned their Address; so the Senior Constable, Henry Blackman, accompanied Kemp to Court and was knighted for his pains. In March 1784 Kemp and the

Captain were re-elected, after Blackman withdrew having polled seven votes. From the hustings he denounced "The Apostasy of my Friends", and singled out his proposer Thomas Harben (the ironmonger) as a double-dealing "Brazier" whose business methods were also crooked. Though Harben retorted, "I used to gather rabbit skins too!", the populace paraded him in effigy on an ass, with his face towards its tail, "showing him every mark of malevolence".

Kemp then supported William Pitt 1784-1801, though the new Prime Minister's scope for Reform was limited by George III's innate Toryism; whereas Lord Pelham and Captain Henry, former allies of Lord North and the Court, with a phalanx of loyal Lewes tenants and tradesmen to command, now backed the eloquent Whig champion, Charles James Fox. These paradoxes prompted an electoral alliance at Lewes in June 1790: William Campion proposed Kemp and seconded Captain Henry, whom Sir Ferdinando Poole (now reconciled with Stanmer) proposed, while also voting for Kemp. This overwhelmed a Whig challenge from Henry Shelley (1767-1811) resident on St Annes Hill, a Guards officer and friend of Miss Thrale, educated at Westminster School and Christ Church. A forbear had been a Borough MP during the Great Rebellion; another shielded local Dissenters after the Restoration. Shelley garnered 89 votes (including 44 plumpers), Kemp 149 and Captain Henry 154. The campaign saw "much feasting and some fighting", but "great temper and moderation" prevailed at the hustings. Beforehand the *Star* and 41 other freeholds, amassed by Thomas Sergison, were sold to a "variety of purchasers". Though only loosely controlled from Cuckfield, and no match for Lord Pelham's "Brick and Mortar Interest", their dispersal increased the Independence of the Borough.

Clio Rickman in Revolutionary garb

The Constitutional Revolution effected in France by 1791 heartened British Reformers; in February "not a dissenting voice" was heard at a Lewes Town Meeting demanding the Abolition of the Slave Trade; and in 1791-2 Tom Paine completed *Rights of Man* (which rejected Edmund Burke's attack on Democracy) while lodging in London with Thomas Clio Rickman who so defamed Elizabeth Plumer. Clio had settled there as a bookseller after trading Thomas Harben's tinplate at Barcelona, which yielded local colour for his three-volumed drama *The Atrocities of a Convent*. A zealous Radical, he named his sons Paine, Washington, Franklin, Rousseau, Petrarch and Volney.

But the success of Paine's book, the spread of Corresponding Societies, and the growth of Jacobinism in France, caused Pitt to curb the more advanced British Reformers. In July 1792 a County Meeting in Lewes heard Lord Sheffield deplore the Societies as Democratical. It welcomed a new proclamation against "seditious writings", and tore up a letter from Paine, setting out his "firm and open" attempts to promote Justice and Liberty while resident in Lewes. Anti-Radical sentiment hardened when priests, nuns and gentlefolk, fleeing the September Massacres in France, landed at Brighton and Eastbourne. Terrified and penniless, many paused at Lewes en route to London, and at the *Star* Lord Sheffield chaired a meeting to assist those "who by unexampled barbarity are driven on our Shores". From South Street Dr Delap chipped in with SEDITION, a satiric ode denouncing Paine.

As the Terror took hold in France, hysteria mounted in Sussex. Effigies of Paine were gibbeted at Seaford and burned at East Grinstead fair. The *Journal* fretted that two men "with large wallets on their backs" were selling cheap editions of his works in the shire. In December 1792 a Lewes branch was formed of the Association "for preserving Liberty and Property against Republicans and Levellers". A keen member, George Shiffner of Coombe Place, immediately noted down two "riotous" Radicals, Drowley and Dunvan, who publicly opposed it, and seemingly they became marked men. James Drowley, the General Baptist lay-preacher, migrated by 1794 to New York State, where he bought land at Sing Sing and laid out the town of Sparta, also known as the "English Jacobin colony" because so many fellow-Radicals settled there. Paul *Dunvan*, whose *History* appeared anonymously in 1795, also quitted Lewes. In January 1793 the Association's committee "accused" William Elphick, breechesmaker to the Prince of Wales; but he stayed put on School Hill.

Listed (allegedly) in Pitt's own Black Book, as a "dangerous demagogue", was the Baptist school proprietor, John Button, an exuberant Philosophical Radical who read the *Examiner* and admired

Charles James Fox. But when his boarders drained away because Tory parents took fright, he denied being a Leveller or Republican, and confirmed his loyalty to the Constitution shaped by the Glorious Revolution of 1688. Though he did belong to a Lewes Society of Dissenters which met at the *White Hart* to petition against the Test and Corporation Acts, that too distanced itself from Extremism. Its leaders met in the vestry room at Westgate to declare that the Constitution offered "the means both of Reform and Improvement". Joseph Middleton's Baptists even claimed to "affectionately esteem the mild government of George III". Taking cover too, the Lewes Library Society now bought books only of the blander kind.

Yet popular opinion turned against Pitt when the war with Revolutionary France brought Repression and Distress. In June 1794 customs officers at Newhaven ransacked the luggage of "industrious" craftsmen and their families, who had barged down-river from Lewes to board the American ship *Mohawk*, bound for the "new city" of Washington. The officials seized or surcharged the hammers, bellows and vices; and they rifled through Radical pamphlets, including Paine's *Age of Reason*, to which their rapacity doubtless gave new cogency. That year Pitt suspended Habeas Corpus, and when his Gag Acts hampered public meetings and all expression of opinion, the *Journal* exclaimed "the Brand-Iron of Despotism will assimilate Englishmen to the debased subjects of their Imperial Alliances".

The re-formed Volunteers also acted as Policemen; hence Lord Sheffield's praise for his Yeomanry Cavalry in July 1794: "each troop in its district to prevent the beginnings of mischief". But a few weeks before the Army itself had sparked unrest at Lewes. While the Herefordshire Militia paraded the High Street with its band playing, the drum major swopped high words with William Kennard, a Whig baker from Keere Street. When Lord Bateman, the officer commanding, tried to "collar" Kennard as an agitator, soldiers and civilians came to blows. Watchmaker Comber fell to the ground; the Senior Constable Arthur Lee tried to restore the Peace; Bateman threatened to clear the High Street at bayonet point; and Private Davies struck the Constable unconscious. Later in the Court of Common Pleas the choleric Bateman was fined £40 for the assault on Lee, and for inciting soldiers to "break ranks" and "drive the town". Besides Repression, the war brought crushing taxes and dear bread, which bore heavily on "industrious" artisans and small tradesmen. During the bitter winter of 1794-5 a thousand Lewesians resorted to the pea-broth donated by Thomas Kemp. The following spring saw bread riots at Brighton and mutiny at Seaford. Joseph Middleton's Baptists thought "the scene of providence is truly awful: God is doing his strange work"; no longer did they esteem so "affectionately" the government of George III. In January 1796 Kemp's pea-broth bubbled again, fortified with nourishing beef.

Like James Drowley, his disciple John Burgess, the General Baptist leather-worker, migrated to New York State, in 1794. His letters home to Ditchling praised a "New World of Liberty", very different from Pittite Sussex:

> we converse upon what subject we please, political, Morral, or Religious, without any person to Controul us. Ah I would not Exchange This Natural Right, the great source of human Happiness, no not for all the riches in Ditchling... Women never ware any Stays.

He poured scorn on England's Ancien Regime, its Church fees, its Licences and Stamps, Game Laws and Workhouses:

> Rates Next to Nothing, and No tythes at all...No Such a set out of Marrying hear. No Liceance nor asking at Church. No Expenc of a ring...if we Can Bye a Hide we Can dress it as we please without Consulting the devil or any of his imps...Shooting and fishing is as much for one as for other, all free...a Man by industry may provide for himself and family, without any fear of having his dear Children taken away from him, and put into a Workhouse to be made Slaves to the Avarice of parish office, Fatgut Farmers, Butchers and Publicans...in England I was poor and Consequently dispised by allmost all Except a few friends that knew Common Sence [a reference perhaps to Paine's pamphlet].

War, Hunger and Repression polarized Borough politics. In December 1795 Thomas Kemp, now disillusioned with Pitt, presented to Parliament a petition against the Gag Acts, signed by nearly 300 residents. This deprived him of Treasury funds. But by then the Stanmer Pelhams had broken with Charles James Fox, and once more upheld the Established Order. Lord Pelham's eldest son Thomas, a Sussex Knight of the Shire, praised the Acts as a "necessary restraint on Coffee-House Idlers and political Clubs", and because consumptive Captain Henry was too ill, Thomas presented a counter-petition signed by 63 householders. Despite this ideological divide, the Kemp-Pelham electoral alliance still held in May 1796 when John Cressett Pelham (c1769-1838) from Catsfield, a faithful Pittite, replaced the dying Henry. 143 electors voted for Pelham and Kemp, whereas only one plumped for Pelham and eight for Kemp. Gossip blamed the continuing alliance on Mrs Kemp who prized the Stanmer connection because she "had sprung and vegetated in a low farm house in the Boeotian air of Romney Marsh"; Thomas being "a matrimonial Sans Culotts in her presence".

However an Advanced Radical also stood. Justice William Green (c1734-1820) was a military engineer, long resident in Lewes, who eloped with a co-heiress, Jane Collier, while building a fort at Hastings. He mapped the remnants of St James's Hospital, and helped to realign the pier at Newhaven harbour. Also very precise was his manifesto issued in January 1796. He pledged Immediate Negotiations with the French Republic, A Reform in the Representation, A Repeal of the Test Act, The Abolition of the Slave Trade, and The Restoration of that Inherent Birthright of Englishmen, Freedom of Speech and Public Discussion, a pillar of "our invaluable Constitution", wrenched away by Pitt. He also promised a keen response to "the Suggestions and Instructions of my Constitutents".

"Citizen" Green's manifesto delighted the Radical Whigs who gathered weekly at a new Independent Club. They attacked the Pelhams for supporting Repression, and the suspension of trial by jury in Ireland, "contrary to the Sense of the Town...and the Welfare of the Country", and for manipulating a Brick-and-Mortar Interest in the Borough. Attorney William Cooper deplored the low rents they allowed, which increased the rate-burden on other residents. He urged Lewes builders to erect new homes, fit for independent electors to live in; and being an active property-developer, he pledged to commission 50 dwellings. Clubman John Kennard was a miller, related to the Keere Street baker who so incensed Lord Bateman. In January 1796 John clashed in the *Journal* with Lord Sheffield, refuting his "shallow delusions" that greedy millers caused high bread prices; all too often their charges reflected the high rents exacted by GRIPING landlords. The Club invited in Mr Hanson, an intrepid Sussex freeholder who had denounced the Gag Acts at a County Meeting. This "Patriotic Stranger" assured members that Englishmen would always use "rational liberty" wisely, whereas the minds of Frenchmen had been "degenerated" by years of Priestcraft and Despotism. Members themselves safeguarded Reason by drinking only the mildest porter at their meetings, which rotated between the *Stag*, the *Lamb* and the *White Lion*, taverns owned by William Cooper's cousin, the brewer Robert Chester. Between the rhetoric and songs toasts were drunk to Lord Egremont and the Duke of Bedford, to Equal Laws and Rights for every Man.

Even before the poll in the Sessions House tensions rose, because the attorney John Hoper, a keen Pittite, suggested (without success) that "gentlemen" be excused the oath forswearing bribery. When polling began Club members saw the alliance between Cressett Pelham and Kemp was holding, despite the ideological chasm between them. This "despicable and unnatural" coalition caused miller Kennard to explode "like a full bottle of ale, tightly corked up". Ripping off Kemp's favour and trampling it underfoot, he plumped for Green, as did other Clubmen not closely pledged to Kemp. William Campion, a leading Loyalist, then rebuked Green as "a well-known supporter of Jacobins and a great admirer of French politics". Uproar ensued; and a hostile source later compared the "round and brainless" head of the ex-Lisbon wine merchant to "one of his Portugal onions"; his Jacobite ancestors at Danny Park were also raked up. Amid the rancour 51 electors plumped for Green; 64 opted for Green and Kemp; and 12 intrepidly polled for Green and Pelham. So Kemp gathered 215 votes, Pelham 156 and Green 127, a narrow enough defeat for Green to claim it, almost plausibly, as "a death-blow to aristocratic influence".

Supporting Green were many Dissenters opposed to the privileged Anglican Establishment, with its income from tithes and church rates, its control of charities and graveyards, grammar schools and universities. They included Pastor Evan Davies at Westgate who seconded Mr Hanson's attack on the Gag Acts at the County Meeting in November 1795; also his Westgate hearers Joseph and William Ridge, Samuel Snashall, Thomas Johnston and William Elphick; the General Baptists, Henry Browne and Aaron Lempriere; the Quaker miller, Thomas Rickman; the Middletonian Baptist and school proprietor, Edward Pugh; and the maverick, Thomas Mantell. Doubtless they spearheaded the Society of Protestant Dissenters, leagued against the Test and Corporation Acts. Not obvious Dissenters however were the attorneys William Cooper and William B. Langridge, the printer Arthur Lee and the explosive John Kennard. Support came too from the builders Daniel Leggatt, Isaac Piercy, Amon

Wilds, Thomas Boxall and John West, whose new terraces in East Street and Bow Windows Row were diluting the Pelham's Brick-and-Mortar Interest in the way Attorney Cooper wanted. Also Greenites were the landlords of the *Stag*, the *Lamb* and the *White Lion*.

After 1796 Repression, Taxation and Hunger were little diminished. In May 1800 Middleton's Baptists bemoaned "the enormous price of provisions and the calamities of war"; and in December the *Journal* reported petty tradesmen and mechanics in the town "tottering amidst their half-starved families". In January 1802 60 stones of beef and over 20 chaldrons of coals were distributed on behalf of Cressett Pelham. But he was now insane; so in July 1802 Lord Francis Godolphin Osborne (1777-1850) stood instead, sponsored by his Tory brother-in-law Thomas Pelham (now Home Secretary), even though he had Whig leanings, and attended Charles James Fox's funeral in 1806. Kemp stood again, and so did a third Whig, Henry Shelley, back home at St Annes Hill after serving in Holland as aide-de-camp to General Hulse. And because the "unnatural" Coalition still held, Tories like John Hoper and William Campion found themselves among 114 electors voting for Osborne and Kemp, both Whigs. 31 Pelham tenants voted with them, but 16 others were among 90 electors opting for Osborne and Shelley. These also included former Clubmen like Thomas Mantell, John Kennard and Amon Wilds, who remembered Kemp's betrayal of Green. William Cooper and Pastor Evan Davies were among 35 electors plumping for Shelley. Only 44 electors polled for Shelley and Kemp. From the confusion, after a scrutiny, Osborne emerged with 208 votes, Shelley with 169 and Kemp with 164.

Undaunted, Kemp celebrated his defeat with a tea-dance in the castle grounds. Four years later, after Lord Osborne decided to contest Cambridgeshire next time, he finally broke with Stanmer and coalesced with Shelley. Thomas Pelham (now second Earl of Chichester) then offered to back George Shiffner of Coombe Place, a sturdy Tory, pleasing to Loyalists and pliable tenants. But an informal canvas disheartened them, so they let Shelley and Kemp be returned unopposed in April 1807. And because the Earl's Brick-and-Mortar Interest was now a wasting asset, as new terraces and streets were built, he sold his Lewes houses in November 1807, giving his tenants first refusal at a surveyor's valuation. Like the sale of Sergison's freeholds, this dispersed ownership, leaving the Borough without a major landlord.

Heartened presumably by the Earl's retreat, the Borough Whigs used a Town Meeting in April 1809 to deplore the Duke of York's corrupt practices as Commander-in-Chief (aided and abetted by Mrs Clarke), and to demand such Reforms in the election of MPs "as will enable them sufficiently to Speak the Sentiments of the People". A Meeting in March 1811 advised the Prince Regent that Reform of "the defective Representation of our order in the State" would bring him new ministers, wedded to "Conciliation, economy and reform", and better fitted to justify the "sacrifices of Liberty and Property" needed to defeat Napoleon. In May 1811 Dissenters met to deplore the Home Secretary's proposal to outlaw itinerant preachers with no settled congregation. Pastor Kerby (Cliffe), Pastor Parker (Westgate), and Friend Marten co-ordinated 400 petitioners against this threat to Gospel Evangelism in the name of Social Policing.

When the Whig petitions were presented to the Regent in March 1811, "severe Indisposition" prevented both Kemp and Shelley from escorting the Senior High Constable, William Madgwick. Instead Thomas Read Kemp (1782-1844) "very handsomely afforded him the Use of his Chariot and accompanied him to Court". Thomas Read was his ailing father's political heir apparent, a moderate Whig, "a Friend of Parliamentary Reform", a foe of sinecures and army floggings. With a Cambridge degree in Theology, an estate at Herstmonceux Place, and a banker's daughter, Frances Baring, as a wife, he almost contested Sussex in 1807. So when Kemp died at Coneysborough Park in May 1811, most Lewesians were ready "to testify their Respect for him" by electing his son. And aware that Shelley was failing fast, with no son to succeed him, George Shiffner and the Borough Tories let the by-election pass uncontested. In January 1812 some 2000 mourners duly attended Shelley's funeral, and Shiffner was nominated. The Borough Whigs fielded Colonel Macaulay (Indian Army), an uncle of the historian, and a "stranger" to the town. But "the Shew of Hands" being so much in Shiffner's favour, Macaulay declined "giving him or the Borough any further Trouble". Endorsed by Lord Chichester and Tory-Anglicans, Shiffner also pulled some weight as a local landowner and Yeomanry officer.

At a general election in October 1812 313 of the 320 Burgesses who polled voted for Kemp, the Borough's favourite son. But Shiffner only just defeated a handsome Whig barrister, James Scarlett (1769-1844) of Abinger Hall in Surrey. Though a "stranger", his eloquent advocacy of Reform polarized the Borough. 157 electors voted for Kemp and Shiffner, 153 for Kemp and Scarlett; three plumped for Kemp and seven for Shiffner. Undaunted by so narrow a defeat, the Whigs formed a Roast Beef Club, to champion the lost Liberties of England and dine annually at the *Crown*, while Shiffner privately bemoaned the expense of victory: "had I been aware of this, I certainly should have kept out of the business altogether".

Despite the Peace Rejoicings on The Wallands in July 1814, Napoleon's defeat heralded a slump throughout the economy that lasted into the 1820s. Ideological divisions deepened in 1815 when Lord Liverpool's Tory government 1812-27 amended the Corn Laws to exclude foreign and colonial wheat until British grain reached 80s a quarter. Town Meetings denounced this Protection of "a few landowners" as "injurious to the manufacturing, commercial and all other classes". The price paid for bread by industrious artisans would be "artificially" raised to inflate the rent-rolls of the gentry and the tithe-income of parsons. The Laws showed the influence in Parliament of "great landed proprietors", whereas Manchester, Birmingham and Leeds were denied "immediate representation". During this bitter debate Scarlett returned in March 1816, after Kemp resigned his seat to become a Dissenting Minister. The Tory candidate, Sir John Shelley of Maresfield Park, was a remote cousin of the deceased Henry on St Annes Hill. His proposer was whist-loving Archdeacon Raynes; his seconder John Hoper who funded Beddingham Sunday School and worried at the castle's decay. Though Shelley won, amid much "rowing", by 219 votes to 200, the Whigs again chose to rejoice, with processions, bands, flags and banners. At the Roast Beef Club Scarlett attacked the use of the army for civil policing, and Tory support for the Inquisition in Spain and Reaction in France. Responding Sir Henry Blackman, now a veteran Whig, gave him a golden snuff box, and pledged to print the names of his 200 voters, in scarlet.

As in 1812 the Whigs rejoiced at the impact of a Reformer, without the local roots of a Shelley or Kemp, fighting the full weight of Tory-Anglican influence: the clerics, Archdeacon Raynes, Parson Gwynne, Parson Crofts and Headmaster Merriman; the Justices of the Peace, Henry Jackson, Jonathan Harrison and "onion-headed" William Campion; the Bishop's Registrar, Josias Smith, and nine other attorneys who, then or later, staffed the County Bureaucracies: Messrs Gell, Gwynne, John Hoper I and II, Kell, King, Langridge,

Turner and Verrall; also Physician Lowdell, Surgeon Hodson and Surgeon Crockford, Banker Whitfeld and Banker Dicker. In their genteel wake swam a shoal of the dependent and deferential: servants, grooms, ostlers, waiters, postmen, sheriff's officers, land surveyors, an Artillery Clerk, an artist, and the "stooping" dancing master Thomas Nicholson. Tory too were most tradesmen reliant on upmarket or rural custom: corn-chandlers, horse-dealers, chinamen, blacksmiths, saddlers, John Chatfield and six of his tanners.

Scarlett's weightiest supporters were often Dissenting tradesmen: Thomas Johnston, Thomas Fisher and William Elphick at Westgate; Henry Browne at Eastport Lane; and the Founding Fathers of Tabernacle, George Adams, Nehemiah Wimble, George and Charles Wille, who were seceding from Cliffe Chapel while the election raged. Among humbler tradesmen, shoemakers were Whig by 22 to ten, bakers by six to two, and butchers were Tory by only nine to six. Their custom often came from back-street households dependent on the booming construction trades, where 41 out of 61 carpenters, bricklayers and sawyers (small masters and journeymen) polled for Scarlett. Many of these worshipped at Tabernacle, Foundry Lane, Bethesda or Jireh. Pastor Gibbs and Pastor Vinall, both shoemakers, supported Scarlett; indeed Gibbs denounced "the Forestaller and Monopoliser" for using the corn trade to induce "artificial famine". Also for Scarlett was John Dudeney, the Self-Improving schoolmaster and Wesleyan lay preacher. However at Cliffe Chapel Pastor Kerby and leading hearers like Charles and Latter Parsons were Tory.

A few leading Whigs had no obvious Dissenting links: the printers Arthur and William Lee; the antiquarian-botanist Thomas Woollgar; the attorney Thomas Cooper (William's nephew) who enlisted the landlords at the *Crown*, the *Stag* and the *White Lion*; and the watchmaker John Holman, who painted his window-frames scarlet and his door-scraper purple, "so that he might scrape his shoes on his enemies' colours". Entirely secular were the politics of Gideon Algernon Mantell. His father, an enterprising shoemaker, named him after Algernon Sidney, a Whig aristocrat executed by Charles II, and sent him to John Button's liberal academy. Despite his great skill as a surgeon, Mantell always believed his "humble" birth barred him from "the first circles in the neighbourhood". Hence his sympathy for the under-dog: the farm labourers kept "in a state of positive ignorance and slavery"; the rebels at Naples; the soldier, so tormented by a sergeant, that he "loaded his musket, and shot him dead". Hence too his contempt for the genteel graveyard-tyrant, Parson Crofts.

Henry Blackman junior (1775-1856), like his father, was also a secular Whig. As an Old Etonian who renounced the Law to enter the family wine firm, he mingled patrician disdain with dialectical thrust. From 1807 his trenchant Resolutions at Town Meetings savaged Tory measures; in January 1821 he castigated the entire British Establishment. As a "modern Demosthenes", "the Great Cicero of Lewes", he reinforced his Resolutions with rhetoric, and founded the Roast Beef Club. He was too a bold tactician: in 1818 during a County Election at Chichester he nominated Sir Godfrey Webster at the very last moment, while Edward Burtenshaw was fumbling to buckle on his sword as an elected Knight of the Shire. At the same venue in 1820 he asserted, amid uproar, that the Cato Street Conspiracy was "hatched at a Police Office".

Shaken by Scarlett's near-victory, Shelley and Shiffner united in June 1816 to rally local Tories with cricket and feasting at Houndean Bottom. They distributed coal in winter, and heavily patronized loyal tradesmen. Moreover at the general election in June 1818 Scarlett abruptly withdrew, sensing a third defeat (however glorious). The Borough Whigs then fielded two "strangers", Thomas Erskine (a future Bankruptcy Court judge), and Henry Baring, a relative of Mrs Thomas Read Kemp. Both polled a token Whig vote, hoping to unseat Shelley and Shiffner afterwards for bribery; a tactic that fizzled out. At Chichester, though, Sir Godfrey Webster was elected a Whig Knight of the Shire, thanks to Blackman's last-minute nomination.

Amid renewed Distress and Repression came the Peterloo Massacre, achieved at Manchester in August 1819 by Yeomanry Cavalry. It provoked Gideon Mantell to compose Resolutions that echoed the "best English authors" studied at Button's academy:

> [this Meeting] reprobates in the strongest terms of indignation, the Magistrates that directed, and the Yeomanry Cavalry that executed, the wanton, barbarous, and illegal attack on the peaceable and constitutional assembly at Manchester, by which men, women and children, were sabred without discrimination and without mercy.

A subscription for those "maimed, wounded or unjustly imprisoned" was begun by four Whig Dissenters: Friend John Marten, Joseph Maxfield (Bethesda), Henry Browne (Eastport Lane) and Nathan Hammond (Foundry Lane). Hammond, a baker, also helped reform the Roast Beef Club as the Bundle of Sticks Society (equipped with Roman-style fasces), which invited down a London barrister, Michael Bruce, before the general election in March 1820. But he declined a poll, so Shiffner and Shelley were re-elected after the "most economical, quiet and sober" campaign ever known. However at the County Election Charles Compton-Cavendish of Eastbourne almost defeated the Tories. So heralded by banners and music, he entered Lewes in an open landau, and feasted at the *Crown* and the *Star* with local Whigs.

They also championed Princess Caroline, the Prince Regent's estranged wife. After a "hopeless exile in a Foreign Land", she was barred from the Coronation in 1820, and then accused of scandalous conduct in a Divorce Bill which, as Lewes Whigs pointed out, ignored "the moral conduct of the Husband", and relied on evidence from the Tory government's network of "Espionage". For her part Caroline compared the king's ministers to "a Canker worm upon the noble Trunk of the National prosperity". When the Bill failed in the Lords, Lewesians in general rejoiced (so unpopular was the king): Gabriel tolled briskly; the church bells rang; the Town Band paraded; Burgesses sported red roses; hucksters adorned their mules with laurel; and Mantell's drawing-room window displayed an apt transparency:

> the imperial crown surmounting a garter on which was inscribed "Dieu protege le droit"; in the centre Caroline regina; at the base a Hercules club on which was written "vox populi", and a dead serpent twined round the club had the word "Calumny" written upon it: the whole surrounded by a wreath of oak and laurel.

Local Whigs also rejoiced when Thomas Read Kemp exhausted his Evangelical zeal, returned to Politics, and began nursing the Borough with gifts of tea, and treats at the *Crown* and the *Star*, though he was already so popular that even Tory True Blues toasted him, gathered in their Porter Club at the *Pelham Arms*. His nomination caused Shiffner to retire at the general election in June 1826. Shelley was longer in the purse and less Ultra, willing to abolish a few Placemen and Rotten Boroughs, yet as to Peterloo he believed the Manchester Magistrates "deserved praise instead of blame".

Besides Kemp, Shelley faced Alexander Donovan (c1770-1846), a Whig barrister of Celtic Irish descent. With his third wife, wealthy Caroline Vanneck from Heveningham Hall in Suffolk, he bought the

Framfield Park estate in 1817. An ardent member of the Southdown Hunt, he often led the field on his powerful stallion *Hector*; with equal panache he collected paintings ascribed to Rembrandt, Raphael, Tintoretto, Rubens, Claude and Poussin. But somehow his ebullience offended the Borough's Whig elite. After dismissing him as "a complete Irishman, thorough blunderer, all blarney and botheration", Mantell abstained from voting, along with George Adams, Henry Browne, William Elphick, Henry Blackman etc.. Sir Henry plumped for Kemp. Thomas Cooper, Thomas Johnston and William Lee opted for Kemp and Shelley.

Their defection prompted the horse-dealer George Drowley, while addressing the Porter Club, to condemn Donovan's "Lewes friends" as "scum who would suck him dry". Yet they mounted an effective campaign. The master tailors William Herridge and William Wright, the master bootmaker Richard Willard and the watchmaker Isaac Gold staged his first "recruiting" dinners at the *Crown*, the *Stag* and the *Lamb* in October 1825. (In 1830 Gold chaired William Cobbett at the Public Temple, and drafted a fraternal Address to the Citizens of Paris praising the overthrow of "their late imbecile Ruler" [Charles X]:

> Your Glorious Revolution will be a lesson to all Ages in the future pages of History, in that lesson they may study the sublime duties of heroism.)

After the dinners Donovan distributed tea, coal and 500 snuff boxes, adorned with a view of the castle and with the legend "May the Electors of Lewes ever be at liberty to take whatever snuff they please". Though The Bundle of Sticks Society gingerly endorsed him, his devotees formed a Pink and Strong Club, where Black Strap was drunk and defiant verses sung:

> In vain the boasting of the lofty Few!
> Who brag, and tremble, 'neath the banner blue;
> The Serif Erin, with his hosts so free,
> Will nobly fight and gain the victory.
> Proudly the standard of the Pinks shall wave,
> And prove their Captain bravest of the brave.

And indeed the Pinks might well have won, had not the Whig elite defected. 289 electors chose Kemp and Shelley, 273 Kemp and Donovan. Including the plumpers, Kemp garnered 569 votes, Shelley 306 and Donovan 279. So keen was the battle that only about 20 electors went unpolled. Artizans and petty tradesmen rallied as strongly to the Serif Erin as they had to Scarlett, among them John Bates (c1792-1881), a journeyman whitesmith, who later managed the gas works, endorsed the People's Charter, and embraced Gladstonian Liberalism. Local strikes the year before may have stoked this Radical militancy: carpenters gained an "advance"; but tailors were sacked, and two spent eight weeks on the treadmill for "intimidation". Yet a few Dissenters did thinly veneer Donovan's cause with Respectability. His proposer, the Unitarian rentier Benjamin Ridge, was to rebuff Justice Harrison's claim in 1830 that the Borough had no prescriptive right to levy a Town rate. His seconder, Pastor Thomas Horsfield, chaired the Bundle of Sticks Society, fostered the Mechanics' Institution, and drew venomous abuse from the Tory *Brighton Gazette*. They were reinforced by Pastor Denham (Eastgate), John Dudeney, Charles Wille, Joseph Maxfield and the stationer R.W. Lower. During the campaign sectarian tension also rose. The Nonconformist British Society, led locally by Dr King the Brighton Co-operator, opened an infant school in the castle yard (probably in Kemp's disused chapel). This provoked Parson Shiffner and Parson Scobell to extend the catchment of an Anglican school serving All Saints and Southover. (In 1841 such rivalries were to close the non-sectarian Lancastrian Subscription School, opened in 1806).

On behalf of the near-victorious Pinks Pastor Horsfield presented a golden snuff box to Donovan, who went on nursing the Borough, sponsoring Monsieur Tistot the Manipulatist at the theatre in September 1828. When Kemp's daughter married in 1829, the taverns were "thrown open" and free coal cascaded. Shelley meanwhile scattered £2000 a year among Borough tradesmen, and his Lady began a Penny Clothing Society. But the political flux that followed Lord Liverpool's heart-attack in February 1827 proved tiresome for Shelley. In March his partisans at the True Blue Club derided the Pinks as "ignorant and prejudiced plebeians" who disrupted parish vestry meetings with quibbles over poor rates and assessors. Many True Blues could not tone down such rhetoric, even after a coalition-government of Tories and Whigs was formed at Westminster. So Shelley, mindful he was a liberal Tory, disbanded their Club in November 1827. Then in January 1828 his friend and political idol, the Duke of Wellington, headed a new Ultra-Tory government, which averted near-anarchy in Ireland and ushered in Catholic Emancipation by repealing the Test and Corporation Acts.

The prospect of Catholics holding Public Office appalled Shelley, as it did most Tories and some Whigs. It was a Unitarian, Thomas Johnston, who in 1815 provided the first place for Catholic worship in Georgian Lewes. Yet when Thomas Illman followed suit, his fellow Baptists at Foundry Lane tried to "reason" him out of it, such was their dread of "Romish superstition". Dunvan's *History* attacked Catholic priests as "blasphemous jugglers" who "pretended to dispense the blood of their God, like a chemical liquid". In 1812 the *Journal* commended Lewes landlords for refusing fish on a Friday to Catholic soldiers, whose "stomachs soon got the better of their scruples". "Superstition" apart, Catholics were seen as a threat to the Constitution. The Bonfire rituals reminded Lewesians of past Deliverance from Popish plots; and a petition lodged at Jireh chapel in 1813 argued that the admission of Catholics to "all Offices of Trust and Authority, both Civil and Military", would destroy that Protestant Ascendancy "to which the People of this Country are indebted under Providence, for the Establishment of their Liberties on a firm and solid basis". Yet though Wellington delivered Catholic Emancipation in 1829, despite outrage among High Anglicans and High Calvinists, Shelley still clung to him at the general election in June 1830 after George IV's death. And because the elite Whigs still boycotted Donovan, Shelley and Kemp were again returned. However Wellington's capitulation to Irish Catholics damaged Tory morale, and a Whig resurgence carried a Reform Act in 1832, which heralded sweeping changes to Local Government, Poor Relief, the Established Church, and the Corn Laws. At Lewes the elite Whigs reunited with Radical artisans and tradesmen, and dominated the town's politics between 1845 and 1872.

*

Lewes Whigs also yearned to reform the Borough's own administration. In 1799 the Senior Constable, William Lee, argued that the Jurymen of the Court Leet were the modern "Representatives" of The Twelve, a prescriptive, self-perpetuating body which till the mid-1660s had chosen the Constables and Headboroughs, the crier, the bellman and other minor Borough officers, without reference to the Manorial Steward. Lee failed to win the Jury these lost Functions and Franchises, but he did assert some control over billeting soldiers: "the Military having practised great impositions on the Inn Keepers". Besides finding quarters for 7000 men, he reviewed the "few Remains of the Town's Property" that had survived "the Hands of Fraud and Official Negligence". Trust deeds were located or renewed, for Steere's Houses, the Town Brook, Hangman's Acre, the Pest House, the old Grammar School site at Southover, and 40 acres "more or less" in East Chiltington called The Godfreys. The deeds of Blunt's Houses (leased out for 150 years in 1758) were unavailable; but his tomb in St John's churchyard was rescued from its "mouldering state". Lee ensured too that the Town Brook, Hangman's Acre and "the Sweepings of the Streets" were let at a public auction. He noted that no interest had been got since 1751 on a bond for £80 dated 16 October 1707. He established a Pound on the Borough Waste, and fitted a Lock-Up into the east wing of the new Market Tower. He also revived the Perambulation of the Borough boundaries "by Land and Water", and paid William Figg for a large-scale survey of it on vellum, "in a Tin Case painted, with a green Baize Bag". He had the heraldry on various staves of office re-emblazoned, and updated the Borough Inventory, itemizing the Deeds and Bonds; the Public Acts and Town Books; Thomas Blunt's cup (wrongly inscribed); 523 dusty volumes bequeathed by Parson Graves; a portrait of Nelson; two brass seals; a set of standard weights, scales and measures; Gabriel, the Great Bell; the Town Clock, and the Market Clock; the accoutrements of the Town Crier and the Bellman; a hammer for sealing leather sold in the market; two fire engines "of the fourth Size", with their pipes, hose and buckets; some arm-chairs and chamber-pots; a dustpan and endless keys to the Town Brook, the Town Stocks etc..

Later Whig Constables were also Reformers. Arthur Lee and William Kennard (both heroes of the 1794 Riot) overhauled the Town Tower in 1807-8. They raised Gabriel (its gudgeons tightened) so it was better heard. They let the space below the bell loft, and removed the Niche near the entrance, previously a great Nuisance. In 1813-4 John Holman (with the scarlet window frames) and John Ade tried to stem the still "shameful" loss of Borough Deeds, by fitting the Town Chest with two patent locks: each Constable keeping one key. In 1815 George Stanford (whose funeral Donovan attended) and William Elphick (the Prince of Wales's "seditious" breeches-maker) regulated the two Borough Feasts : they were to rotate between the *White Hart*, the *Star*, the *Pelham Arms* and the *Crown*; the free Liquor was to be funded from the rent of the Town Brook, and from the largesse of the Leet Steward and the Borough MPs; after "the removal of the Cloth" each diner was to pay for his meal.

As William Lee had noted in 1799, the Borough Engine House in the castle grounds, though "presented" by Thomas Kemp in 1784, had not been legally conveyed. Thomas Read Kemp duly claimed it back in 1816, after Amon Wilds showered the engines with Dust and Mortar while fitting up a chapel for him nextdoor. So the Borough built an Engine House and Record Room in Fisher Street, snugly equipped by 1823 with chairs, tables, fire irons, candle snuffers, spittoons, a tobacco pot, and "A MOREEN WINDOW CURTAIN...with Japanned Pole, Brass Ends and Ornaments". To help liquidate the mortgage, Parson Graves's "mouldering" library was sold; an expedient the still vigilant William Lee deplored. Other Reforms in the 1820s included the Bellman and the Crier being allowed a new coat and hat every two years, "not oftener"; and The Godfeys being perambulated every seven years, which revealed that two Borough oaks had been mistakenly felled on George Shiffner's authority.

11
A Showcase of Building: Masons and Architects, Materials and Styles

Daniel Defoe thought early Georgian Lewes a "fine" town, "well built, agreeably situated". Dean Milles in 1743 found it "very neat, dry and pleasant". Mr Whaley noted "a great many good Houses"; Parson Burton judged them "gracious, numerous and outstanding" (though the public buildings were shabby and mean); and with almost pardonable exaggeration Mr Cox in *Magna Britannia* (1730) described the town as chiefly composed of Gentlemen's Seats "with their Gardens adjoyning". Yet between 1714 and the late 178Os the built-up area grew but little, being still contained within a medieval framework. New ground was broken below Brack Mount for the *Lewes Arms* and St John's poor-house; near Eastgate for Arthur Morris's stone-works; off Fisher Street for a Riding School; near All Saints church for houses promoted piecemeal by Thomas Sergison to accommodate Tory tenants (12-18 Lansdowne Place); and for a block of back-to-back cottages on Timberyard Green off South Street. There was much rebuilding, of course, including the terrace later known as Russell Row (7-17 Fisher Street), erected about 1738 for William Kempe where the tithe-barn of Malling Deanery had stood. And a few dwellings were demolished, to expand the precincts of St Annes House, The Shelleys and The Grange.

The fine houses the tourists admired belonged to rentiers, professional men and "eminent" tradesmen, who had replaced, or at least refaced, their timber-framed residences, to conform with a Rule of Taste, Dutch in origin, but fully Anglicized by 1714. These new genteel facades neatly balanced the doorway and windows, the plinth, plat-bands and cornice. The Friars, built in 1673 for the rentier-merchant Thomas Pellatt, had given a lead, though its pilasters were still a shade Mannerist, and being six-bayed its doorway was off-centre. Entirely correct was pedimented Newcastle House, perhaps built in the 1680s by Thomas's brother William, which stretched unadorned

The Friars (Horsfield's History)

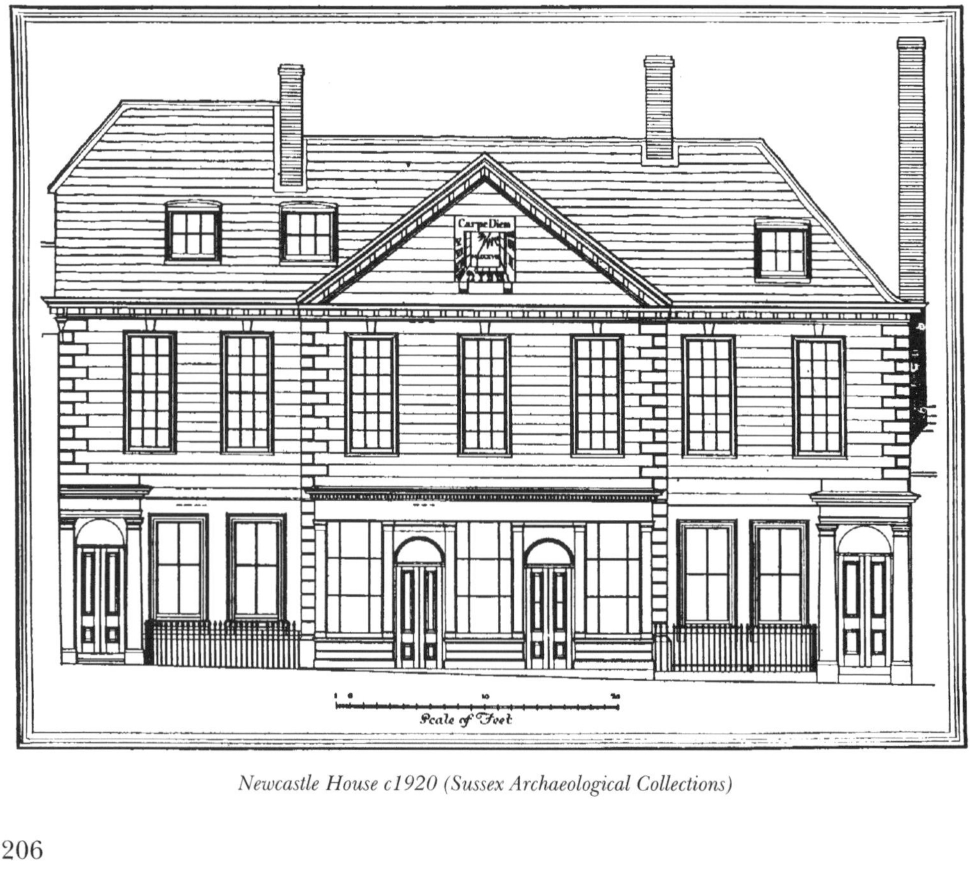

Newcastle House c1920 (Sussex Archaeological Collections)

across seven bays; ironmonger Court added a sun-dial in 1717. Both facades were of Caen stone, taken maybe from the friary site. It was also used at pedimented Dial House (220-1 High Street), built about 1740 (Pevsner suggests) for the rentier Thomas Brown, and at St Swithuns House (now Lloyds bank), owned by the Registrar William Michell (1708-71), and advertised in 1773 as "new built", after Lord Napier rented it.

However most new facades were composed of Wealden bricks; and Alec Clifton-Taylor has celebrated Lewes's "prolonged love affair" with them. When sand-faced and hand-moulded, they have "those slight irregularities and subtle colour variations which add liveliness and interest even to the plainest wall". In 1710 Malling House was stretched "comfortably" across nine bays for John Spence, the Radical-Whig landowner. St Annes House was rebuilt in 1719 for the rentier John Apsley; 203 School Hill in 1735 for the surgeon John Snashall; Barbican House for the draper Thomas Friend (probably); Old Bank House (now Barclays) for the wine merchant Gabriel Ayres (probably), perhaps in the 1730s; and The Caprons in 1769 for Lord Pelham's estate steward. Being the campaign headquarters of the shire's Tories, the *Star* was remodelled for Thomas Sergison in 1739, with a Venetian window beneath a lunette in a projecting central bay. Also handsome was the arcaded shop-front, pierced by a proud Composite portal, which ironmonger Molineux erected at 61 High Street sometime after 1734. A slight affront to the Rule of Taste however was the off-centre door of five-bayed School Hill House built in 1715 for Dr Peter White.

The bricks used in 1674 for a back extension of Moat House, and reused to front NatWest on the same site, were still narrow and irregular. More uniform were the greys (always headers) employed at Malling House in 1710, and the reds reserved for its cornice, platband and window surrounds. Dr White chose the same colour balance at School Hill House, with its crisply cut window-heads. So did Lord Pelham in 1769 at The Caprons, where the bricks came from demolished Halland House in East Hoathly, and from Mr Vernon who owned Newick Park. At The Shelleys the reds edged the canted bays added to the back in 1763. At Southover the mason William Stephen used reds with greys to form a chequer pattern across the lower storey of the church tower in 1714. At Lewes House reds composed the pedimented centre, and greys the wings, of the garden front, possibly rebuilt in the 1730s for the attorney William Kempe. And reds claimed the whole facade at St Annes House, Barbican House, Old Bank House, and at 135-6 St Annes Hill, remodelled with archaic gables about 1738 for down-market tenants of Thomas Sergison.

About 1750 finely knapped and squared flints were briefly in vogue. They faced in 1748 the rebuilt south aisle at St Michael's, where two Pointed doorways, each with a quatrefoil Rose Window

St Michael's Church (Horsfield's History)

above, neatly flanked three Pointed windows, all framed by a cornice, plinth and quoins, predominantly of Portland stone: a Gothick effect moulded by the Rule of Taste. The "plan" was prepared by Joseph Daw, a Lewes bricklayer (and mapmaker), who claimed to build "in Beauty, Strength and Conveniency". The date was set within a Gothick trefoil, similar to that on the flint porch added in 1749 to Brightling church. Possibly Daw also worked at Offham House in Hamsey, where the rainwater-heads, above a fine seven-bay pedimented facade of knapped flint, also bear the date 1749. Flint too was the south aisle at St Thomas's, renewed in a Gothick style in

1753; the Rule of Taste carried a central porch upwards to merge with a strong cornice. Joseph died in 1752, but may have prepared the "plan"; certainly his family firm installed there a "neat" marble font. Also flint-faced, and perhaps rebuilt about 1760, were 139, 140 and 141 High Street, and the stables behind The Shelleys (now the Paddock Studio). Almost a century passed before flint was again used for prestige work, mostly Anglican in character, for St John's church (1839), the National Schools (1840), St Michael's almshouses (1846) and the Grammar School (1851). Yet because Daw's Gothick lacked High Seriousness, Early Victorians deemed his aisle at St Michael's "miserable", and the porch at St Thomas's "unsightly". "Boulder" flints, smoothed by tidal action and barged up from Newhaven, were mostly used for rough work and cobbles (though they faced 19 Sun Street about 1812). In 1774 the "ancient customary right" of Lewesians to dredge Beach, Gravel and Sand near the river-mouth was upheld at the Assizes.

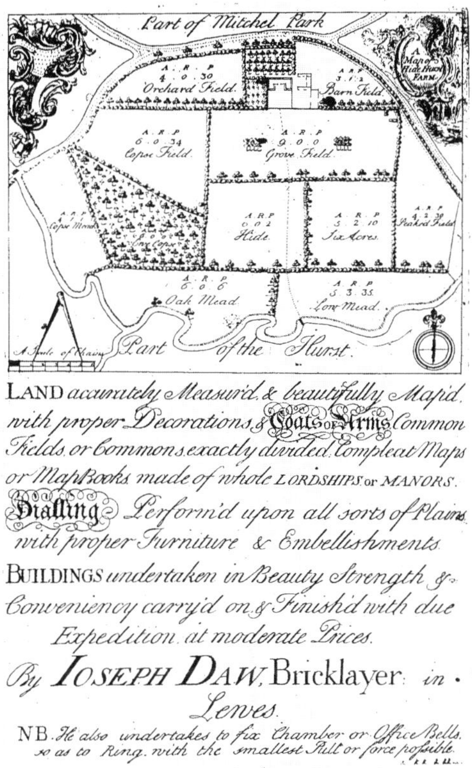

Daw's trade card (Sussex Archaeological Society)

In 1726 James Daw senior built a stable wall at Stanmer Park which collapsed; and in 1739 Thomas Sergison poached James junior from Newcastle's camp, perhaps to work on the *Star*. However as builders they were overshadowed in mid-Sussex by fellow hearers at the Westgate meeting, Arthur Morris (c1685-1744) and his son John. When Arthur became a "foreign" member of the London Masons' Company in 1712, he used a riverside stoneyard at Cliffe, but about 1727 he moved to the opposite bank near Eastgate. In 1715 he built the fine facade of School Hill House. He installed chimney-pieces and a doorcase at Compton Place, Eastbourne, in 1719, and continued there as principal mason to the architect Colen Campbell: his stables survive, and a "Paradice" summerhouse on the hill behind.

From the 1720s he was much used by the Pelham Family. For the Duke he fixed chimney-pieces at Halland and Bishopstone. For Thomas from Catsfield he updated Pelham House at Lewes. For Henry's new mansion at Stanmer he supplied Plymouth marble, Purbeck paving, and stone from Portland, Reigate, Lindfield and Buxted. Presumably Pelham influence clinched his County contracts, to replace Lewes bridge, and to oversee the rebuilding of Horsham Gaol (1720) and Cliffe House of Correction (1740). But he clashed with Nicholas Dubois, the King's Master Mason who designed Lewes bridge and Stanmer House. Dubois denounced him as "intolerably saucy and unruly", ever prone to tricks and lies. Morris (the Westgate hearer) dubbed Dubois "the french son of a Bitch". Pelham patronage possibly lost him one commission: in 1728-30 the ardent Tory Henry Campion used London bricklayers to rebuild the south front of Danny Park to a design by Mr Saunderson. A strong Whig, by contrast, was Parson Joseph Graves at St Anne's; in 1723 Thomas Morris (Arthur's brother perhaps) laid out a Walk in the churchyard and planted 12 limes, trees associated with the Hanoverian cause.

John Morris (1715-92) inherited in 1744 his father's books "treating of Architecture", and his epitaph at All Saints described him as a

The new Sessions House

Mason, Architect and Surveyor, "eminent in his Profession". He both designed and erected the "neat and firm" new Sessions House at Lewes (1761) and, it seems, the "formal and monumental" approach to Glynde Place (1755-60), through a pedimented stable-block crowned by a wooden cupola; he also "worked the stones" for the Great Parlour and Library there. Perhaps he was also the Architect

The Gothick Dovecote (R.Moore)

The Ogival Gothick Temple

The Hermitage

when he built facades at The Hooke (1754-6) and Ashburnham House (c1760), and possibly the entrance front at Firle Place (c1750). He rebuilt Laughton Place (1753) for Henry Pelham the Prime Minister, Glynde church (1763-5), and Laughton chancel with the Pelham vault below (1765-7), but the church's suave Classicism was due to Sir Thomas Robinson, and the chancel's Ogival Gothick to William Robinson whose plan superseded his own. At Coombe Place "Mr Robinson" advised on landscaping the park, and perhaps too on the handsome stable-block, the Gothick Dovecote and Cottage, and the Ogival Gothick Temple (reminiscent of Laughton chancel), which Morris erected there in 1768-78. Doubtless he also built the Gothick summerhouse at Ashcombe for his relative Mr Boys, and possibly The Hermitage in the grounds of Parson Henry Lushington's mansion at Eastbourne (now the Towner Art Gallery); in 1775 he signed an elegant wall-tablet to Henry's first wife Mary in the parish church. He also sent shapely chest-tombs to Glynde and Hellingly, and supplied Portland chimney-pieces for Lord Pelham at Lewes, Bishopstone and Stanmer.

Another fine craftsman was the joiner Robert Burstow (?1685-c1740) who used a yard behind the defunct *White Lion*. He assembled a staircase for School Hill House next door in 1715, and installed windows and wainscot at Compton Place, Eastbourne. For Henry Pelham at Stanmer House he crafted a circular sash-frame for the pediment-window, three wide elliptical arches "with open Pillasters and Keys in the Center" for the inner hall, 20 pineapples for the angles of a dentil cornice, and a splendid cantilevered staircase, designed by Dubois, with "31 steps made of right wainscot...rails and balusters twisted and ramped, the brackets, capitals and pilasters carved". His apprentice Samuel Balcombe settled in Friars Walk, as did Balcombe's son-in-law, William Langridge (c1716-1801), who supplied woodwork to Glynde Place and Glynde church in 1762-5. His premises at Friars Cottage (destroyed about 1930) sported a timbered front with rusticated wooden quoins. When Clerk of the Peace his son, William Balcombe Langridge, could select deals at London for the Shire Hall at Lewes. Another weather-boarded facade with severe pedimented doorways (destroyed in 1965) graced 46-7 North Street Cliffe where lived the Gastons, carpenters and timber-mer-

St. Thomas's altarpiece (Reeves)

chants. However the altarpiece installed at St Thomas's in 1754 came from London, the gift of Mr Stanton the shipbuilder. It had

> 2 pillars in the middle, between which are the Ten Commandments, and 2 pilasters on the outside, all in the Doric order, with Architrave, Cornish and Frize, neatly carved and gilt, and between the Pillar and Pilaster on

the North side the Lord's Prayer, and on the South side, the Creed.

Besides Daw, Morris and Burstow, other Lewes craftsmen worked at Stanmer House in the 1720s. John Kenward built the backstairs. William Attersoll supplied elm for an oval sash, and busied with the well and reservoir. Henry Bean chose oaks at Buxted, and fashioned joists for the pigeon-house and the Family pew (he also made communion rails and a table for St Anne's). George Cooper from his smithy in the Broken Church sent screws, cramps, bars, staples, bolts, grates, tenterhooks, fire-dogs and hanging candlesticks. Thomas Taylor supplied gutters, sash-weights, water-pipes and rainwater-heads; he also pantiled the kitchen, and fixed lead pipes to the well-engine and reservoir. Benjamin Couley painted four sham doors on stucco in the entrance-hall. He also worked at Compton Place and Danny Park; painted the new Lewes bridge; gilded the weather-vane at St Anne's; and recorded Mr Pelham's gift of a fire-engine to the Borough. Despite such industry, his widow and six children were forcibly resettled at Wapping in 1731. Another painter in the 1720s with shipyard links was Robert Smith of Lewes and New Shoreham; he drew and coloured Royal Arms for St Anne's and St Michael's, and possibly for St Thomas's where a robustly fluent composition survives.

Not till the late 1780s did housing boldly overflow the town's mediaeval limits. A sharp rise in its population during and after the American War (1776-83) continued through the 1790s, and the 1801 census numbered about 5200 inhabitants. In 1783 Thomas Standley built 122-5 St Annes Hill for Lord Pelham, the first new terrace since Russell Row, though on an ancient tenement. In the late 1780s low interest rates prompted a national construction boom, and by April 1792 the "rage" for building at Lewes made bricks for a new Market Tower difficult to get. By 1795-6, before the inevitable slump, the nucleus of a New Town had been erected. The coal-merchants John Dennett and John Wimble promoted 8-11 Market Street. The Radical attorney William Cooper (eager to undermine the Pelham Brick-and-Mortar Interest) released Durrant's Field, which re-emerged as 2-15 East Street (Poplar Row), 1-6 Little East Street, and 60-8 North Street (the *Stag* and Bow Windows Row). The banker Thomas Harben bought and partitioned Townsend Field. On it were built 6-10 North Street, the House of Correction, and St Johns Street which included the Theatre, some mortar-yards and lime-kilns, and

Lewes in 1824

UTHOVER, FROM AN ACTUAL SURVEY, BY J. MARCHANT.
REFERENCES
A Black Horse Inn
B St Anns Church
C Southover Church
D Genl Baptist Meeting
E Unitarian Meeting
F St Michaels Church
G The Castle
H County Hall
I Post Office
K White Hart Inn
L Wesleyan Chapel
M Star Inn
NN The Banks
O Crown Inn
P The Market
Q St Johns Church
R Lancasterian School
S Tread Mill
T The Gaol
U Bath
V Theatre
W Record Room
X All Saints Church
Y Quakers Meeting
Z Baptists Meeting
1 The Tabernacle
2 Bear Inn
3 Cliff Church
4 Jireh Chapel
5 Independant Chapel
6 Foundery
7 Gas Works
a Scite of St Peters Ch.
b Do of St Mary in Foro
c Do of St Mary Magda
d Do of Broken Church
e Do of Old Market Ho.
f Do of Old Town Hall
g Do of Old free School
h Do of St James hospital
i Do of St Nicholas hosp.
k Blunt's Charity houses
l Steer's Charity houses
Paper Mill
Brick Yard
Kiln
Town Hall
NORTH STREET
Little East Street
East Street
East Gate
SCHOOL HILL
FRIARS
CLIFF
Cliff Boundary
MALLING
CLIFF
Malling Hill
Spring Ditch
Timber Yard
All Saints Parish
Southover Parish
Chalk Pit
Scale of Yards.
0 50 100 200 300
the Act directs, March 1st 1824.

about 20 houses, descending from Mr Hargraves's demure residence (now 41) to a cramped terrace, Flint Row, alias Botany Bay. William Cooper also demolished the late Samuel Durrant's mansion, to make room for 192-200 School Hill; and a few houses appeared south of Friars Walk, near All Saints church.

The houses built or rebuilt during this First Surge were often faced with cheerily red mathematical tiles. In 1783 they clad the upper storey of Lord Pelham's terrace. At Westgate House, Castle Hill House and 199-200 School Hill, they were suavely combined about 1790 with shallow bow windows, derived locally from Henry Holland's Marine Pavilion at Brighton. They covered the five bays of 213 School Hill which the attorney John Hoper occupied from 1789, and 201-2 School Hill which the fashionable breeches-maker William Elphick owned from 1795. In the New Town they fronted East Street. On 41 St Johns Street and the Quaker meeting-house (1784) the reds were trimmed with black M tiles, which entirely faced the five bays of 120 St Annes Hill, probably built for the rentier William Durrant about 1782, and 13 Western Road which began as a carpenter's shop. Moulded in terracotta were the playfully swagged Borough Arms on the Market Tower, perhaps by Jonathan Harmer of Heathfield. Mildly sportive too was the Tower (1793) that St Michael's Vestry funded to support the clock from the demolished market-house. More sombre of course were the stock-bricks of the House of Correction, with its repressive Cyclopean portal, designed by William Blackburn of Southwark, and erected by John Fentiman of Stoke Newington, who built the other prisons Blackburn planned at Dorchester and Exeter.

The first owner-occupier of 41 St Johns Street was the mason Isaac Hargraves (c1738-1822): indeed carved fragments survive in the cellar. He supplied handsome chest-tombs to Herstmonceux and Glynde (for John and Elizabeth Ellman), and wall-tablets to Stanmer and Horsted Keynes. At Number 41 he kept a lens for viewing his Botanical Journals and illustrated books, a *History* of the cathedrals at Canterbury and York, John Evelyn's *Parallel of Architecture*, and the *Palazzi di Genova* (Antwerp 1622) with plates by Peter Paul Rubens. Lead and plaster statuary in the garden offset his prize tulips and hyacinths. Still vigorous in 1817, he worked on a new wing at the House of Correction.

At the Eastgate yard John Morris junior (1745-1822) joined his uncle John, and carved in 1785 a fine chest-tomb of Portland stone, with black marble panels, to commemorate Robert and Sarah Plumer at Southover. When his uncle retired, he partnered Edward May (c1750-1803), and they built 199-200 School Hill. He then retired, buying 15 acres at Ryders Well in Malling in 1800. From Eastgate Edward May and Latter Parsons (1773-1848) distributed tombs and chimney-pieces across mid-Sussex, and beyond; at Knole near Sevenoaks they repaired the Duchess of Dorset's battlements. Parsons signed wall-tablets to Henry Humphrey (1792) at Newhaven, to Robert Durrant (1799) at Framfield "in the manner of the younger Bacon", and to Joseph Wallinger (1827) at Southover. From 1803 he partnered his brother Charles (1776-1828), and they built the crisp Neo-Classical front of the Shire Hall in 1808-12. The firm dealt widely too in Welsh slate, receiving 104 tons from Port Penrhyn in 1833 aboard the sloop *Gage*.

A builder prominent in the First Surge was Amon Wilds (1762-1833), a native of Hastings. Though a lodginghouse-keeper at Seaford in 1787, he worked as a master carpenter on the Market Tower in 1791-2. Then he occupied a yard on Durrants Field, and built houses in East Street, Bow Windows Row and St Johns Street. In 1806 he both designed and erected the new All Saints church, a red-brick preaching-box with starved cast-iron galleries and plain roundheaded windows, deplored by Mantell in 1846 as "factory-looking". By 1806 a second national building boom was under way, which peaked about 1812, and petered out amid the post-war Depression. At Lewes the boom coincided with a rise in population from about 5200 in 1801 to 6500 in 1811 and 7400 in 1821. The Second Surge increased the inhabited houses from about 800 to 1200, and many were in neat cottage terraces which expanded the New Town. They spilled across Little East Street onto Dobells Field; down North Street and along West Street; onto Black Lion Field to form New Street; across Lancaster Street onto Tanners Field, where Pleasant Place was built near John Gibbs's Refuge Chapel (1811) and the Subscription School (1809); down Sun Street (alias Kemp Street) laid out on Thomas K's field; down Church Street (renamed Abinger Place, to honour the Whig hero James Scarlett); along Mount Place under Brack Mount; down White Hill, and along New Road (alias County Row).

During this Second Surge Amon Wilds built Pleasant Place, the "neat" Refuge Chapel, and houses in Little East Street. He also demolished the Sessions House. However the new Shire Hall was

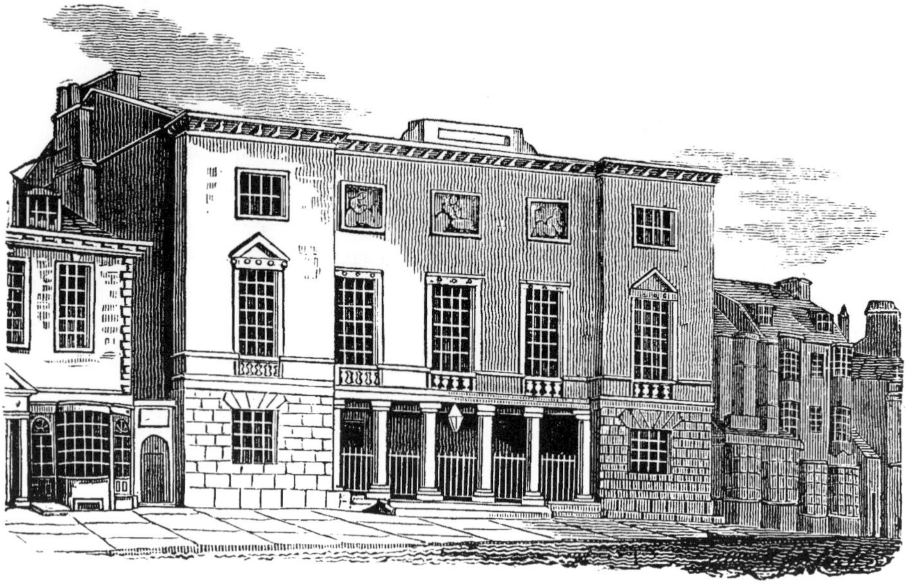

The new Shire Hall (Horsfield's History)

designed by an octogenarian, John Johnson of Leicester, the architect of "elegant Courts at Chelmsford". His chaste Neo-Classical facade of Portland stone carried high-relief Coade-stone panels (cut-price replicas of those at Chelmsford), depicting Wisdom, Justice and Mercy, virtues which rarely sweetened the Assizes staged within. His facade also publicized an upheaval within the Rule of Taste; red bricks and M tiles were out of favour; fashion now demanded cool ashlar or substitutes with a "stone-look", whether stucco, grey headers, or black and gault M tiles. Greys with red brick trim were used to face Lewes House (c1815), and the *Crown* (1811), its Venetian window echoing the *Star*. Black M tiles fronted Bartholomew House (c1813), 27-29 Sun Street and 1-5 North Street, with a squashed bow window, among the last built in Lewes. Yellowish-white M tiles ("gaults") were used on Southover Old House, inherited in 1816 by the attorney James Ingram; whereas in the 1790s nearby Brooklands had been boldly clad with red M tiles. Slates covered the octagonal Subscription School (1809), and were spread, elegantly scalloped, across Samuel Berncastle's shop at 1 Cliffe High Street (1823). Flint boulders, regularly coursed, fronted 19 Sun Street. Even the new cottage terraces mostly sported chequered grey and red brick, in New Street, Mount Place, Abinger Place, and 24-46 Sun Street, the best surviving row.

Amon Wilds probably built Bartholomew House, and soon after, about 1814, he erected nearby 1-4 Castle Place for Thomas Read

Kemp, to replace the defunct *White Horse*. As a tribute to Johnson's Shire Hall, he used greys trimmed with reds; he placed a Coade-stone grinning man as a keystone above the quoined doorways (at least of Numbers 1 and 4); and across the facade he stretched a cast-iron balcony of geometric design, crowned with laurel-wreaths (other Empire garlands dignified the Doric doorway of Southover Old House). However about 1819 he merged 2-3 for Gideon Mantell, artfully creating a three-bay stuccoed facade, rusticated below, crowned by a partly balustraded cornice with shell-patterned acroteria, and flanked with giant pilasters of the Ammonite order (first used by George Dance at Pall Mall in 1789, and feebly copied about 1820 at 14-15 and 37-38 Cliffe High Street). Wilds also added a heavy Ionic porch; and about then presumably another was grafted onto St Annes House, along with a two-tier Trafalgar balcony on the garden front, probably by the Registrar Josias Smith. Severely Neo-Classical was the Engine House and Record-Room Wilds designed for the Borough in 1818. By then he owned a Manufactory near his Hot and Cold Baths at Greenwall which made Mastic, a composition of litharge, pulverized stone, sand and linseed oil. But when John Nash used it to face "the Chinese Pagodas" of the Pavilion, the product "completely failed"; by 1822 the King's costly dining-room was in such a state that Pans were "placed over the Surface, to guard the Interior from the Influence of the Rain".

The Engine House

In 1820, before this debacle, Amon's growing practice at Brighton caused his removal there with his son. Henry Amon Wilds (1784-1857) and his partner, Charles Augustin Busby, designed much of Kemp Town between 1823 and 1825. Henry also built Montpelier Crescent, Park Crescent and a Mughal dome at Western Terrace; he designed Mantell's tomb in Norwood Cemetery; and patented a device for cleaning horizontal chimney flues without recourse to climbing-boys. Amon "resigned" his Lewes business to Messrs James Berry & Son. The father was a timber-merchant and surveyor, James II (1796-1877) something of an architect. Perhaps with Castle Place

Albion Street (Reeves)

in mind, they laid out stuccoed Albion Street (1822), facing a formal garden, and graced by a honeysuckled balcony of cast iron (John Ellman retired there soon after). On School Hill they created a formal approach, using shallow arcades and Greek Key patterning to unify Albion House (now destroyed) and numbers 208-09. After James II married in 1820, he built himself Coombe Cottage near the *Wheatsheaf*, a suave stuccoed villa, with Tuscan columns attached to a central bow. At Ryders Well his brother-in-law Charles Wille occupied a villa very similar in style. Like Henry Amon Wilds, he graduated from Lewes to a nearby resort, laying out for Lord Burlington a New Town at Eastbourne, due west of Sea Houses, between 1847 and 1851.

Albion Street (1822) heralded a Third Surge in building, which slumped badly from 1829. The decade saw inhabited houses at Lewes increase by perhaps 350 to about 1550, and the population rise by perhaps 1500 to around 8900. Cottage terraces broke new ground along Western Road, Western Terrace, Elm Grove, South Parade and Soap Factory Lane. In Southover Spring Gardens and St Pancras Terrace formed "the classic district of Toby's Town". In the New Town Brook Street and Spring Gardens were grafted onto North Street, and on Dobells Field the builder Thomas Smith laid out Wellington Street, Norfolk Street, Bouverie Street, York Street and Queen Street. Because the taste for a "stone look" continued, greys trimmed with reds often ousted grey and red chequer on the new cottages, as they always did on the new, mildly genteel, terraces in Lansdowne Place, Market Street, Mount Pleasant, Fisher Street and Waterloo Place. 19-21 Abinger Place also sported Coade keystones portraying King Alfred, as much a hero to local Radical-Whigs as James Scarlett of Abinger Hall. Greys also fronted houses remodelled in the 1820s at the behest of Improvement Commissioners anxious to ease traffic flows: the neatly rounded *Lewes Arms*; 50 High Street by St Marys Lane; and much of Cliffe High Street on the south side. On the new showrooms at Eastgate yard (1823) the greys were used with finely cut Portland stone (a combination repeated nearby at 16 East Street about 1838). At genteel 53-4 Southover High Street (1825) greys were neatly contrasted with rusticated arcaded stucco below. Fully stuccoed were 108-9 St Annes Hill (1824) and 57-62 Southover High Street with Greek Key patterns and attenuated pilasters. Nearby, The Gables, The Croft and Brookside were refronted with stucco. Red brick was also rejected at the "chaste" engine-house (1833) designed for the Lewes Water Company by William Cubitt with a daring Mannerist portal.

However the builder Thomas Smith went bankrupt by 1830, as a new national slump deepened; thereafter his grid of terraces beyond Waterloo Place took several years to complete. And the 1830s saw the town's own economy falter. Its population rose by perhaps 600 to around 9500, and inhabited houses by perhaps 150 to about 1700. The new terraces were mostly at Malling, at Thomas Street and 50-64 North Street, or at Southover, at 5-12 Eastport Lane, Priory Street and Mount Street, where buff-yellow bricks sometimes replaced greys. In 1830 these were used, to balance a stuccoed base below, at 12 School Hill (later The Dispensary), and again at Priory Crescent between 1836 and 1852. The Crescent's slow completion reflected the town's continuing economic decline. In the 1830s the new householders at Southover and Cliffe were often farm labourers or quarrymen, unable to find homes near their work. In the 1840s and 1850s Lewes's population stalled at under 10,000; the advent of the railway in 1846 brought dislocation, not renewal; and in 1851 the Census spoke of many "young persons" leaving for want of employment. Not till the mid-1860s did house-building cautiously resume, at Wallands Crescent. Yet in 1901 the population was still below 12,000; and the fabric of the town was still much as the Georgian builders had left it. Indeed it remained intact till witless "slum clearance", German bombs and the Great Motor Car Economy arrived to ravage it.

Headstone to Mark Sharp
carpenter, St John's churchyard (Gammon)

References

These are fairly full, but streamlined to give essential guidance only. I have abbreviated the following:

Albery: W Albery: *History of Horsham* (1947). BL: The British Library, Additional Manuscripts. Brandon: P Brandon, *The Sussex Landscape* (1974). Brent: J Brent, The Pooles of Chailey and Lewes, SAC 114. BG: *The Brighton Gazette.* Button: J Button's *Directory of Brighton* and Lewes (1805). Button Poem: JV Button, *Lewes Library Society: A Poem* (1804). Burney: C Barrett ed., *Diary and Letters of Madame D'Arblay* (1904). Byng: C Bruyn Andrews ed., *The Torrington Diaries* (1954). Collier: CL Sayer ed., *Correspondence of Mr John Collier* (1907). Colvin: H Colvin, *A Biographical Dictionary of British Architects* (1978). Dale: A Dale, *Fashionable Brighton 1820-60* (1967). Defoe: D Defoe, *A Tour through the Whole Island of Great Britain* (Penguin 1971). DNB: *Dictionary of National Biography.* Dunvan: Anonymous [P Dunvan], *Ancient and Modern History of Lewes and Brighthelmstone* (1795). Ellman: Rev E Boys Ellman, *Recollections of a Sussex Parson* (1925). ESN: *The East Sussex News.* Farrant: J Farrant, The Seaborne Trade of Sussex, SAC 114. Farrant Rand: J Farrant, Civil Engineering in Sussex around 1800, SIH 6. Gilbert: EW Gilbert, *Brighton, Old Ocean's Bauble* (1954). Godman: S Godman, A Collection of Lewes Handbills 1768-77, SAC 97. Gunnis: R Gunnis, *Dictionary of British Sculptors* (2nd ed). Holman: G Holman, *Some Lewes Men of Note* (1905). Horsfield: TW Horsfield, *The History...of Lewes and its Vicinity* (1824-7). Horsfield Sussex: TW Horsfield, *The History...of Sussex* (1835). Hurdis: Rev J Hurdis, *Poems* (1808). Huzel: JP Huzel, Population Change in Lewes, SIH 3. LBP: *The Lewes and Brighthelmston Pacquet.* Lower: MA Lower, *The Worthies of Sussex* (1865). Lower Handbook: MA Lower, *A Handbook for Lewes* (1846). Lower History: MA Lower, *A Compendious History of Sussex* (1870). LJ: *The Lewes Journal and Sussex Weekly Advertiser.* Mantell: EC Curwen ed., *The Journal of Gideon Mantell* (1940). Mantell Ramble: G Mantell, *A Day's Ramble in Lewes* (1846). Marchant: Rev E Turner ed., The Marchant Diary, SAC 25. Nairn: I Nairn and N Pevsner, *The Buildings of England: Sussex* (1965). Neville: B Cozens-Hardy ed., *The Diary of Sylas Neville* (1950). PRO: The Public Record Office. SAC: *Sussex Archaeological Collections.* SAS: Sussex Archaeological Society. SASN: *SAS Newsletter.* SCM: *Sussex County Magazine.* SE: *The Sussex Express.* SIH: *Sussex Industrial History.* SNQ: *Sussex Notes and Queries.* SRS: *Sussex Record Society.* Town Book: V Smith ed., *The Town Book of Lewes 1702-1837*, SRS 1972-3. Turner: D Vaisey ed., *The Diary of Thomas Turner* (1984). VCH: *The Victoria History of the Counties of England: Sussex.* Wisdom: Memoranda Book of William Wisdom (1756-1843) of Glynde, East Sussex Record Office PAR 347/7/1. Young: Rev A Young, *General View of the Agriculture of the County of Sussex* (1813).

The following archives are in the library of the Sussex Archaeological Society at Barbican House in Lewes: the Attree pedigree; the Baxter Book; the Bax MIs; CP/B; Joseph Daw's prospectus; the Dudeney MSS; Holman's Diary; the Independent Club book (1796); the Norris Book; Woollgar's Spicilegia; or at the East Sussex Record Office in Lewes: A; ABE; ADA; AMS; ASH; BBR; BLE; BLK; BMW; D; DAN; G; GIL; GLE; GLY; HIC; HIL; HOOK; HOP; HOW; LAN; LCG; LEW; LLD; NB; NI; NU; PAR; QAF; QAP; QCC; QI; QM; QO; QR; R/A; R/C; R/L; RAF; SAS/ Acc CO/c DD DM DN E FB G, Gage Acc, GT HC I RF SM WS; SHR; SOF; SPK; TAM; T/CC (County Council deeds); W.

1 The Mart of Mid-Sussex: Catchment and Communication.

Friars Wall: Mantell Ramble 24. 1559 fire: VCH vii 11. ID Margary, Traffic Routes in Sussex, SAC 109. Trampers: PAR 411/9/1. Barcombe bridge: A4113. Sea salt: Horsfield i 207. Lewes bridge: SAC 37 119. Newhaven trade: PRO E190. Downland catchment: Budgen's map of Sussex 1724; LJ 29 Dec 1817, 5 Jan 1818; Marchant passim; DAN 2198-9. Southdown farming: Young 6, 23-4, 311, 348. Johnson: SCM Jly 1943 188. Wheatears: Hurdis 88-9; SCM Apr 1946; LJ 23 Aug 1790. Wealden farming: Young 146-7. Farming boom: Brandon. Southdown yeomen: Lower 85; LJ 10 Aug 1801; S Farrant, John Ellman, *Agricultural History Review* 26; Wisdom; LJ 4 Mar 1805, 11 Aug 1823, 4 Jun 1810; Mrs JA Symonds, *Recollections* (1893) i 10; Ellman 44-5. Southdown population: ASH 933, Jun 1687; G6/1a/8, 347-50; BL 32697 295; SAC 100 26-7; SNQ 2 24- 5. Southover farmers: LJ 20 Oct 1788; AMS 5029; LJ 28 Spt 1801; Ellman 4-5; M Davie ed., *The Diaries of Evelyn Waugh* (1976) 139; Wealden farmers: Brent 77-9; Young 70, 473-81; W Cobbett, *Rural Rides* (1967), 113. Lewes investors: AMS 4599; LJ 6 Jan 1823; Holman 70.

Commercial outreach: Curtis A1896; Turner passim; AMS 5853; RAF/F13/1. The Verralls: Wisdom; Turner 28-9; Ellman 22-3, 28-9. FW Steer, A Catalogue of Sussex Maps, SRS 61. Surveyors: Turner 109; LJ 3 Apr 1780; (Budgen, see printers); Holman 81-4; A6077/12/19; GIL 530/2. Scarp route: ASH 933; BL 32933 90; G White, *The Natural History of Selbourne* (1951), 138, 167, 170; W Johnson ed., *The Journals of Gilbert White* (1970), 18, 156, 416; BG 17 Dec 1829. Juggs Road: Defoe 145; SAC 9 197-8; Dudeney MSS. Mrs Green: Collier 366, 387, 423, 432. Wealden roads: SAC 1 104; Defoe 144; E Straker, *Wealden Iron* (1931), 184; Horsfield i 161. ID Margary, Turnpike Roads in Sussex, SNQ 13. Turnpike roads: SAC 15 146-7; SAC 52 78; BL 32727 432; LJ 11 May 1829, 12 Jly 1813, 26 Dec 1814, 26 Oct 1818. Lewes approaches: LJ 26 Aug 1771; LEW/C3/1/1, Feb 1822; BG 31 Mar 1825; LJ 13 Nov 1809, 13 Nov 1826, 4 Aug 1828, 5 Apr 1830, 11 Oct 1830.

J Batchelor: W Hills, *A History of East Grinstead* (1906), 148-51; LJ 12 Apr, 31 May, 7 Jun 1762, 18 Apr 1763. Passengers: SHR 924; Neville 117-8. Tubb & Davis: LJ 5 May 1788; W/A66/35; LJ 2 Jun 1794, 12 Jan 1795; QO/EW25, Epiph 1777. Lewes bypassed: Gilbert 115; Mantell 99; LJ 15 May 1809; BG 10 May, 24-31 Aug 1826; LJ 5 Apr 1830; Ellman 68-9, 99-100; SE 19 Feb 1861. Ades: LJ 2 Dec 1822, 6 Oct 1823, 23 May 1825; BG 10 Feb 1825. Star: SAC 52 78; LJ 23 Aug, 20 Dec 1784, 3 Feb 1794, 29 Dec 1823. White Hart: W/INV 2697; A Haly ed., *William Verrall's Cookery Book* (1988); Neville 117- 8; Byng 125, 127. Carriers: SHR 1620; Dunvan 254-7; *A Complete Guide to London* (1740); Hook 16/14, 1763 Almanac; Button; John Baxter's *Compendium* (1826); LJ 14 Dec 1829; Farrant. J Greenwood, *The Posts of Sussex.* Postmasters: BL 32694 314, 32935 63, 32969 131, 351; QR/E538/86; LJ 30 Dec 1822, LJ 27 Jan 1823.

Newhaven harbour: LJ 7 Mar 1825; Mantell 44; Brandon 116-8; VCH vii 63-4; BL 33058 144; LEW/C2/1/1, Jan 1715; Farrant Seaborne Trade, & The Evolution of Newhaven Harbour, SAC 110; LJ 18 Spt 1790; Horsfield i 335-8; LJ 9 May 1814, 7 Jly 1823, 22 May 1826. Navigation hazards: LJ 8 Jun 1761; SAC 37 122; GLY 2768; LJ 29 Jan, 5 Feb 1776; HOOK 16/26; LJ 21 Mar 1814; A5120/85/1; GLY 2774. Lower Ouse Navigation: Farrant Rand; LJ 26 Oct 1795; Wisdom; LJ 10 Feb 1834; BG 11 May 1826, 16 Aug 1827, 30 Apr 1829; LJ 27 Jan 1834, 20 Aug 1838. DF Gibbs & JH Farrant, The Upper Ouse Navigation, SIH, 1 & 2; LJ 22 Nov 1813, 6 May, 4 Nov 1811, 3 Oct 1825; BG 10 Nov 1825. Barges: QR/E375; QI/EW5/34 36; LCG3/EW2; LJ 21 Aug 1815; LLD/E5; LAN 15; SAS/I312.

Wrecks: QM/EW7 Jan 1735; QO/EW18 Jan 1745; PRO E190; SCM Apr 1927. AMS 2132; R Armstrong, *The Beachy Head Light*; LJ 1, 22 Jan 1787, 26 Dec 1791, 27 Jan 1800, 8 Nov 1802, 10 May 1803. E Morris: AMS 5569/65 1837. Privateers: LJ 11 Jan 1779, 5 Nov 1781, 5 Spt 1796, 1 Dec 1800, 10 Jly 1780; SPK/M9. Royal Navy: LJ 6 Jan 1800; *Calendar of State Papers Domestic, Charles II (1672)* 450-1; LJ 5 Jan 1801; BL 32697 255; HOOK 16/26; BG 21 Dec 1826. Fleet size: JH Andrews, *The Maritime Trade of Kent & Sussex*, London PhD 1954; Horsfield Sussex i 194. Shipowners: PRO E190 754/18, 784/21, 785/10, 818/26, 812/2; A5697/4; SHR 2721; LJ 22 Dec 1777, 16 Oct 1786; AMS 6041; LJ 20 Aug 1792, 26 Dec 1796, 20 May 1811. Hurdis 117-8, 94. Shipyard: MR Bouquet, *No Gallant Ship* (1959); LJ 2 Oct 1758, 9 Spt 1782, 12, 26 Jly 1784; AMS 6041; LJ 16 Jly 1832. Cliffe shipwrights: LJ 20 Aug 1838; SIH 1 33; BL 32688 56; W/SM/D7/194-6; PAR 415/9/16.

2 The Mart of Mid-Sussex: The Exchange of Local Produce.

Market house: SAC 19 164; LEW/C2/1/1; LJ 6 Mar 1775, 11 Mar & 23 Dec 1793. Farrant Seaborne Trade. Tidemills: S Farrant, SAC 113; A3632 May 1766. Barcombe mill: AMS 6041; LJ 13-20 Jly 1795; D380; BG 12 Feb 1829. Catt: SAC 19 186; SNQ 14 245. Watermills: SAC 13 23; Dunvan 414-5. Windmills: SCM Nov 1941; LJ 10 Mar 1760; W/SM/B7/7; LJ 11 Spt 1798, 4 Jun 1832, 21 Jan 1825, 13 Feb 1826; BG 10 Aug 1826; LJ 8 Feb, 3 Mar 1802; Mantell 12; AO Bell ed., *A Moment's Liberty* (1990) 80, 84. Packham: HIC 1029; *The Illustrated London News*, 11 Mar 1848. Medhurst: SIH 17 27-35. Hubbard: R/A2/516 (12). Hurdis 91. Chalk: LJ 26 Apr 1773; Mantell Ramble 127-8; LJ 1 Jly 1804, 12 Apr 1819, 20 Feb, 27 Mar 1826, 13 Aug 1827, 6 Mar 1809; SHR 824; SIH 15 15-18.

Hops: Andrews *Maritime Trade*; ADA 45; LJ 30 Jly 1838; E190/772/12; LJ 5 Feb 1759; AMS 5569/28. Dunke: E190/770/18. Verralls: AMS 6306; Ellman 29-30; SE 14 Jan 1892. Rickmans: TAM 4/1/3/6-8, 4/1/4/1; LJ 3 Nov 1817; SE 27 May 1876; *Ringmer History Newsletter* 31. Berry: LJ 16 Jly 1821, 8 Feb 1830, 12 Apr 1842. Fisher St brewery: HIL 6/16; Wisdom; LJ 12 Spt 1796; BBR, introduction. Castle brewery: R/C4/2/1; LJ 12 Feb 1787, 21 Oct 1793; BL 32690, 471; LJ 4 Spt 1809; DNB Mrs Clarke; LJ 12, 26 Spt 1825. JJ Cartwright, Dr Richard Pococke (*Camden Society* 1889). Friend: Turner 208, 210; VCH vii 255; SAC 82 4-5; LJ 14 Dec 1761. Kemp: Dale 49-50; Young 353; LJ 2 Spt 1771, 5 Jan 1778. Wool fair: SAS Acc 1326; LJ 24 Jly 1780; Young 356-7, 362-3; LJ 22 Jan 1787, 30 Jly 1792, 1 Aug 1796, 3 Aug 1818, 12 Nov 1792.

Sheep fair: ASH 1178/259-60; Dunvan 311, 313-4; Horsfield i 291-2; LJ 6 Oct 1783, 25 Spt 1786, 24 Spt 1787, 5 Oct 1789, 7 Oct 1776, 3 Oct 1791, 8 Oct 1798, 7 Oct 1805, 29 May, 5 Jun 1809, 24 Spt, 8 Oct 1810, 28 Spt 1812; SAS/HC 343. Selmeston: Young 431; LJ 25 Spt 1826. Cattle: CP/B131/20; Byng 124; ASH 1178/259-60; SAC 106, 153. Cliffe fair: LJ 6-13 May 1793, 4 May 1818, 10 May 1819. Whitsun fair: LJ 31 May 1779, 20 May 1793. Cattle market: LJ 26 Mar, 2 Apr 1810, 29 Apr 1811, 12 May 1823. Horse-dealers: W Thackeray, *Vanity Fair* (Penguin) 263; LJ 30 Apr 1821, 25 Aug 1823, 31 Aug 1835. Vets: SHR 1378: LJ 2 Aug 1824; Pigot's *Directory* 1829. Butter: Marchant 172; Turner 198, 341; LJ 10 Nov 1828. Provision market: Neville 117-8; Town Book 79, 88-90. Cliffe market: Dunvan 313; Horsfield i 291-2.

Agricultural Societies: LJ 6, 26 Aug 1771; SHR 1379; Young 466; LJ 24 Oct 1796, 3 Apr 1797; SHR 823; Button 49-50; LJ 5 Aug 1805. Soap: LJ 12 Dec 1770; Turner 44; HOOK 16/20; LJ 29 Mar 1824; Ellman 121; LJ 5 Mar 1811; LS Davey, *Street Names of Lewes* (1970), 51. Tanning:

E190/810/28; A4600/7; A2220; LJ 26 Oct 1761; SAC 13 99; W/A64/263-9; SAC 29 162; W/A73/612-5; A2220; LJ 13 Mar 1820. Wealden leather: QR/E95/15, l6; LEW/C2/1/1; Matthews & Tuke, *A History of Barclays Bank* (1926), 192; Town Book 104-5. Gilbert: A4113; LEW/C5/3/5a-b. Breechesmakers: AMS 5853; LJ 13 Aug 1790, 26 May 1823, 6, 27 Nov 1826; TA Burnett, *A Regency Dandy* (1981), 4; Ellman 47. Saddlers: DAN 2198; LJ 22 Jly 1822, 24 May 1830; Ellman 36; LJ 28 May 1838, 8 Oct 1781; Turner 36, 218. Shoemakers: LJ 11 May 1778, 15 Mar 1779, 31 Mar 1828. Rope: A4600/7; Curtis A1896; LJ 19 Spt 1836, 2 Jan 1837. Basketmakers: LJ 21 Jan 1833, 30 Jun 1777, 12 Nov 1781, 2 Apr 1810. Hats: LJ 7 Jun 1802, 30 May 1803. Weavers: LJ 27 Feb 1769; BL 33338.

Wealden timber: SRS 34, 125; QI/EW3/87; W/INV 1903; Lower History i 183; LJ 8 May 1837; E190; BL 32692 11; GLY 2769; LAN 14; Farrant. Tan: E190/811/26. Wealden iron: E190; Straker 61-2; SRS 165-6, 279; TAM 4/1/3/3; SAS/G13/53; BL 32692 13; GLY 862; LJ 24 May 1762; GLY 2772; LJ 21 Jun 1762, 15 Mar 1773; SAS/E 15-20. Guns: BL 32688 371-2; SAS/RF15/25/732-3; SAC 67, 44, 51. Fish: SAC 13 26; Gilbert 51; LJ 22 Jun 1801, 7 Spt 1829, 19 Apr 1830, 1 Spt 1823, 28 Aug 1826; BG 3 Jan 1828; LJ 18 Jun 1792, 16 Oct 1775; Young 393; Marchant 167-8, 178.

3 The Mart of Mid-Sussex: Out-County Commodities and Credit.

Button 47. Softwoods: E190/797/40; Farrant; SAC 100, 6, 8; CP/B129/21; SAC 23 68; A3632; LJ 28 Jan 1771, 28 Jly 1777; SAS/WS207; A 2220; LJ 26 Mar 1787. Coal: Farrant; GLY 2767; HOOK 16/6; AMS 5853; LJ 23 Jan 1792, 30 May 1796, 14 Apr 1823, 10 Jly 1780. New wharfs: LJ 8 Jun 1778, 25 Jun, 27 Aug 1792, 2 Apr 1810. Iron: E190/797/28, 803/30; Farrant. Court etc.: QI/EW/6/96; R/C4/19; SAC 8 262; SAC 92 11; A4600/7; QO/EW/16; CP/B129/30; DAN 2199; SAS/DD129; A3632; LJ 31 Aug 1812, 23 Aug 1824. Roase etc.: DAN 2201; LJ 24 May 1762; Turner 97; LJ 4 Dec 1769, 17 Dec 1770, 17 Feb 1772, 28 Nov 1774, 11 Jan 1779, 2 May 1796; SAC 1 97; HIL 2/3; LJ 10 Feb 1834; Town Book 272-7; SAS *Guide*, Anne of Cleves House. Foundry: LJ 6 Jan 1800, 29 Feb 1808, PAR 236/9/1; R Gilbert, E Morris & Son, *Sussex History* Mar 1976; *Southover Parish Magazine*, Mar 1988. Machinists: Turner 15; LJ 12 Spt 1796, 10 Oct 1836, 10 Jun, 1 Jly 1833, 4 Aug 1834. Clockmakers: EJ Tyler, *The Clockmakers of Sussex* (1986); SAC 4 99; LEW/C2/1/1; LJ 28 Aug, 2 Spt 1820, 1 Jun 1772; Ellman 120-1; SHR 1374; LJ 16 Spt 1822, 6 Jun 1831; Mantell 31; *Transactions of the Jewish History Society*, 30, 106-7. Pipes: E190/809/1; QR/EW116/39; SNQ 15 & 16; Turner 2; LJ 12 May, 23 Jun 1828.

Consumer goods: E190/811-2, 796-7; Farrant; LJ 30 Nov 1772, 22 Dec 1777; Kelly's *Directory* 1845. Galloways: A4113; SAS/G13/53; H Cleere & D Crossley, *The Iron Industry of the Weald* (1985) 193, 309; TAM 4/1/3/1, 3; A4600/7; DAN 2199; QO/EW 16 & 17; SAS/RF/25/84. Cardin & Jarvis: SAS/RF/25/168, 254. Whitfeld: SAC 39 76; SAS/E 15, 16, 18-20; SAS/RF/25/255; GLY 862; Wisdom; SAC 7 124-5. Grocers: Ellman 181. Newton: E190/761/6. Paine: Wisdom. Johnston etc: LJ 24 Feb 1783, 2 Dec 1793; LAN 1 & 121/2; ESN 24 Feb 1888; SE 25 Feb 1888. Ayres: CP/B129/26; DAN 2199; BL 32688 620-1. Bean & Barbados: Farrant; SAS/DM 281; SHR 2721-7; A5697/4; A3632. Blackman etc: HOOK 16/20; SHR 13/76; Horsfield i 201, 213; LJ 16 Feb 1795; SAS CO/c 196; SHR 444; Independent Club book. Drapers: SRS 68, 120-1, 124-5; DAN 2198; Turner 215; (for Martens, see Quakers); LJ 7 Jan 1828; HOOK 16/24; BL 32877 476; LJ 16 Oct 1769; Wisdom. Manchestermen: Turner 15, 245; BL 32890 462. Egles: Lower 332; LJ 27 May, 10 Jun 1793; Button; Horsfield ii 232; BLK 77/3-4. Dyers: W/A8/164; LJ 21 Jan 1828, 11 Aug 1788;

LEW/C5/3/5a-b. Tailors: SRS 68, 132; SAS/Gage Acc 741; SHR 1373. 9 Cliffe: LJ 29 Jan 1770, 25 Jan 1773, 23 Dec 1793. Ellis: LJ 19 May 1788. Barbers: W/INV 244; PAR 413/1/1/2; LJ Aug 1774; HIC 1166; Turner 259, 292; SHR 1376; LJ 28 Jly 1823; Ellman 21. Paper: A4113; E190/797/28; SNQ 13 8; LJ 8 Feb, 20 Spt 1802, 1 Apr 1805; BMW/C15/4/15; LJ 24 Jly 1809; Horsfield ii 142; BG 24 Mar 1825.

Money: SHR 1608; Turner 211; DAN 2199; A3632; Turner 150, 177, 330, 341-4; Dunvan 407-9; LJ 23 Dec 1782. Harben: JA Chamberlain, *Notes on the Families of Chamberlain and Harben* (1915); H Browne, *Joseph Chamberlain* (1974); SHR 1375; LJ 1 Jan 1772, 10 Jun 1776, 23 Dec 1782, 19 Jan 1784; AMS 5853; LJ 25 Dec 1786; Byng 127; LJ 18 Spt 1786, 26 Dec 1794, 9 Jan 1792, 29 Mar, 5 Apr 1784; HOOK 16/33; Wisdom; LJ 15 Apr 1793, 24 Feb, 29 Dec 1794. New Bank: Matthews & Tuke 192-5; PR Jenkins, *Sussex Money* (1987); LJ 26 Dec 1825, 3 Apr 1826; Ellman 53-5, 171. Hard Times: LJ 7 Oct 1816, 4 Oct 1817; Brandon 198; LJ 29 May 1820; Town Book 279-80; LJ 23 Aug 1830. Fairs: LJ 28 Spt 1829; BG 26 May 1825; LJ 3 Aug 1818, 1 Aug 1825; BG 24 Jan 1828. Shows: LJ 14 Aug 1820, 1 Dec 1823. Markets: BG 8 Jan 1829; LJ 4 Jan, 1 Mar 1819, 8-15 Dec 1828. Overpopulation: BG 18 Feb 1830.

W Crosskey: LJ 30 May 1874. Cheales: ESN 17 Jun 1887. Chatfields: SE 2 Jan 1866, 14 Oct 1876, 25 Jan 1879. R Hillman: SE 30 Dec 1884. E Morris: ESN 12 Oct 1888. Everys: LJ 9 Mar, 25 May 1835; J Gay, *Cast Iron* (1985), 17. J Broad: ESN 3 Aug 1900. A Russell: SE 14 Nov 1874, 12 May 1888. W Verrall: SAS/Acc 1244/7. Southdown & Harvey's: LJ 14 May, 31 Dec 1838.

4 The County Town: Bureaucracies of Church and State.

A Descriptive Report on the Quarter Sessions, and other official and ecclesiastical records in the custody of the County Councils of East and West Sussex (1954). S & B Webb, *English Local Government* (1906).

King's Peace: Holman's Diary; Hurdis 125: LJ 12, 26 Spt 1825, 30 Jan 1826; Town Book 114. Bonfire: LJ 8 Nov 1773, 5 Nov 1785, 6 Nov 1797, 5-12 Nov 1798, 19 Jan, 9 Nov 1807, 9 Nov 1808; QR/E710; SHR 825; LJ 7 Nov 1814, 24 Dec 1827: BG 16 Nov 1829. Roads & bridges: Marchant 194; Town Book 102, 111- 2. Corn supplies: Turner 82, 84, 143; LJ 5-26 Jan, 20 Apr, 2 Spt 1795, 8 Feb 1796; BL 33059 255; NBl/1/1a; LJ 24 Feb, 24- 31 Mar, 15 Spt, 20 Oct, 22-29 Dec 1800, 2, 23 Feb, 2, 16-23 Mar 1801, 8 Feb 1802; Town Book 112. W Hay: DNB; Webb 362-3. Poor Relief: Marchant 167; LJ 9 Jan 1826; Turner 266; Holman's Diary; QO/EW16; QR/E388/16. Clerks & Treasurers: SNQ 13; SAC 100 1-11; QR/E362, 366, 450.

Assizes: Albery; PRO ASS 35; LEW/C2/1/1; BL 33085 90. Judges: LJ 20 Jly 1789; BL 32949 294; Turner 11, 107, 188; LJ 4 Aug 1806; BG 27 Jly 1826; Lower Handbook 49; SNQ 40 282. Trials: LJ 4 Apr 1836; Ellman 33-5; LJ 7 Aug 1826; BG 11 Aug 1826; Mantell 78. Executions: Albery passim; LJ 19 Jly 1799, 6 Apr 1807, 21 Aug 1820, 8 Aug 1822; SAC 52, 179; Jacobs Post; LJ 5 Apr 1790; Albery 263-5. Pressing: LJ 13 Jan 1806; SAC 19 121-5. Gallows Bank: Town Book 116; Horsfield i 316. Whippings: LJ 11 Jan 1790, 23 Jly 1792, 10 Jun 1793, 10 Aug 1795, 19 May 1817, 21 Aug 1828. Stocks: Ellman 27: BG 30 May 1826. House of Correction: PAR 415/12/1; LJ 5 May 1788; BL 32961 362; LJ 23 Jly 1792, 4 Dec 1782; Dunvan 345; Button 39; LJ 16 Dec 1793, 24 Spt 1798. Treadmill: QAP2/E14(19); BG 4 Jly 1829. Inmates: LJ 1 Jun 1801, 9 Jan 1826, 6 Apr 1807; BG 29 Apr 1830.

County Court: VCH vii 15-6; BL 32697 352. Coroners: the Attree Pedigree; BL 32958 411-3,

32960 110, 246; HOOK 16/34; LJ 26 Feb 1785, 16 Oct 1809, 21 Jly 1817; QCC/E2. Inquests: QR/E590-704; Turner 284. County Elections: BL 32919 371, 32735 219; Turner 219-20; BL 32979 117, 158, 32980 1; GLY 2772; LJ 28 Jun 1790; BL 33059 46, 96, 32697 280. Contests: Horsfield Sussex ii app 24; SHR 1613a; LJ 24 Oct, 21-28 Nov 1774, 3 Jly 1826; Wisdom; SAC 10 36-52; LJ 18-25 May, 1 Jun 1807; Town Book 166-7; SHR 825; A2300; Wisdom; Mantell 17; SAC 100 34-5; LJ 15 May 1820, 17 Jly 1826. Sheriffs: BL 32875 441; Ellman 34; LJ 3, 17 Aug 1789, 10 Jan 1791, 28 Oct 1822; Marchant 18; SNQ 2 58; SAS/RF15/25/78; BL 32718 55-60, 74. Revenue: D472 Misc; LJ 18 Jun 1787; Wisdom; M Foot ed., *The Thomas Paine Reader* (1987), 40, 51; LJ 11 Oct 1773. Smuggling: BL 32719 17; Albery 479; LJ 12 Dec 1774, 29 Jan 1787, 11 Spt 1797; BL 32712 330; AMS 5853. Stamps: Horsfield i 343; Byng 13, 127.

Militia: SAC 30 152; BL 32892 203, 32893 132, 289; HOOK 16/20; LJ 13 Apr, 8 Jun 1778; Eastbourne Library, Elliot MSS; Centre for Kentish Studies, U269c 46/7(64); Burney i 220, 223. Army: LJ 19-26 Jan 1747; Dunvan 269-70; GLY 2770; BL 32694 458, 32858 203; LJ 6 Jun 1763; BL 32951 375; LJ 17 Jan, 26 Jun 1780. Military build-up: LJ 28 Apr, 23 Spt, 14 Oct, 18-25 Nov 1793, 5, 19 May, 3 Nov 1794, 24 Aug, 26 Oct 1795, 18 Jan, 5-12 Dec 1796, 23 Oct 1797, 9 Spt 1799. Invasion scare: LCG3/EW2; LJ 13 Feb, 22 Aug, 24 Oct 1803, 1, 15 Feb 1804; Ellman 18; LJ 18 Nov 1805; JV Button, *Exercises on Elocution* (1805) 229-31. Barracks: Spicilegia 1790 survey; LJ 4 Nov 1793, 12 Spt 1796, 9 Jan, 24 Apr, 15 May, 1-8, 29 Aug 1803; Attree's *Topography of Brighton* (1809) 45; J Evans, *An Excursion to Brighton* (1821) 103; LJ 13 Mar 1809, 7 Spt 1807, 14 Oct 1811; AMS 5809/19; Wisdom; LJ 10 Apr 1826, 5 Nov 1810, 13 Jly 1812. Peace: LJ 11 Apr 1814; Town Book 199-201; LJ 24 Jly 1815.

Spiritual Court: A3632; Turner 89-91, 226-7; Huzel 5; PAR 247/4/1; LJ 26 Mar 1827. Archdeacons: Turner 100-1, 158, 297; *Gentleman's Magazine* 76 589; LJ 5 Feb 1770, 3 Mar, 5 May 1806, 26 Jan 1824; Ellman 41. Bishops: Turner 11; LJ 19 Jun 1758, 30 Jly 1792, 13 Aug 1798, 10 Jly 1820, 19 Aug 1823, 22 Jun 1829; Ellman 55, 137-8. Archbishops: Spicilegia ii 335: Dunvan 315-9; LJ 12 Jly 1792, 16 Jly 1810.

5 The County Town: The Learned Professions.

Michells: BL 32939 89, 32946 228; Lower 229-30; A Wagner & A Dale, *The Wagners of Brighton* (1983). Hoper: Ellman 22-3; LJ 26 Mar 1827. Smith: Horsfield i 308. Gilbert: SAS GT l/1/1-2, 1/2/1-2. Langridge: LAN 1. Burtenshaw: A3632; LJ 6 Mar 1775; Turner 305-6. Tabor: SAS/HC 591, 605-6; Lower 61. White: SHR 1613a, 1641-53; Marchant 172, 179, 187, 191; Lower 298. Russell: DNB; Gilbert 56-62; SAC 36 246; BL 33058 70, 32697 464, 32688 198; Turner 1; SAC 131 note. Poole: BL 32900 256, 32961 62; LJ 3 Mar 1760; Turner 213-6; GLY 2770. Barham: T/CC9l38; LJ 3 Apr 1769. Frewen: DNB; Lower 198-9; QR/E483/104-5; SHR 1377. Blair: Ellman 30; SAS/Gage ACC 141; Mantell 3. Hospitals: LJ 18 Jan, 25 Mar, 5 Dec 1796, 4 Dec 1797, 13 Mar 1826; Gilbert 70-4, 85. Baths: LJ 8 May 1809, 19 Nov 1810, 10 Jun 1811, 5 Oct 1818.

Surgeons in 1720s: SRS 28 112, 174; XSP 26; CP/B1299; DAN 2198; BL 32688 185; Dunvan 269-70; LJ 19, 26 Jan 1747; SAC 93 31; SAS/I302-3. Surgeons in 1760s: SRS 28 52, 125, 193; A3632 Spt 1765; SHR 1374; HOOK 16/37; LJ 3 Oct 1791, 4 Feb 1793, 19 Mar 1827. Rickmans: DNB; SAC 58; LJ 30 Jan 1775. Hodson: LJ l Jun 1778, 29 Spt 1794, 30 Nov 1801, 6 Mar 1826, 19 Apr, 10 May 1841; Ellman 30. Mantell passim; S Spokes, *Gideon Algernon Mantell* (1927); LJ 23 May 1814, 1 Dec 1817. Smallpox: W/INV 130; Society for the Propagation of Christian Knowledge,

Misc. Abstracts to 1722; PAR 411/13/1/1; LEW/C2/1/1; QO/EW17; BL 32697 281. Pesthouse: Horsfield i 209-10, 311; Town Book 37-8; Dunvan 372-3; PAR 415/12/1. Inoculation: GLY 2772; LJ 9 Apr 1770, 21 Jun, 6 Spt 1773; Town Book 94-6; LJ 27 Jan, 17-24 Feb, 24 Mar, 14 Apr 1794, 4 Feb 1796; Dunvan 278-9. Vaccination: LJ 21 May 1804, 13 Jun, 4 Aug 1800. Pesthouse: Town Book 164-5, 169; LEW/C3/1/3-4; LJ 14 Oct 1811, 24 Feb 1817, 7 Oct 1822, 12 Apr 1830. Agues: ASH 933; Wisdom; BL 32929 52; LJ 21 Jan 1782; BG 22 Nov 1827; Dunvan 320-1; Horsfield i 292-3. Elixirs: LJ 23 Aug 1762, 24 Jly 1789; SAC 36 170. Healers: LJ 20 Apr 1761; Godman. Chemists: LJ 28 Aug 1820, 30 Dec 1821, 18 Feb 1828; Ellman 31; LJ 12 Nov 1832: GLE 2/1.

Grammar school: VCH ii 411-5; Horsfield i 308-11, 327-8; Spicilegia i 181-4, 275; BL 4321 102; LJ 3 Feb 1783; BL 32688 522, 558, 32729 1. Pupils: BL 32916 340; A 2462/1/1; *Alumni Cantabrigiensis* 525; D Higginbotham ed., *The Papers of James Iredell* (1976); J Sunderland, John Hamilton Mortimer, *The Walpole Society* 52; LJ 7 Jly 1788; Ellman 6-8, 36-7. Steere's Exhibition: Town Book; Horsfield i 311-2. Rand: Farrant Rand; R/L11/7/6; LJ 25 Nov, 2 Dec 1771, 20 Apr 1772. Button: Dunvan 373; LJ 11 Jly 1791, 7 Jan, 15 Jly 1793, 29 Dec 1794, 4 Jan, 11 Jly 1796, 19 Jun 1797, 20 Dec 1802, 25 Jun 1810, 9 May 1825; BG 1 May 1828; SE 22 Feb 1862, 6 Jan 1883; Mantell Ramble 123. Raymond: LJ 16 Jly 1787, 13 Jan 1789, 1 Aug 1791, 11 Jan 1796; Byng 126. Dunn: LJ 6 Jly 1807, 1 Jan 1821, 1 Dec 1823, 9 Jly 1827, 26 Jun 1837; BG 3 Jan 1828. Roscorla: LJ 11 Jun 1821; HOP 77/1. Carleton: LJ 23 Dec 1822, 29 Jun 1829, 14 Oct 1833. Dudeney: Lower 343-4; SAC 2 253-6; Dudeney MSS. Philpot etc: SAS/RF/15/28; BL 32703 162; SAS/I 302-3; Brent 79; Collier 446-7, 449; LJ 10 Dec 1770, 21 Dec 1772, 24 Dec 1787, 23 Dec 1793, 6 Jan 1797. Adams: LJ 25 Nov 1782, 20 Jly 1789, 4 Jan 1791, 24 Jun 1793; FL Jones, *The Letters of Percy Bysshe Shelley* i (1964); T Medwin, *The Life of Percy Bysshe Shelley* (1913) 13-14; Miss E Hitchener, *The Weald of Sussex* (1822) 67.

6 The County Town: Sense and Sensibility.

Rowe: SRS 34. Tabor: Horsfield i 33, 35, 53-4. Austen: Horsfield i 300; SNQ 16 194-8; W Page, *Guide to Lewes* (1853); PAR 411/13/2; Dunvan 358. Elliot: Lower 329; Dunvan 343-5; Horsfield i 9-12, 61, 71, 272-5, 295-6, 322, 327-8. Burrell: DNB; SRS Jubilee 1951 vii-ix; Horsfield i 115-6; Nairn 371. Dunvan: Lower 333; SHR 820; AMS 5853; Dunvan History passim. Horsfield i passim. Ruinous churches: Horsfield i 278, 283-4, 288, 294; PAR 414/9/2; SNQ 9 122; PAR 415/9/16; Spicilegia ii 248; Byng 126; LJ 28 Oct 1805. Redundant churches: SAC 13; Dunvan 297-8, 335, 357; LEW/C3/1/2; Mantell Ramble 24; LJ 5 Apr 1819. Priory: Mantell Ramble 31, 57, 64-5, 69, Horsfield i 247-51, SAC 40 270-1; LJ 13 Aug 1804; Button; Lower Handbook 39; LJ Jly 1836. West Gate: Dunvan 349; SHR 939; Spicilegia 1790 survey. Earthworks: Horsfield i 272; Mantell Ramble 117; Dunvan 415, 306-7. Artefacts: Horsfield i 31, 36, 42. Excavations: Dunvan 370-1; LJ 14 Jan 1788; W Hay, *Mount Caburn. A Poem* (1730) 13; LJ 24 Mar 1800; Horsfield i 44-5; LJ 30 Jly 1810. Cripps: LJ 8 Jun 1812; DNB (Edward Clarke); Lower 271-2; Button: LJ 1 Jun 1818, 13 Aug 1827. Mantell's fieldwork: Horsfield i 46-8, 74-6; Ramble 104; Journal 76. His Geology: DNB; White's Selbourne 167-8; Dunvan 304-5; Ramble 60-1; Journal passim; Holman 34-6; Lower History xxiii; W Feaver, *The Art of John Martin* (1975) 146-9.

His Romanticism: Journal passim. Hurdis: Poems; DNB; J Betjeman, *First and Last Loves* (1960) 18; Lower 161-2; Button Poem; SAC 19 186. Castle: SASN 52 12-3; LJ 27 Aug 1770, 27 May 1771, 12 Spt, 10 Oct 1803; Byng 125; Dunvan 353; Button; Horsfield i 256. Baldy's Garden: Spicilegia ii 249; Dunvan 318-9; PRO Prob 11/1099; A6077/12/19. Lambert I: Dunvan 323-5; Lower 39; AMS 2132; PAR 378/9/2; HOOK 16/17; GLY 2769; SHR 1373; LJ 9 Dec 1771, 23 Feb

1789; SAC 90 102- 52. Lambert II: W/SM/D10/258, 422; GLY 2938a; SRS Jubilee 1951 viii-ix; Nairn 484; LJ 18 Nov 1805; Mantell Ramble 124-5. G Baxter: DNB; Holman 71-6; *Centenary Exhibition Catalogue*, Lewes Aug 1967. Henwood: SASN 54; LJ 29 Spt 1828; GB Hughes, Hob-nob goblets of the Georgians, *Country Life* 10 Spt 1970. Clio: DNB; *Poetical Scraps* (1803); Holman 65-8; Horsfield ii 127. Delap: DNB; Lower 328; Burney i 223, 227-8, ii 126; LJ 14 Jan 1805. Thrales: SHR 819, Feb 1791; LBP 24 Spt 1789; Lower History 22.

JH Mortimer: Sunderland; B Nicolson, *JH Mortimer* (1968); Lower 159. High Art: Horsfield i 276, 284-5, 288, 296; Nairn 552, 554; SCM 19 257; LJ 21 Jun, 9 Aug 1762. Norman: LEW/C2/1/1; QO/EW16. Lee I: LEW/C2/1/1; A Beckett, The First Sussex Newspaper, SCM 15. Lambert: SHR 1373; LJ 19 Jun 1758, 20 Oct 1760, 11 Apr 1774. Lee's press: RJ Goulden, ESTC British Library; LJ 8 Oct 1781. Fibbing: LJ passim; Ellman 52; Mantell 69, 76, 88. A Lee: Holman 39-46. The Pacquet: LJ 26 Jan 1789. J Baxter: Holman 68-71. Circulating Libraries: BL 32877 476; Button; LJ 12 May 1823, 20 Jun 1836; Holman 56-7. Library Society: Horsfield i 342-3; R/L11/7/6; Button Poem. Philosophical Society: Dudeney MSS; Mantell 5, 27.; DNB Joshua Mantell; LJ 15 Dec 1817, 9 Spt 1822; Horsfield i 343. A Tynan, Lewes Mechanics' Institution, *Rewley House Papers* iii 4. Lectures: LJ 7 Nov, 12 Dec 1825, 20 Feb, 25 Spt 1826, 8 Mar 1827, 22 Dec 1828; BG 30 Nov 1826, 19 Nov 1829.

7 The County Town: Sport and Amusement.

The races: VCH ii 454-5; SNQ 20 227; Marchant 183; BL 33085 25, 90; SAS/RF15/25/80; SAC 8 261. Newcastle: BL 32926 42. Auctions: A3632 Jly 1763. Fagge etc: Wisdom; SAC 8 267; A3632 Jly 1763. The races: BL 32948 177, 187; LJ 16 Oct 1769; HOOK 16/20; LJ 30 Jly, 6 Aug 1770, 1 Aug 1774. Cumberland: LJ 23 Spt 1782. The Prince: LJ 2-9 Aug 1784, 6 Aug 1787, 10 Aug 1789, 2 Spt 1793, 15 Aug 1803; Holman 39. Barrymore: LJ 9 Aug 1790, 16 Jan 1792. Minuets: LJ 10 Aug 1789. Umbrage: Town Book 171-2; LJ 1 Jly 1816, 13 Jan 1817.

Poole: R Mortimer, *The History of the Derby Stakes* (1973); LJ 13 Apr 1801; Albery 297; LJ 16 Jly, 6 Aug 1804; HOOK 22/5/19; Holman 40; HOOK 22/5/1. Pelham Arms: LJ 18 Apr 1770, 19 Dec 1763, 20 Apr 1761, 25 Apr 1763, Dec 1821. Running Horse: LJ 27 Apr 1789; Wisdom. Black Horse: LJ 16 Oct 1809, 5 Nov 1827. Lade: Spicilegia, 1790 survey; VCH ix 207; LJ 19 Jly 1784. Rider: W/A67/744; LJ 3 Spt 1798. Brown: 14 Apr 1823, 27 Jly 1829, 26 Aug 1833, 24 Jan 1842. Riding School: QAF/2/1/E1. Lawrence: LEW/C2/1/1; BL 32688 584-6, 32692 146. Cricket: SASN 54; SCM 19 256; BL 32697 388; Turner 61; LJ 6 Jun 1763, 18 Aug 1788; GP Burstow, Cricket in the Lewes Area 1814-1818, SNQ 15; BG 10 Jly 1828.

Wagers: LJ 27 Jun 1763. Bowling: *The Game of Bowls at the Tilting Green, Lewes* (1968); SHR 1373-4; QR/E44/1 (1639); W/A62/56; LJ 15 Jly 1771, 14 Dec 1772. Paine: LJ 13 Jan 1794. Robust usage: SHR 822, 4 Mar 1797; LJ 13 Apr 1795, 23 May 1803; BG 2 Aug 1827. Cock-fights: LJ 11 Jan 1773, 22 Jun 1778, 22 Apr 1771; Turner 250; BG 17 Jun 1830; LJ 14 Apr 1830. Bull-baits: LJ 9 Apr, 17 Dec 1781. Prize-fights: Marchant 191; LJ 19 May 1788; LBP 22 Oct 1789; QR/E 704; LJ 3 Apr 1797, 9 Aug 1790, 13 Aug 1792. Egan: DNB; LJ 1 Dec 1823; Holman 40. Violence: Dunvan 359-60; A3632 Aug 1763; Albery 256-9. Hunting: [J. Macky] *A Journ y through England in Familiar Letters* (1714) IV, 2 Sept 1713. Brookside harriers: SAC 29 162; LJ 28 Mar 1763, 10 Oct 1791; LBP 5 Nov 1789; LJ 3 Nov 1823. Fox hounds: LJ 13 Aug 1821; BG 17 Apr 1828, 2 Apr 1829, 25 Mar 1830; Ellman 74. Shooting: Macky; LJ 26 Dec 1796, 16 Jan 1826, 29 Mar 1830; Byng 127-8.

Fishing: LJ 1 Spt 1800, 12 Nov 1763, 25 Feb 1805, 6 Jly 1761; Dunvan 28. Quarries: GLY 51 (1762); PAR 411/9/1; Dudeney MSS; Wisdom.

Urban gentry: BL 32707 437; Ellman 22-5, 41-2; LJ 2 Aug 1790. (Strife in 1730s, see chapter 9). Renewed gaiety: SHR 919; Collier 387, 391-2. Verrall: BL 32699 419, 32965 286; LJ 29 Dec 1794. Star coffee-house: LJ 12 Apr 1779, 23 July, 24 Spt 1781, 26 June 1809, 18 May 1835. Other coffee-houses: BL 33086 21; LJ 21 Dec 1761, 18 Apr 1770, 10 Feb 1783. Assemblies: LJ 1 Nov 1790, 5 Jan 1795. Jane Austen, *Lady Susan, The Watsons, Sanditon* (Penguin Classics). Shire Hall: LJ 27 Jly 1812; Lower Handbook 46-7; Gunnis 209. Musicians: Godman; BL 32703 162; LJ 25 Nov 1793; the Baxter Book; LJ 21 Jun 1802, 21 Aug 1820. Cliffe organ: Spicilegia ii 239; Horsfield i 288; LJ 20 Oct 1760, 25 Mar 1782, 20 Spt 1802; PAR 492/9/3. Other organs: LJ 19 Oct 1829. Southover peal: Dunvan 421; SAC 37 197; LJ 20 Jly 1778, 15 Jly 1822.

Early players: J Winston, *Theatric Tourist* (1805); LJ 24 Feb 1752, 30 Oct, 13 Nov, 18 Dec 1758, 14 Aug 1769. Johnson: LJ Oct-Dec 1770; Godman; LJ 1 Mar 1773. Castle Yard theatre: HC Porter, *The History of the Theatres of Brighton* (1886); The First Playhouse in Lewes, *Southward Ho* 1, 201; LJ Jan-Mar 1775, 14 Jun 1779, 10 Jly 1780, Aug-Nov 1786, 23 Jly, 20 Aug 1787. West St theatre: Colvin; Holman 40-1; LJ 1 Jun, 10-17 Aug, 28 Spt, 21 Dec 1789, 30 Aug 1790, 24 Oct, 12 Dec 1791, 16 Jly, 13 Aug, 22 Oct 1792, 19 Aug 1793. Jonas & Penley: LJ 16 Nov, 21 Dec 1795, 29 Oct 1804, 7-14 Jan 1805, 7 Jly, 4 Aug 1806, 8 Jun, 10 Aug 1807; LJ 1807-12. Pic-Nic: ADA 160/363; Holman 41-2; LJ 10 Jly 1815, 15 May 1826; BG 31 Jan 1828; SE 26 Jan 1850; Ellman 51-2.

Novelties: Godman; AMS 5853; LJ 24 Oct 1795, 31 Mar 1800; Mantell 37, 89; LJ 4 Spt 1826; BG 16 Nov 1826. Watson: Lower History 94-5; Mantell 82. Townshend: LJ 13 Jan 1823, 6 Feb 1837; BG 17 Dec 1829. Electricity: LJ 5 Oct 1761, 23 Spt 1805; Godman; Horsfield i 211; Dunvan 305-6. Showmen: QR/EW/11/7a/49; LEW/C2/1/1; LJ 29 May 1820. Cliffe fair: HIC 1166, Spt 1698; LJ 6 Mar 1769, 28 Spt 1812. Southover fair: LJ 7 Apr 1823. Race fair: Dunvan 359-60; LJ 16 Jly 1804, 15 Aug 1808, 23 Mar 1829. Assemblies: BG 23 Nov 1826; LJ 11 Jan 1830. Races: VCH ii 455; LJ 26 Jly, 16 Aug 1824, 13 Aug 1827, 14 Jly 1828, 9 Aug 1830; BG 5 Aug 1830; Mantell 82; LJ 21 Aug 1837, 16 Aug 1841. Theatre: LJ passim; BG 8 Jan, 31 Dec 1829, 7 Jan, 4 Feb 1830; R/C 4/2; Mantell 15; Horsfield i 342. Fairs: LJ 29 May 1820, 22 Spt 1828, 19 Apr 1830. Race fairs: LJ 12 Aug 1816, 6 Aug 1821, 13 Aug 1827, 13 Aug 1832.

8 The Zion of Mid-Sussex.

Anglicanism: Christ Church College, Oxford, Wake MS 20 letter 557; Ellman 5-6, 40-2, 46-8, 122-3; Mantell 71. Clerical poverty: BL 32687 81, 32703 17-18; Lower 324-5; Mantell Ramble 28; Dudeney MSS; Horsfield i 288-9; LJ 29 Jun 1807; BL 32,692 266; LJ 19 Feb 1749; PAR 411/9/1. Tottering fabrics: Horsfield i 271, 278, 283-4, 288-90, 294-5; Spiciligia i 406; PAR 414/9/2; LJ 18 Jly 1808; BG 9 Apr 1829; CR Davey, *St Michael's and the Oxford Movement,* 2.

Old Dissent: Wake MS Letter 557; N Caplan, Religious Dissent in Sussex in 1717, SASN 21. Westgate: NU1/1/1, 2/1; JM Connell, *The Story of an Old Meeting House* (1916); T/CC 11,661; JE Ray, Lewes Nonconformity in the Early Eighteenth Century, SAC 51; Notes on the Ridge Family, SAC 37. Johnston: Horsfield i 303; A5697, Jan 1749; NU1/2/1. Watkins: Horsfield i 304. J Goring, A Sussex Dissenting Family: The Ridges of Westgate Chapel, Lewes SAC 129. Napier: LJ 26 Apr 1773; MA Lower, Memorials of Seaford, SAC 7 124. Horsfield: BG 19 Feb 1829; NU1/6/1; 1829

Return of Nonconformists, QCR/1/11/E1. Southover meeting: Horsfield i 304-5; Connell 93-4; NU1/10; LJ 1 Jly, 7 Oct 1811; the Norris Book; RA Armstrong, *Henry William Crosskey* (1895); A Briggs, *Victorian Cities* (1963); AMS 5853. Quakers: D Hitchin, *Quakers in Lewes: An Informal History* (1984); SOF/1/1; Dunvan 275; LJ 30 Aug 1819; AE Marten, The Family of Marten of Sussex, SAC 68; AMS 5849/44.

Selina's Mission: N Caplan, The Calvinistic Methodists and the Work of the Countess of Huntingdon in Sussex, *Sussex Genealogist & Local Historian* 1; LJ 15 Spt 1760, 6 Nov 1769, 17 Aug 1772, 6 Aug 1771, 29 Jan 1770; NB1/1/1A; E Keeble, *The Story of the Lewes Baptists* (c1934); LJ 29 Jan 1776; AMS 5569/48-9; NI/1/27/1/2; NH3/1/12. R Chambers, *The Strict Baptist Chapels of England: Sussex* (no date). Jenkins & Huntington: T Wright, *The Life of William Huntington S.S.* (1909); LJ 14 May 1798, 8 Jly 1805, 3 Spt 1810, 12 Jly 1813; JS Reynolds, Providence Chapel Chichester, *Chichester Paper* 19. Vinall: E Vinall, *Memoir of the Rev John Vinall* (cl860); Reynolds 22-9. Gibbs: NI/3/2; LJ 7 Oct 1811, 30 Dec 1821. Cliffe chapel: NI/1/27/1/2. Rowland Hill: DNB; LJ 5 May 1806, 18 Apr 1808, 8, 22 May 1809. Tabernacle: NC2/9/2; AMS 5722; LJ 13 Apr 1818, 29 Jan 1817, 20 Nov 1830. Kerby: the Baxter Book. Apostasy: AMS 5569/64.

Arminian Methodists: R Swift, *Methodism in Sussex*, Sussex University MPhil (1984); LJ 13 Apr 1807, 19 May 1788, 25 Jan 1796; Dudeney MSS. Bible Christians: LJ 31 May 1824, l7 Nov 1828; Holman 43. Kemp: Dale; LJ 15 Jly 1816, 9 Spt 1816, 2 Dec 1816; Town Book 215-18, 221-4.

9 Political Nerve-Centre: the Duke of Newcastle and his Legacy.

For elections and MPs see the volumes of *The History of Parliament* by B Duke Henning 1660-90 (1983), R Sedgwick 1715-54 (1970), and Sir L Namier & J Brooke 1754-90 (1964); also Newcastle's letters, BL 32686-32,992; and M Cramp, *The Parliamentary Representation of 5 Sussex Boroughs*, Manchester University MA (1953). For the Pelham Family see N Thompson's contribution to *A House in Town* (1984); and for Borough politics 1642-89, C Brent, The Neutering of the Fellowship, SAC 121, and Lewes Dissenters outside the Law, SAC 123.

1705 election: Spicilegia ii 14-16; NU1/1/1; R/C 4/19; Caplan, Religious Dissent; ABE 34C/13; SNQ 3 251. The Pelham Family: DNB 702-6, 689-92; Brent; RF Dell, *The Glynde Place Archives* (1964) xx-xxvii. 1722 election: BL 33058 258-66. Spence: NU1/1/1, baptism 1698. Excise Crisis: BL 33058 331, 32688 56-7, 236-7, 257-8, 246, 269, 303, 371-2, 379-80, 423.

1734 election: LEW/C5/3/5a & 5b (with massive appendix on disputed votes); B Williams, The Duke of Newcastle and the Election of 1734, *English Historical Review* 12. Tories: BL 32688 passim, 32689 7-8, 19, 49-50, 134-5, 33058 331. Garland: BL 32688 59, 173, 242, 257-8, 558, 604, 32689 130, 134-5, 33058 331. Thomas & Turk: BL 32688 522, 526, 584, 627, 32689 7-8. Lieutenants: BL 32698 310, 32688 275, 595, 32693 102. Custom: BL 33058 343. Charity school: BL 32689 128-9. Floating voters: BL 32688 584-6, 603, 32689 7-8, 13, 15-16, 86, 90-1, 96, 99-100. Cliffe freeholders: 32688 56-7. C Brent, The Selection of High Constables at Lewes 1733-40, SAC 122. Poor rates: BL 32688 599, 32689 110-11, 128-9, 144- 5. Pamphlet-war: LEW/C5/3/5a & 5b.

Reorganization: BL 33058 364-6, 375, 378, 32690 470-1. Patronage: BL 32692 318, 32696 285, 32700 260, 32698 106, 265, 32699 119, 32697 169. Clock: BL 33058 360-1. Organ: BL 32695 16. Rate subsidies: GLY 772. Houses in 1767: GLY 775. Newcastle House: BL 32689 411.

Sergison's campaign: BL 32692 180, 32692 266. Whitfeld & Kempe: BL 32690 473, 32692, 148, 180. 1738 by-election: BL 32691 37. The Club: BL 32695 67. Dissensions: BL 32695 371, 383, 385, 401, 455, 479, 32698 481-2; West Sussex RO, Goodwood MS 1160/32. Whitfeld restored: BL 32696 137, 184, 259. 1741 election: BL 32696 408; Goodwood MS 1160/36; Spicilegia ii 19-21. 1742 by-election: BL 32699 121. Double by-election 1743: BL 32699 25, 32,701 58; Wisdom; BL 32701 97, 107, 113-14, 154-5, 168, 32701 273-6.

Reconciliation: BL 32704 passim, 32708 35, 203, 32712 379, 32703 17-18, 327. 1754 election: BL 32735 94. 1761 election: BL 32919 460-1, 32920 110-11, 333, 33059 17. Patronage: BL 32861 236, 32708 387, 32925 221, 32724 93, 32879 446, 32727 400, 32946 179-81, 32726 369, 32932 263, 32863 278, 32866 182, 32924 284. Ploughmen: Wisdom. Apogee: BL 32894 120, 135; Turner 188; Hurdis 58. Purges: BL 32946 123-4, 179-81, 220, 32969 8. 1763 by-election: BL 32946 394-6, 32947 33, 51; LJ 21 Feb 1763. Plate: BL 32948 177. Beef: GLY 2772. 1768 election: BL 32979 300, 32983 220, 32989 9; GLY 781-3; Hampshire RO, Broadlands MS V/4/14, 15; LEW/C5/3/6. Reprisals: BL 33059 73-5, 83.

1774 election: Horsfield Sussex ii Appendix 46; LJ 10-17 Oct 1774; LEW/C5/3/7. 1780 election: LJ 18 Spt 1780; LEW/C5/3/8; BL 33,059 92; LJ 25 Dec 1775; GLY 792; Hook I6/35, Feb 1786; SHR 303; LJ 20 Nov 1780, 26 Mar 1781. Anti-Court feeling: LJ 27 Aug 1770, 9 Aug 1773, 29 Aug 1774, 12 Spt 1775, 27 Jly 1778, 22 Feb 1779.

Paine: LJ 11 Spt 1769, 4 Feb 1793, 8 Jly 1793, 25 Jly 1808, 19 Mar 1827. Business failure: LJ 11-18 Apr 1774, 13 Jun 1774. Social life: LJ 13 Jan 1794, 17 Oct 1811, 22 Aug 1825; Holman 47. Letter: LJ 11 Oct 1773; PAR 414/32/3/12.

10 Political Nerve-Centre: The Battle for Reform

For elections and MPs see RG Thorne, *The History of Parliament 1790-1820*, and Horsfield Sussex ii Appendix 46-8.

Reform hopes: LJ 1 Apr 1782, Town Book 69-70. 1784 election: LJ 29 Mar 1784, 5 Apr 1784; HOOK 16/33; Wisdom. 1790 election: LJ 14 & 21 Jun 1790; LEW/C5/3/9 (Pelham 154, Kemp 149, Shelley 89: P&K 121, P&S 26, K&S 22; plumpers, P 7, K 6, S 41; voters 223, abstainers 16). Sergison's houses: LJ 6 Jun 1774, 22 May 1780, 22 Mar 1784, 14 Dec 1789, 24 May 1790.

Slave trade: LJ 13 Feb 1791. Clio Rickman: DNB; LJ 21 Spt 1789; AMS 6041. French Revolution: LJ 9 Jly, 10-24 Spt, 15 Oct 1792. Abuse of Paine: LJ 17-31 Dec 1792. Loyalist Association: HOP 30; SHR 820, 6 Dec 1792, 17 Jan 1793. Button: LJ 17 Dec 1792. Retraction: LJ 31 Dec 1792; NB1/1/1A, 3 Jan 1793; R/L11/7/6. Repression: LJ 30 Jun, 7 Jly 1794, 16 Nov 1795, 7 Jly 1794. Lord Bateman: LJ 26 May 1794, 27 Apr 1795; QR/E/660. Baptists: NB1/1/1A, May 1795. Burgess: AMS 5853. 1795 petitions: LJ 30 Nov, 7-14 Dec 1795. 1796 election: LEW/C5/3/10; the Independent Club book; AMS 5745/1; Collier v-viii; Horsfield i 300; Farrant Rand 8; LJ 4, 18-25 Jan, 30 May 1796.

Distress: LJ 11 Jan 1802. 1802 election: LEW/C5/3/11; 6 Spt 1802. 1807 election: SHR 825, Mar 20-22 1806; LJ 27 Oct 1806, 11 Apr 1807. Chichester's sale: LJ 9 Nov 1807. Mrs Clarke: Town Book 171-2; LJ 24 Apr, 1 & 15 May 1809. Defective Representation: Town Book 180-2; LJ

18 Mar 1811. Sidmouth's Bill: LJ 27 May 1811. TR Kemp: Town Book 182; Dale. 1811 election: SHR 826, 3-10 May 1811; LJ 6-13 May 1811. Jan 1812 election: LJ 6-13 Jan 1812; Town Book 185; SHR 826, 8-13 Jan 1812. Oct 1812 election: LJ 5-12 Oct 1812; SHR 320 & 826, Oct 1812. Roast Beef Club: LJ 26 Apr 1813, 18 Apr 1814. Corn Laws: LJ 13 Jun 1814, 20 Mar 1815; Town Book 197-9, 203-5.

1816 by-election: LJ 4-18 Mar, 10 Jun 1816; SHR 321. Holman: LJ 8 Dec 1855. Mantell: Mantell 10, 16, 19, 26, 35, 47, 71, 75, 82, 88. Blackman: LJ 5 Feb 1856; R/L11/7/6; LJ 27 Mar 1820; Town Book 236-8; LJ 21 May 1832, 3 Apr 1837. Tory coalition: LJ 24 Jun 1816, 9 Mar 1818, 16 Jan 1826. 1818 election: LJ 1-29 Jun, 6 Jly 1818. Peterloo: 4-ll Oct 1819; Mantell 12-13. Bundle of Sticks: LJ 20 Aug 1821, 25 May 1826. 1820 election: LJ 6-27 Mar, 15 May 1820. Caroline: Town Book 227-31; Mantell 28. Kemp's return: BG 3 Feb 1825, 11 May 1826. Shelley's views: 13 Mar 1820.

Donovan: Horsfield ii 103-5; LJ 6 Oct 1828; Mantell 81. 1826 election: LEW/C5/3/15; LJ 12 Jun 1826; BG 18 May 1826; LJ 17-24 Oct 1825. Gold: BG 21 Oct 1830; Town Book 267-9. Snuff boxes: LJ 12 Dec 1825, 9 Jan 1826. The Pinks: LJ 21 Nov 1825, 15 May 1826. Bates: ESN 1 Apr 1881. Strikes: LJ 14 Mar, 6-13 Jun 1825. Ridge: Town Book 260-1. Horsfield: LJ 29 May 1826; BG 15 Jun 1826. Schools: LJ 5-19 Dec 1825, 30 Oct 1826, 29 Jan 1838, 26 Nov 1838, 25 Jan 1841. Nursing the Borough: LJ 2 Oct 1826, 14 Jan, 22 Spt 1828; BG 22 Jan 1829, 27 May 1830. True Blue Club: BG 15 Mar, 20 Nov & 13 Dec 1827. Anti-Catholicism: NB1/1/1A; 30 Jan 1817; Dunvan 420; LJ 11 May 1812. 1813 petition: SHR 1351-2. Protestant outrage: BG 17 Apr 1828, 19 Feb 1829. 1830 election: LEW/C5/3/16.

Lee's campaign: Town Book 103-7, 109-27, 136-42. Later campaigns: Town Book 169-70, 201-2, 206-7. Engine House etc: Town Book 215-18, 221-4, 246-50.

11 A Showcase of Building.

For Lewes's architecture see I Nairn and N Pevsner, *The Buildings of England, Sussex* (1965); A Clifton-Taylor, *Six More English Towns* (1981); W Figg, Memorials of Old Lewes, SAC 13; and WH Godfrey, The High Street Lewes, SAC 93 (1955). The discussion of house-building has drawn on parish land tax and poor rate lists, Borough surveys made in 1790 and 1812 (Spicilegia), the minute-books of the Borough Improvement Commissioners (LEW/C3/1/1-3), and deeds held in public or private hands.

Tourists: ESRO transcript XE6; SCM 19; JH Farrant, SASN 52; T Cox, Magna Britannia v (1730) 512. New building: ADA 159/ 51 (Lewes Arms); ADA 159/78 (Poor-house); HIL 6/28c (stone-works); BL 32692, 13-14 (Sergison's houses & Russell Row); LJ 24 Spt 1764 (South St). Houses demolished: AMS 5745 (St Annes Ho); AMS 3022-23 (The Shelleys); A2327/3/1/2 (The Grange). The Rule of Taste: Spicilegia ii 248-49 (The Friars); ASH 933 (Newcastle House); LJ 20 Jly 1773. Wealden brick: SHR 1641-53 (School Hill Ho); BL 33339, AMS 2132 (The Caprons); SAS/DN 184 (The Shelleys); BL 32692 180 (The Star); WH Godfrey, 173 High Street Lewes, SAC 68; LS Davey, *Lettered Stones and Inscriptions in Lewes* (1974); BL 32692 16 (135-36 SAH). Flints: PAR 414/9/2; Joseph Daw prospectus; PAR 415/9/16. Victorian Taste: SAC 13 15; Mantell Ramble 123. Boulders: LJ 24 Aug 1774.

The Daws: BL 33085 294, 32692 366. A Morris: Gunnis; A5120; SHR 1613a; CP/B129; C

Hussey, *English Country Houses: Early Georgian* (1955) for Compton Place; BL 32692 148 (Halland); BL 32688 384 (Bishopstone); AMS 5569/48 (Pelham House); A4600/7 (Stanmer); QR/E396/15 (bridge); QO/EW/16 (Gaol); QM/EW/8. N Dubois: Colvin; BL 33085 59-60 351. Mr Saunderson: Colvin; DAN 2199. Graves: QR/E221/2. T Morris: PAR 411/9/1. J Morris: Gunnis; Colvin; HIL 6/28c; Bax MIs; Dunvan 345-6; Brent 79; A6077/22/8 (Laughton church); SHR 1375 & 1379 & photos in SCM 2 386-94; Horsfield ii frontispiece (Ashcombe); *The Hermitage*, Eastbourne BC (1990); SAS/FB 113 (Laughton Place); AMS 2132 (Lewes & Bishopstone); A6077/22/11 (Stanmer). W Robinson: Colvin. Burstow: W/A48/238; SHR 1617; CP/B129; A4600/7; SRS 28 10. Langridge: GLY 2768; LJ 8 Jly 1765. Friars Cottage: SAC 72 278. Altarpiece: PAR 415/9/16; Defoe Tour 7th ed (1769). Stanmer craftsmen: A4600/7. St Anne's rails: PAR 411/9/1 (1720). Couley: CP/B129; DAN 2199; QO/EW/17; PAR 411/9/1 (1723); LEW/C2/1/1 (1727); QR/E408. Smith: PAR 414/9/2 (1720); PAR 411/9/1 (1723).

First Surge: AMS 2133 (122-5 SAH); LJ 2 Apr 1792; BLE/C2/8, 16-17, 20; T/CC 6239. EW O'Shea, Mathematical Tiles in Lewes, SASN 37. Clock Tower: PAR 414/10. Prison: Colvin; QAP2/E12; LJ 7 Aug 1789. Hargraves: Gunnis; LJ 4 Mar 1822; QAP2/E13. J Morris jun: SAS/I/276; AMS 5569/48; LJ 6 Jan 1823. May & Parsons: LJ 10 Apr 1797; 24 Oct 1803; AMS 5836/2. Parsons: Gunnis. A Wilds: Colvin; Dale; LJ 4 Aug 1788; Lewes DC deed 26 (1791); Lewes DC deed 56; LJ 23 Jun 1806; Mantell Ramble 27-8; LJ 11 Jun 1810. Johnson: Colvin, Architects; SAC 100; A Kelly, Mrs Coade's Stone (1990); LJ 29 Feb 1808. The Crown: LJ 21 Oct 1811. Berncastle's: LJ 26 Jan 1824. A Wilds: SAS/SM 40, SAS/HC6 93 (Bartholomew Ho); Town Book 222; LJ 27 Oct 1817; J Summerson, *The Life and Works of John Nash Architect* (1980), 107-8.

HA Wilds: Colvin; Dale; N Bingham, *CA Busby* (1991). Berry & Son: LJ 15 May 1820; AMS 5569/3, 48-9, 74; LJ 15 Dec 1823, Ellman 62 (Albion St); LJ 12 Nov 1821 (School Hill); D Cannadine, *Lords and Landlords* (1980). Third Surge: LJ 9 Jun 1828 (South Parade); LJ 14 Aug 1826, SE 8 Nov 1870 (Toby's Town); LJ 22 May 1826, HOP 28-9, HOW 45/9 (T Smith). The "stone look": LJ 19 Mar 1827 (50 High St); LJ 5 Apr 1824 (108-9 St Annes Hill); LJ 21 Oct 1833, 11 Aug 1834, H Hobhouse, *Thomas Cubitt* (1971), plate 22g (engine-house). Buff-yellows: LJ 12 Apr 1830 (12 High St); LJ 14 Nov 1836, HOW 97/1 (Priory Crescent).

Subject index

Persons Index

T. Henwood del^t